TALKING ON AIR

A Broadcaster's Life in Sports

by
Ken Coleman and Dan Valenti

Foreword by
Ted Williams

SPORTS PUBLISHING INC.
WWW.SPORTSPUBLISHINGINC.COM

Director of Production, Book Design: Susan M. McKinney
Cover design: Christina Cary
Proofreader: Paula Erwin
Production assistant: Crystal Gummere

ISBN: 1-58382-062-0

Library of Congress Catalog Card Number: 00-100047

SPORTS PUBLISHING INC.
804 N. Neil
Champaign, IL 61820
www.sportspublishinginc.com

Printed in the United States.

To my grandchildren: Chelsea, Kayla, and Casey James

—Ken Coleman

To my wife Paula and to Teddy Ballgame

—Dan Valenti

Also by Ken Coleman:
So You Want to Be a Sportscaster

Also by Ken Coleman and Dan Valenti:
Diary of a Sportscaster
The Impossible Dream Remembered
Grapefruit League Roadtrip

Also by Dan Valenti:
Red Sox: A Reckoning
From Florida to Fenway
Cities Journey
Cactus League Roadtrip
Clout!
TJ: My 26 Years in Baseball (with Tommy John)
December Sunlight
The Gunny (with R. Lee Ermey)
A Man Like Him (a stage play)
You Never Know When You'll Run Into God

Contents

Acknowledgments

We'd like to acknowledge all the gifted people over all the many years who by their endeavors and exploits both on and off the athletic fields of this land have made this book—as Yogi Berra might say—necessary. Particularly, we'd like to extend our deepest thanks to Ted Williams, hitter, and Jim Brown, ball carrier.

There were also numerous mentors, role models, and kind people along the way for both of us—parents, teachers, colleagues, friends, family, and loved ones who by their influence and example inspired us to become, well, "us." They got us started in some cases; they kept us going in others. Still others will see us through. They know who they are. To these beautiful people, we can only express our endless gratitude.

Now go out and enjoy a game, everybody!

— Ken Coleman and Dan Valenti, January 3, 2000

Foreword

—————————

by
Ted Williams

When it comes to hitting a baseball, some people think it's just a matter of good eyesight and a good swing. It's much more than that. It's practicing until your hands bleed. It's studying the opposing pitcher. It's knowing what the count is and what pitch to look for, and it's being patient. Basically, hitting is hard work that to the fan may look easy. In fact, hitting a baseball is the single most difficult thing to do in sports.

I like to listen to baseball on the radio, and I had one of the best describing my games in Curt Gowdy. I never got to hear Curt that much, because when he was broadcasting I was playing. But his record speaks for itself. He was a great one.

I've heard Ken Coleman do hundreds of games, and he is also one of the best. When I was up in New England in the summertime, he boomed in loud and clear and his descriptions were always accurate and concise. What sets Ken apart in my book are his knowledge of the game and his remarkable recall when it comes to the history of baseball. That tells me something about how hard he has worked in his trade.

Most Red Sox fans know Jack Fisher of the Orioles was the last man I faced in my career. Not many know that Red Ruffing of the Yankees was the first. Coleman knows. Not many know I played in a game with Babe Ruth, who managed a Major League All-Star game during the war to raise money for the military. Coleman knows.

That's why I'm looking forward to reading his book. I know it will be honest, accurate, and enjoyable, because he is. I also know that Ken and his collaborator Dan Valenti have an excellent track record. This is their fourth book together, and once again they have touched all the bases.

— *Ted Williams, December 16, 1999*

CHAPTER *1*

Openings

To Travel Hopefully

I'm an avid reader and I've read many "life stories"—some good some bad, some great some awful. People interest me. I enjoy reading about them and how they tend to the problems attached to this strange yet exhilarating business called living. There's no "one way" that works for everybody, and yet at the same time, each of us has to find our way—the way that works for us. That's why it's not just entertaining to read about someone else's life but also instructive as well.

As you will see, this book is not an autobiography *per se*. Rather, it's a selective account of my life "in the toy store" of professional sports, the account of a man who was afforded the deep blessing of broadcasting sports for more than 50 years. There is, of course, a heavy autobiographical overtone to all of this, since I'm describing things that I've seen and that have happened to me. In that sense, I guess you could say it's an autobiography if you allow for that broad understanding.

I present my life obliquely, as it unfolded around my job as a sports broadcaster. The story begins in boyhood and continues through to my start at a small Vermont radio station. It eventually leads me into a Major League broadcasting booth and through to my days broadcasting to the entire nation watching and listening intently to a World Series game or an NFL championship match. It also leads up to the last day I had the privilege and high honor of being the "Voice" of a Big League ball club. My account continues to the present moment, where you will find a man who has been gifted with the tremendous blessing of being able to look back on his career and feel good about it. For me, broadcasting was like walking on air, only I did it by "talking on air."

Along the way, I served as the "Voice" of some of sports' most storied franchises. These included the Cleveland Browns, when they were a football power; Ohio State football; Harvard football; the Cleveland Indians, baseball's Big Red Machine in the mid-70s; and for 20 years in New England as the Voice of the Boston Red Sox.

I started as a young man full of dreams and prepared to walk an uncertain path. Initially, as many young people would admit if they could, I lacked confidence and took each unsure step not knowing where it would lead. I left the broadcasting booth older and much wiser, a man fully engaging his talents, going off the air for the last time in a Big League baseball game knowing full well that the circle was left unbroken.

The circumstances surrounding that last broadcast troubled me for some time after, as you shall read, but now I know that endings happen the way they do for reasons we can't always control. I'd like to tell you the full story of my exit from the game, and it's the first time I've told it, other than to my collaborator Dan Valenti.

This also marks the first time I've dealt extensively in a book with my years in Cleveland, both with the Browns and the Indians. I'm delighted to be able to reminisce and share with you, my reader, some of the happiest and most fulfilling years of my life. Again, knowing I couldn't tell everything, I selected certain personalities and moments to stand in for the rest. With the Browns, I focus on legendary coach Paul Brown, the great running back Jim Brown, and the championship years in the mid-60s under Blanton Collier. In discussing the Indians, I find my focus essentially in the dramatic story of Herb Score—the best pitcher of a generation whose career ended prematurely.

In many ways, the real story of my life as a broadcaster deals with the players and teams that made my job such fun. In this book

I want to talk about some of them. Again, you shouldn't be looking for an exhaustive treatment, but rather highlights.

There are many ways to "play" a book like this—I'm not sure there's any right or wrong way. But when I discussed what I had in mind with Dan Valenti, I realized I didn't want to "take inventory" of my life as a broadcaster by attempting to recall every single person, event, or incident. First, it couldn't fit in one book. Second, it really couldn't be done. You inevitably leave people out. Third, such an exercise would become presumptuous. Fourth, by focusing on highlights, I can indirectly but more effectively cast a light on the sum of my experiences.

In this book, you will meet a few of the many people who have touched my life. The intersection of their lives with mine has helped color me and make me the person I have become. In that sense, I'm as much a work in progress 53 years after the fact as I was when I first got my professional feet wet, and I hope I never forget that humbling thought.

From all of my professional life, I have learned two overriding things: first, be yourself. There's no substitute for personal integrity. The second is this: to travel hopefully is a better thing than to arrive. Robert Louis Stevenson wrote that, and it's true. Life is a sojourn in which the journey means a lot more than the destination. This book is an account of some of my traveling. I'm delighted to take you with me.

As for the end, well, I'm not quite there. There are, as Robert Frost once wrote, miles to go before I sleep. There are many more people, many more events, and the future is still where it's always been—one day away.

A Series of Snapshots

I chose not to write a straight autobiography for several reasons. For one thing, too many of these strike me as exercises in ego. I have no desire at this stage to put myself in that kind of limelight. Moreover, because autobiography is probably the most self-indulgent literary form, the tendency is often to present a revisionist view of one's life. This can quickly become a great pressure. In a sense, the autobiographer is in a lose-lose situation—if he tells his life with unblinking candor, he will invariably hurt some people. That's just the nature of life. Even the most harmonious existence has conflict, and even the most friendly and loving people have made enemies. These I'd rather pass over. If, on the other hand, the author rewrites personal history by glossing over the rough spots and inflating what he has done and who he is, he cannot be true to himself. That's why I've taken the approach of this book.

Another point about autobiographies is that many fall short because they lack "character" (an odd failing for this genre, which at its best should allow us to get inside another person's life). By that I mean the person failed to convey his or her "essence." I can't exactly define "essence" here, except that it means about the same thing as "substance," even "soul." Essence is what makes you "*you*"—your interests and concerns, your habits and idiosyncrasies, what brings you joy and what ticks you off.

Now I realize it's impossible for a person to say everything about him- or herself. Thankfully so. For one thing, such an account would be too long, too tedious to read. But more importantly, it would lack the discrimination on which good life stories thrive, those *selected* events and vignettes—both little and great—that define someone's life.

Again, that led to the structure of this book. We wanted to present some of these selected moments in my life not because you're necessarily terribly interested in Ken Coleman, but because presumably you're interested in where I've been and what I've seen and who I've met in the sporting life.

As you will see, this book has almost a kind of scrapbook feel to it. My life, even this highly selective version of it, can be presented best not as a dry chronology or a straight timeline, but as a series of snapshots (some literal, some not) that check in on my life at various times, at various stages. Sometimes, a picture with a mere caption will do. Other times, I have to tell you a full story.

In fact, when we first thought about doing the book, Dan and I considered doing it as a scrapbook, literally—just a lot of pictures, mementos, and snapshots, short on the text, long on images. We've retained some of that flavor, but then realized that nothing beats the word—both written and spoken—when it comes to recreating or sharing the nuance of people, places, events, and things. Dan's a writer who does some broadcasting; I'm a broadcaster who does some writing. We both love and respect the power of words.

An analogy to this kind of life chronicle would be a director editing a film. From the miles of footage, the director selects the scenes and images that are meaningful in presenting his theme or controlling idea. That's what the "scrapbook" format does for me. It allows me to develop and share the themes of my life in a way that not only makes sense in terms of this book but also that reflects what I feel is the *true* me. If I cannot feel this way about a telling of my life, there's no point in writing a single word.

Life "in the Toy Store"

I want you, the reader, to understand not so much the dates and events, the "this happened, then that happened." Rather, I want to give you some sense of really knowing me through some of the things I have experienced. How do I react to situations? How do I feel about people? What is important to me? What's not? What caught my eye about a certain player or event?

At the same time, I don't want to club you over the head with it. I'd like to show as well as tell. Though this account is "word rich," I've tried to include a fair amount of photographs and visuals. These visuals are the people and events that have intersected with my life. They each tell their own story. I won't tell you that a picture is worth a thousand words—or ten thousand, for that matter—but I will say that when you see an image, much of the ambiguity goes away. You can see an actual moment frozen in time.

I hope you will find this account of my life in sports interesting. The people are sometimes famous, the places often noted, and the events frequently important. At other times, the people are not so well known but still significant; the places obscure but meaningful; the events small yet revealing. The famous will interest you by the sheer power of their attraction, people like Ted Williams, Jim Brown, Vince Lombardi, and Carl Yastrzemski. As for the rest, they too have something important to say.

An Aftertaste of the Person

As I write this, I have beside my bedside a book called *It Ain't Over*, an account of his life by my dear friend Yogi Berra. Yogi's book is interesting and enjoyable to me, and because I've known Yogi for such a long time, I can see its truth—in addition to the humor one would expect from Lawrence Peter Berra. I see and hear Yogi on every page of that book; that's what I meant before when I referred to "essence." Yogi didn't tear anyone to shreds in his book. He just told his story. Is the *person* there in the pages? Do you find Yogi? If you answer "yes," we can say that the book has succeeded. By that measure, I hope you can honestly see me when you read these pages.

Other autobiographies with "essence" are Dom DiMaggio's book with Bill Gilbert, *Real Grass, Real Heroes,* and Katherine Hepburn's *Me.* These books leave a kind of aftertaste of the person, even after the reading is over. You feel as if you know the person. That's what I'm after in this book. It would be like the two of us meeting and sitting down and swapping stories over a couple of beers.

A lot of autobiographies try to impress people by dropping names. That's a disservice to readers. Readers can sense that, and I think it turns them off. The really great ones don't have to make themselves important. They *are* important. For example, in a book like *My Turn At Bat* by Ted Williams, Ted comes off larger than life because that's the way Ted is. Ted Williams has nothing to prove. He doesn't need to *seem* important. He is, as Reggie Jackson said at Ted Williams Night at the Jimmy Fund in Boston, "a national treasure."

I quite obviously am not. But I've done the best I could in life, and I'd like to think that my being here made a difference somehow. To the millions of fans throughout the nation, but particularly in New England, I know I have made a difference. I know because they have told me and tell me even today. It still gives me the chills when someone will come up to me at a Jimmy Fund golf tournament or after a speaking engagement and tell me that I served as the soundtrack of his or her summers.

I almost don't know how to properly answer when they say "thank you" for that. I feel I should be thanking them for tuning in and for continuing to remember.

Of course, if you're in my line of work, which is broadcasting, you'd better have an ego. There's nothing wrong with that. As Yogi says, the best thing a man can say about himself is this: "There is nothing he would rather be than what he is." The trick is not to let ego get in your way to the point of shutting out or running over other people. I'd rather have dug ditches than let that happen.

I've written this book with the hope that it will entertain and inform people about my professional life in sports, and by extension, to share my life with readers, many of whom were probably my listeners and viewers in my 53 years as a radio and television broadcaster. I'm not writing the book to toot my own horn. I'm not writing to make a lot of money. I've never had a lot of money. Therefore, I don't need it. I'm not writing to impress anybody, nor am I writing to grind any axes.

I'm writing to give people a sense of what it's been like to be me, to have been fortunate enough to broadcast professional sports, to associate with gifted people, to mix with famous ones, to be touched by so many wonderful ones. I want to write about sports, about friends, about . . . living. I've done a lot of it. Some of it is here.

"Regrets, I've had a few. But then again, too few to mention."

I can hear the spring-green voice of Frank Sinatra singing that signature line. He articulates the words in a way whose total effect is quite hard to describe, but it's warm, poignant, and honest. Soft, too, like the pockets in a pair of cotton pants. This signature line could be my own. There's been joy, tranquility, anger, disappointment, anxiety, tragedy, grief. Like anyone else, I've made mistakes. But regrets? Too few to mention. So I won't.

I want to share a taste of my life "in the toy store" with you. I hope you enjoy it.

CHAPTER 2

A Career Gets Under Way

PORTRAIT OF THE BROADCASTER AS A YOUNG MAN

Lost Vision

Let me take you back to a cool November day in 1939, the day my life changed.

I'm 14 years old, in the eighth grade, doing what a lot of kids do in New England at that time of the year—playing field hockey with a friend.

We're in the driveway of my home. Jack McNally's in goal; I'm taking shots. After a while, we switch and I'm the goalie. We're just a couple of youngsters having some fun in the innocent times of the late 1930s in the safety of our Irish Catholic neighborhood in North Quincy, Massachusetts. It was a time of security, when people knew and helped each other. It was a place of stability, where no one moved, where we were proud of our heritage, and where growing up—even through the Depression—was just a joy.

We were having a lot of fun that day in November. I was probably pretending I was Milt Schmidt or Bobby Bauer or Woody Dumart when taking shots, or Frankie Brimskek when playing goal. But on that gray afternoon, there was to be more shooting than just the tennis ball we used for a puck.

As our little game of field hockey ended, my life would never be the same.

One of the guys in the neighborhood had a new BB gun and was trying it out. Unfortunately, Jack McNally was the target. He didn't like getting peppered in the fanny, and neither did I, seeing it happen, so I decided to take the gun away from the culprit. I started across the yard to do it. A bronze blur whizzed toward me. I tried to duck, but I couldn't move fast enough. The BB penetrated my left eye and split the pupil. From that moment on, I was blind in that eye.

I immediately fell to the ground, holding my eye. Jack came over, telling me it would be all right. I remember lying on my back, the cold penetrating my bones. I kind of blacked out after that, not out entirely but in a daze. Jack helped me inside the house, and later at the hospital I learned the hard truth about my lost vision.

Stumbling into a Calling

Prior to that day, I had exceptional eyesight and could hit a baseball hard and often. But let me not delude myself. The odds that I could have been a professional baseball player were slim to none. However, following my injury, there was a less than zero chance. After the accident, I spent a lot of time at home recovering. For the next couple of months, I would sit in the breakfast nook in the kitchen and play a homemade game of dice baseball and broadcast the game aloud to myself, much to the amazement of my mother, Frances (Grady) Coleman.

Those were the first games I called. You know what? I made an amazing discovery.

I found I could string the words together into a flow. I had no trouble with the continuity of saying something. I had stumbled onto my "gift," or what writer Alice Walker once labeled "the work your soul must have." What a tremendous thing to have happened, and I often wonder: if I hadn't had the accident, would I ever have made it into a broadcasting booth?

My mother was born and raised on Mission Hill in Roxbury, which in those years was practically all Irish. Her husband, my father William Coleman, also was from Mission Hill. He worked as a salesman for a number of tire companies in his younger years, but as he came toward the end of his abbreviated life, the government froze rubber as World War II broke out. Shortly after the government's restrictions on rubber, designed to appropriate as much of the commodity as possible for military use, my father found himself out of work. He eventually became the night watchman on the construction job at the Squantum Naval Air Station.

Then my life changed again, in one instant.

On September 10, 1942 at 7 a.m., the first day of my senior year in high school, my mom and sister Ruth woke me up. They told me as best they could that dad had come home from work and died on the kitchen floor of a cerebral hemorrhage. He was 54.

It was a tremendously difficult thing for her to have to tell a young man, and it was even more difficult to hear. How do you lose your father? How do you say goodbye and let go?

I didn't realize this until I was much older, but my reaction at the time was one of shock. My first response was to take a long walk. I didn't really feel much of anything for some time. I felt emotionally numb or neutral. I understand now that this type of reaction is the way people often cope with overwhelming sorrow. Your body and soul get anesthetized, so to speak, to prevent you from feeling the full brunt of the blow too quickly, and it's this numbness that allows you to carry on with your normal day-to-day life. It's healthy and necessary, as long as you process the grief at some point, which I later did.

At the wake, which was held in our home as was the custom back then, I went through two days and nights of anger. All of dad's old drinking buddies were in the kitchen drinking beer and eating the mounds of food sent over by concerned neighbors.

They were telling jokes, laughing, and carrying on, and I had a very hard time with that. I just didn't understand that these were nice people who didn't know how to deal with their sadness and sense of loss any better than I did. I realized that much later.

My dad and I had been close, and we were close because of baseball. Until I started playing ball in the eighth grade for the Sacred Heart CYO team, our typical summer Sunday consisted of 9 o'clock Mass, a big breakfast, a packed lunch from mom, and a doubleheader at either Fenway Park or Braves Field. We would be there when the gates opened at 11 a.m. to watch batting practice, infield practice, the throws from the outfield, the pitchers warming up. Then we would stay for both games. We never had the thought of leaving early, no matter how one-sided the game.

All of it was special to my dad and me, and baseball became our bond. I remember the day we watched Johnny Vander Meer at Braves Field in the start after his two consecutive no-hitters. Johnny went into the fourth inning pitching hitless ball before Debs Garms, who played outfield and also a little third base, singled.

Over the course of broadcasting Major League baseball for 34 years, I can't tell you how often I thought of my father and how so very dearly I had wished that he could have been with me. Dad would have enjoyed meeting the men we had watched together, players like Bobby Doerr, Bob Feller, Lefty Grove, and the kid named Ted Williams. He would have been pleased to learn what fine men they were.

I'm sorry we missed all that, but I will forever be grateful that he loved the game of baseball and that he passed that love along to me.

When I lost the sight in my left eye, my dad—who ironically had lost the sight in his right eye, though I never found out how—would say: "You watch your half and I'll watch mine, and we'll tell each other about it." Such is the dry wit of the Irish.

My mother didn't care that much for baseball, but she used to take me in as a child on Ladies Day (ladies free; children 10 cents). She might not have understood the nuances of baseball, but she sure liked Jimmy Foxx and Joe Cronin, a couple of strapping matinee idols.

One of my regrets in later life, especially when I started broadcasting for the Cleveland Indians in 1954, was the feeling of how much my father would have loved his son being associated so closely with the game and making his living from it. Dad had been a big fan of Al Lopez during his playing days, and Lopez was the manager of the '54 Indians. Dad also liked Tony Cuccinello and Mel Harder, and both were coaches on that team. He had seen Bob Feller pitch, and Feller was still on the Tribe that year. He would have loved the chance to meet and talk with these people, but that chance never came.

It brings to mind the words of Henry David Thoreau, words that have always given me hope and courage: "However mean your life is, meet it and live it. Do not shun it and call it hard names. It is not so poor as you are. It looks poorest when you are richest. The faultfinder will find faults even in Paradise. Love your life."

I don't recall that my dad read many books, but he was a bright man, intelligent, and outgoing most of the time. I never knew how far he went in school. He never mentioned it, nor did he ever discuss high school sports or his buddies with me. It might have happened if he had lived longer.

Mostly, we talked baseball and boxing. Dad would let me stay up late to listen to the fights on the radio. I'll never forget the Joe Louis-Max Schmeling fight (the second one). We were living in an upstairs flat. I can still see my father near his pipe stand with those half-dozen pipes and his Prince Albert tobacco (I used to wonder why he smoked Prince Albert and not Kentucky Club that announcer Fred Hoey used to talk about on the radio when he broadcast baseball games). I remember dad going into the kitchen for something, and when he came back, he asked me if the fight was ready to start, and I said:

"Louis just knocked him out. Two minutes and four seconds of the first round."

He never even got to light his pipe.

"Love your life," Thoreau advised. Well, my father loved his life, and when he died, the people he worked for at the Edmund J. Rappoli Construction Co. did a nice thing. My brother Bill was in the Marine Corps. He had enlisted on December 8, 1941, the day after Pearl Harbor. And so the construction company offered me my father's job—seven nights a week, four until midnight, $1 an hour, $56 a week. I took it, gladly. My mother and I needed the income.

Reporting at 4, I would start at 5 p.m. to clean out the offices, which took until about 8. I'd then get in a pickup truck and put the incendiary gas bombs on the construction sights. From 9:30 p.m. until midnight, I'd gab with the Marine on duty or occasionally even do some homework.

Throughout those years I also played baseball. Even with my left eye sightless, I could still hit some, but I soon turned to pitching. While I didn't have much beyond a big jug-handle curve and a less than average fastball, I had pinpoint control. In pitching, control and location are everything, and so I had some success. Academically, I was an indifferent student. I got by but didn't work hard.

In order to play ball during my senior year, I would trade off with the midnight-to-8 a.m. watchman. His name was Eddie Spitz, a gruff, elderly man, but nice enough when you got to know him. He smoked Turkish cigarettes. Eddie would cover for me whenever I had a game.

On graduation day in June of 1943, every boy in the senior class went into the service with two exceptions. The first was John "Banger" Randolph, a tackle on the football team who unwittingly drank a Coke just before his urine test. They found sugar in his blood and he was classified 4-F. He later went into service.

I was the second 4-F because of my blind left eye. Nonetheless, I wanted to serve. That's how most of us felt about the country back then. We felt it not only to be a duty but also an honor to help actively with the war effort. I kept bugging the draft board, and eventually in November 1943, I entered the Army on what was called "limited service." Limited service was just that: you served in a reduced capacity and would never get close to the theaters of action.

Nonetheless, it got my foot in the door and from there I kept putting in for a regular military commission. My persistence paid off. I finally got waived from my "limited" classification, and the Army sent me to serve in the China-Burma-India Theater with the 472nd Quartermaster Truck Regiment, which drove the Burma Road. I was in Headquarters Company, and we were called the Shamrock Regiment because of our leader, Col. Ireland.

Later I was assigned to the postal unit at Chabua Airfield, about 30 miles from Burma in the Province of Assam. While part of that unit, I was offered the chance to work at the Armed Forces Radio Station in the area and turned it down for a very good reason. The thought of speaking into a microphone to the troops petrified me.

You're laughing, I suppose, at the idea of Ken Coleman being afraid of a microphone, but I was. The experience taught me a valuable lesson. I learned about the nature of fear. Fear bothered me. It gnawed at me, and I became determined to overcome it. For some people, fear cripples. In my case, fear of speaking into a broadcast microphone fueled my desire to succeed. The microphone fascinated me no end.

Walking on Air

That fear and fascination of the microphone prompted me into action. When the war ended, I came home, and in 1946 enrolled to take broadcasting courses at Curry College, now located in Milton, Massachusetts. At the time, the school was located in Boston at 251 Commonwealth Ave. My first day of school was memorable. I walked around outside for a very long time and almost walked away. I tried to talk myself out of it. But something wouldn't let me do it. I was literally at a crossroads. Young Ken Coleman was *that* close to quitting, and you never would have heard a peep from me.

Finally, I gathered my courage, walked in, and made up my mind I would give broadcasting an honest shot. It's true: courage is not the absence of fear; rather, it's acting in spite of being afraid. Once inside the school, I resolved I would not do what I did in high school and slack off with my studies. This time I would work hard. After all, I had my mother to support.

There isn't any map to success in life. Everyone has to find his or her own way, and life's lessons continued. The year I spent at Curry College taught me I could overcome my fear. I learned that fear is a bully, and like most bullies will push you around as long as you submit to the treatment. However, look a bully in the eye and say, "Okay, you want to fight? Let's go," and what happens?

The bully backs down.

I also learned that success in life comes from doing what you can do well. As I had discovered when recovering from my eye injury, I had the gift of gab—I could describe the pictures and accounts of a baseball game, albeit an imaginary one. Deep inside, I knew I could do it for real. More importantly, I enjoyed the daylights out of going on the air for an audience. That's not to say I didn't get nervous—I did then and still do to some extent today.

But I took my inner trust and combined it with hard work. I studied and studied. I constantly practiced my delivery. It paid off.

After one year at Curry College, I got a job at radio station WSYB in Rutland, Vermont in 1947. I got the job at WSYB after doing a guest spot on Art King's show at WEEI in Boston. The show basically aired as a "job center of the air" for returning veterans.

At WSYB, I did it all—newscaster, disc jockey, copy writer, and serving as the voice of the Rutland Royals in the Northern League (similar to today's Cape Cod League). The manager of the Royals, later a catcher with the Boston Braves, was Ebba St. Claire. We also had a young pitcher in junior high school out of Rochester, N.Y., named Johnny Antonelli, who of course later went on to great success in the Majors with the Giants.

Mt. Pelier had a pretty good pitcher of their own, a kid out of Michigan State by the name of Robin Roberts. Yes, the Hall of Famer Robin Roberts. As you can see, it was a good league, and it provided invaluable experience to the novice sportscaster.

After a year at WSYB, I moved on to WJDA in Quincy back in my hometown, where I stayed for three and a half years. I served as a sports announcer and program director from 1948 to 1951. Again, it would be more accurate to say I was the station's all-around guy, its utility man. I did a little bit of everything, from football games to news casting to disc jockeying.

My next stop was at WNEB in Worcester for one year to the day, where I got the job broadcasting Boston University football. In those days, the Terriers had All-American Harry Agannis at quarterback, who in my view was the greatest college quarterback of all time.

In each of those early radio jobs, I tried to learn as much as I could. I asked questions, observed other broadcasters, volunteered for assignments, and went on the air as much as I could. Those years of paying dues led to my first big break. In my 11th month in Worcester, I got a call from WJDA's Charlie Glass, one of the announcers at the Quincy station.

The Big Leagues Call

It is customary in my kind of work to get lots of mail. The bulk of it consists of press releases, which, after a perfunctory look, usually get tossed in the wastebasket. Well, a letter had come addressed to me at WJDA. Fortunately for me, Charlie was looking through my mail and noticed that the letter appeared a little different from the usual press releases and junk mail. It was from an advertising agency in Cleveland, Ohio. My name had been cleanly typed on the envelope, instead of the mass-produced and often smudged mimeographed address labels. It looked like a person-to-person letter, an important letter, so instead of tossing it into the trash Charlie called me at WNEB in Worcester. I asked him to open it and read it to me.

The letter had been sent by Al Fisher of the Lang, Fisher, and Stashower Agency in Cleveland. It said the agency was actively looking for a play-by-play radio announcer for the Browns of the National Football League. Mr. Fisher told me I had been recommended by Tom McMahon of N.W. Ayer, a New York ad agency that placed a lot of sports ads for the Atlantic Refining Company. Mr. Fisher asked if I would be interested.

Would I be interested? He didn't have to ask twice.

He requested that I send him a play-by-play tape as a sample of my work. Unfortunately, I did not have a play-by-play tape of any of my work. So I did the next best thing. I improvised. I sent them a "letter" on tape, telling them I would like consideration for the job. The tape would let them hear what I sounded like, and at the same time would allow me to submit my qualifications in my own voice.

Actually, it worked in my favor. I think they were struck by how unique my presentation was. All the others who applied had done the usual demo thing; they all ended up looking and sounding the same. My taped "letter" stood out. They invited me out to Cleveland for an interview. I had $85 in my savings account, and that was enough for a round-trip ticket by train. I said so long to friends and loved ones and headed way out west—at least it seemed "way out west"—to Cleveland.

I met with Al Fisher at 1010 Euclid Avenue, home of the agency, and we went down to the Leader Building, the headquarters of the

Cleveland Browns. There I met Paul Brown, the famous football coach who had a lot to say in the selection process. We talked football and family for more than an hour, and then as Fisher and I were leaving, I was excused. Al and Paul talked alone briefly. The job had come down to Lindsey Nelson and me.

"The Job is Yours"

They made up their minds quickly and didn't leave me in suspense for long. On the way back to the agency, Al stopped in a drug store doorway and said: "The job is yours. We can pay you $10,000 a year."

Ten thousand dollars! To broadcast professional sports! For a team that two years before had been NFL Champions and the year before played in the championship game as Eastern Division kings! I couldn't believe it. I never imagined I would someday be making five figures. I also had no clue that Al Fisher would make the offer then and there. It was like being in a dream.

I immediately accepted the offer. I never had an easier decision in my life.

I was about to start on my second major voyage. My only other journey had been in the military. I was just an 18-year-old youngster when I went on that one, proud to serve my country. But this was different. At age 27, I was in the Big Leagues. I would be the radio voice of one of the best teams in football, the Cleveland Browns.

So I loaded my Nash Rambler in Worcester and took off for Ohio in mid-July, 1952. The next day, I arrived at Hiram College, about 30 miles southwest of Cleveland.

As I went to sleep that first night, my mind reeled. I knew this was a huge opportunity for me. Sure, I felt apprehensive, but I was determined to succeed.

I actually tried not to think about success or failure. Rather, I remember telling myself that the only thing I could do was my best. The rest would take care of itself.

CHAPTER 3

Into the NFL

HIS NAME: COACH PAUL BROWN

"You Can Call Me 'Coach' or 'Paul'"

Paul Brown was then and remains today one of the pivotal figures in National Football League history, a man whose remarkable lifetime record (213-104-9) is but a partial reflection of the profound influence he would have on the league and continues to have to this day.

I knew I would be working with a man regarded as best of the best in football. I was excited, nervous, and absolutely determined to try to "raise my game" to meet Paul Brown's extremely high standards.

The Browns were quartered in the girls' dormitory at Hiram College. The morning after we arrived, Monday morning in July, 1952, the team had its first meeting. I will never forget the man who spoke.

Paul Brown was a giant of a man who stood five feet eight inches and weighed 150 pounds. He was bald, slender, and soft-spoken but a man definitely in charge. He looked like an accountant but had the power and demeanor that said Authority, capital "A". You knew that immediately upon meeting him. Off the field, he enjoyed golf, gin rummy, and listening to music. On the field, he was all football.

That initial meeting lasted three hours, with a couple of breaks in between. Paul would have his speech prepared and typed out on papers which he kept in front of him. He started out by saying that there was only one reason for everyone to be gathered in this room, and that was to win the championship of the National Football League. Period.

"Anybody who does not share that goal and is not fully dedicated to that goal is welcome to leave right now." Long pause. Paul Brown's voice then sharpened.

"There is absolutely no reason for such a man to be in this room," he said. You could see the players taking the words in, looking at each other, and realizing that this man meant business.

Paul's tone then became gentler, though still firm and businesslike.

"My name is Paul Brown. You can call me coach or Paul, whichever you're most comfortable with. And when you refer to your teammates, I would prefer that you call each other by your first names. It's warmer that way. It's better to say 'Otto' and 'Lou' than to bark out 'Hey, Graham,' or 'Hey, Groza.' I think you'll agree with me."

He then introduced every man in the room.

"This is Otto Graham, candidate for quarterback, from Northwestern. This is Lou Groza, candidate for offensive tackle and place kicker, Ohio State . . ." Everyone, from star on down, was introduced as a candidate.

He went through every man in the room, with all of the players and practically all of the Cleveland media present.

"This is Lenny Ford, candidate for defensive end, Michigan."

Then he got to me.

"This is Ken Coleman. He's our radio announcer. Ken comes to us from Boston."

I was seated next to Ford, a mammoth man, one of the biggest defensive ends in the league. Ford leaned over to me and said: "I figured you for a defensive back."

I whispered back, "Hope I didn't scare you, pal."

After the introductions, Paul said in regard to the newspaper, radio, and TV people: "I want you players to realize that the gentlemen from the press have a job to do. I want you to cooperate with them. But don't ever say anything that will hurt our football team."

Paul pronounced "football" as "foo-ball," one of the few oddities of speech by an extremely articulate man. He explained that the team would start with two-a-day practice sessions and hold classroom meetings at night. Before each practice there would be a meeting to explain what the session was for, what that particular practice was meant to accomplish.

Paul would deliver his welcoming speech in even, matter-of-fact tones, which had the effect of making the words sound even more serious than they might have with an over-the-top delivery:

"We don't want any butchers on the team. No T-shirts in the dining hall. Don't eat with your elbows on the table and eat quietly. We all eat together, every meal, and I want no cliques. I want you to eat at different tables each meal. There is no excuse for missing a meal unless it comes from me. Not an assistant coach or any other official, but from me. I will be at each meal, and I expect you to be.

"We intend to have good people because that's the kind who win the big ones. If you're a drinker or a chaser you'll weaken the team, and we don't want you. We're just here for one thing, to win. If I hear you've been drinking, I'll ask you in front of the squad. If you have, you're through. If you have and deny it, you've branded yourself a liar in front of the team.

"You are to watch your dress, your language, and the company you keep. When we're traveling, stay away from that stranger who may want to take you to dinner or talk to you in the hotel lobby. Maybe he isn't a gambler or after information, but stay away from him anyway.

"The rules for training camp and on the road are simple. In your room at 10 and lights out at 10:30. Sometimes the coaches make a bed check. There is an automatic fine of $500 for any player who sneaks out after bed check. That sticks, too. I have had to levy fines in the past, and I have never rescinded one for subsequent good behavior or meritorious performance."

Paul also talked about the Browns' play book. When teaching a new play, he made every player write down in longhand, not only his part of the play, but everybody else's as well. A player had to learn what every teammate would be doing on a particular play. This was true for every play in the book. Brown was just a meticulous man who as a coach thought of everything. And I mean everything—he even mentioned to the players where the pencil sharpeners were located so everyone would know and not waste time searching for the sharpener.

"I want my players working on the play books," Paul would say. "If they save a minute or two because they know where the pencil sharpeners are, they can invest that time in studying their assignments."

As I say, he missed nothing.

The next day, the team began workouts. Paul Brown's actual practice sessions were brief, usually under two hours. This was one of his many innovations. He felt that if he worked the team beyond two hours, little could be effectively done either physically or mentally. He abhorred coaches who held long practices, with the accent on the physical. He felt a boot camp-type practice was a waste of time. Paul wasn't into that sort of macho display. Moreover, the Browns didn't scrimmage much in practice, either in camp or during the season, except for an annual intrasquad meet that was open to the fans.

During training camp, Paul would divide the team into four units, each working under an assistant coach. In the regular season, he held practices at the time the games would be played. Most coaches practiced in the morning, but Paul figured practicing at the same time as games would give the Browns an edge that was as much mental as it was physical. That was Paul Brown—always looking for anything that could give him a slight edge.

Paul Brown wanted winners, and he had a definite idea of what a winner played like, looked like, and acted like.

"A few years ago we once had a big end," Brown once said. "I heard he chewed tobacco and spit it on the wall next to his bed. Can you imagine that? I went to his room. I told him that I would fine him $500 if he didn't wash down the walls. Then I stood and watched him wash them. Can you imagine living with an animal like that?" (Maule 38).

He also didn't like complainers or whiners. Bellyaching, he felt, was extremely detrimental to a team.

In those early meetings, I had the opportunity of sitting in with the assistant coaches and their people, men like Blanton Collier, Weeb Ewbank, Fritz Heisler, Paul Brinker, and Ed Ulinski—some of the best football minds ever assembled. I say "opportunity." The better word is privilege. Paul expected me to sit in with the coaches. As he put it, "If you're going to broadcast our games, we want you to know our brand of football."

It was enthralling. I can't tell you what that meant to a young broadcaster trying to build his self-confidence. Paul knew that as a member of the broadcasting team, I would have a tremendous influence on "selling" the Browns. He wanted me to feel like part of the team. The ensuing PR benefit to the ball club would then take care of itself. He left nothing to chance.

The Great Innovator

Paul was one of the game's great innovators. He was the first coach, for example, to use a messenger (rotating guards) in and out of the huddle to bring in the offensive play. He also designed the first face bars for helmets, an innovation that prevented countless serious injuries. The draw play? Running pass patterns to specific areas of the field? The development of a taxi squad? A full-time scouting system? They were all Paul Brown's ideas. He was also the first to employ assistant coaches year-round.

Under Paul, the Browns had as many as 32 scouts—mainly college coaches and former players—who were paid to file at least two reports a year that, when cross-tabulated, would include information on every team from every conference in the country. Thus, each year Paul would acquire information on more than 1,200 college players—all this was done long before personal computers, which today make such a job simple. The Browns' full-time scouts would then cull all the material and narrow it down to the best dozen players in the country.

Paul was also the first coach to make extensive use of films to evaluate not only his players but also the opposition. In fact, he was the first to emphasize classroom learning as a part of both training camp and practice. Paul once even experimented with putting a headset receiver into the quarterback's helmet.

Paul was also the driving force in building up a nationwide TV network for the Browns. By 1959, the Cleveland Browns games were shown on 84 TV stations and heard on 43 radio stations throughout the country over Sports Network Inc. Compare that to 1950, when a lone Cleveland station broadcast the six road games.

Dick Bailey, then president of Sports Network, described the potential TV audience for the Browns on a typical Sunday as "astronomical. Easily, 25,000,000 per week can see the Browns." (Scholl).

Paul Brown's use of rotating guards to bring a new play in the huddle changed the game. It took control out of the quarterback's hands and put it where Paul thought it belonged—with the head coach. This set off a debate that raged for years and to some extent continues to this day—should the quarterback or the coach call the plays?

"The quarterback on the field has plenty to worry about without calling plays," Paul once said. "When I assume that responsibility, he's free to concentrate on his passing, his ball handling. I have a lot of help during a game—the other players, a spotter upstairs, the other coaches. I should be able to tell what the situation is much better than the man playing the game" ("NFL Debate..." 80).

When the Browns traded quarterback Milt Plum to Detroit for ex-Brown Jim Ninowski, Jim expressed concern about returning to Cleveland because of what he thought was Paul's restrictive approach in terms of play calling and audibles. By that time, almost every coach in the league allowed their quarterbacks to check off, or go to an audible, if they saw something in the defense they really didn't like. Paul, however, did not allow audibles. Paul thought that over time, a quarterback calling his own plays would become too predictable.

As a player, you didn't lightly disagree with Paul Brown. Once, Paul sent backup quarterback George Ratterman in for Otto Graham when the Browns had a big lead over the Eagles late in the game. George started driving the team downfield for another score when Paul sent a guard in with the next call.

"That one won't work," Ratterman barked. "Go back to Paul and get another one."

The dumbstruck guard just stood there with his mouth open. You never, ever, went back to Paul Brown like that.

"Go on," Ratterman shouted. Finally the guard started to trot reluctantly back to the bench. "Hey, get back here!" Ratterman said. "I was only kidding. What do you want to do, get us both fired?"

Sometimes, Graham would dare to run an audible or call a different play than the one sent in by Paul, but as he said, "When I pulled that stuff, it had to work or Paul wouldn't like it."

New League, Same Results

Under Paul's tutelage, Otto Graham was one of the men—along with Sammy Baugh, Sid Luckman, Frankie Albert, Ace Parker, and Bob Waterfield—who helped turn the forward pass from an oddity into a potent offensive weapon. Protected by the imposing presence of fullback Marion Motley, Graham stretched out opposing defenses with long passes to receivers like Dante Lavelli, Mac Speedie, and Dub Jones.

In 1952, my rookie year as voice of the Browns, my first interview was with Otto Graham. Not long before, I had watched him win the championship against the Rams. I was extremely nervous, and my first question was typically brilliant:

"Otto, how do you feel about this year?"

"Better than you do," Otto answered. "I'm not as nervous as you are."

That broke the ice, and I've always appreciated that. Great athletes transcend eras. Certainly, there were guys who played with and against Otto Graham who couldn't make it in today's NFL, but Graham could play today and he'd be as big a star as he was in his own era. In fact, Graham was the best all-around athlete I ever saw. Besides starring in football, he was a scratch golfer, and he even played for Rochester in the NBA.

You can talk about great quarterbacks like Unitas, Starr, Marino, Montana, Staubach, Young, and so on, but the bottom line is that only one ever got his team into the championship game 10 times in 10 years, and that was Otto Graham. He could feather the short one, throw a bullet over the middle, and launch the long bomb, all with equal finesse. Otto's breathtaking athletic skills coupled with the innovations of Paul Brown simply proved to be more than anybody in the league could handle.

Otto was a superb talent playing for a man who was perhaps sports' all-time great perfectionist. That's why the Browns were so successful under Paul and with Graham, first in the old All America Conference and then later in the NFL. In the NFL, the Browns won three world titles in their first five years: 1950 (a 30-28 thriller over the Los Angeles Rams), '54 (56-10 defeat of the Detroit Lions) and '55 (downing the Rams again, 38-14). They also took the Eastern Division crown in 1957.

In 1950, three AAC teams were merged with the NFL, absorbed by the established league as a way to grow—the Browns, 49ers, and Colts. The Browns had immediate success. In their very first NFL game, the league scheduled them against two-time World Champion Philadelphia Eagles. It was the NFL's way of putting the new team in its place. The Browns, who were the cream of the AAC, would be literally "out of their league" thrown in against the *real* champs … or so the league thought.

The final score of that game told the story: Browns 35, Eagles 10, a win that Paul Brown called the most satisfying of his career.

Paul's preparation for that game illustrates how forward thinking he could be, miles ahead of everybody else. Brown noticed that much of the Eagles' success derived from their big five-man defensive line, especially 280-pound middle guard Bucko Kilroy. He therefore devised a game plan to take advantage of that and turn one of the Eagles' greatest strengths into a weakness.

"We began spreading our offensive line a few inches on each play," Brown recalled years later. "Of course, their defensive linemen took post on the shoulder of an offensive man, so they began to spread too. Before long, that big middle guard was isolated over the center with no one in position to help him" (Maule 36).

At season's end, they beat the Giants 8-3 in a playoff for the Eastern Division crown and defeated the Rams 30-28 in the 1950 title game on the frozen turf of Cleveland's Municipal Stadium.

It was an outstanding team. The offensive line of Lou Groza, Abe Gibron, Lin Houston, and Lou Rymkus was one of the best in all of football. The ends were Mac Speedie, a former hurdler, and the swift Dante Lavelli. The incomparable Graham lined up over center, behind him the great Marion Motley at fullback flanked by Dub Jones and Rex Baumgardner.

There's a funny story associated with the Browns' 56-10 defeat of the Lions in the 1954 title game. Lions quarterback Bobby Layne had talked his team into going to bed by 10 p.m. After the pasting, Layne, one of football's all-time great carousers, cited that game as proof why he needed to stay out at night.

The 1955 title contest was especially rewarding because it was the last game in Otto Graham's career. He went out a winner. The '55 Browns had won their unprecedented tenth straight division title (going back to the old AAC) and came into Los Angeles' Memorial Coliseum on December 26 ready to play before 85,693 fans, a championship game record.

Graham had a great day, throwing for two touchdowns (50 yards to Dante Lavelli and 35 yards to Ray Renfro) and running for two more (a one-yard plunge and a 15-yard scramble). Otto's opposite number, Rams' quarterback Norm Van Brocklin, had a terrible day. The Browns picked him off six times, one for a touchdown, in the 38-14 win.

Thus, in two straight years, the Browns won two world titles by a cumulative score of 94-24. So much for being out of their league.

Injuries were never an excuse with Paul. I remember standing on the sidelines once next to Lavelli, whose leg was in a cast from an injury. Brown walked by and said, "How long you going to be in that thing, anyway?" Paul wasn't trying to be nasty; it's just that he had this single-minded pursuit of perfection and had little patience with anything that got in the way. Again, that's what makes a winner. It may not make you as many friends, but it produces results on the field.

For Paul personally, the toughest part of the game, as he once told me, was letting people go. As long as he coached, he said he never got used to releasing players. This is true, I suppose, only of men who honestly care about their players as people, as I think Paul did.

Paul was one of the game's great teachers. From the late 50s through the 1980s and even into the 90s, there were many "Paul Brown men" coaching in the NFL. These were men who had either played for him or were assistant coaches under him, guys like Don Shula, Weeb Ewbank, Chuck Noll, Blanton Collier, and Bud Grant.

The Winds of Change

Paul Brown's last season was 1962. The year before, Art Modell took over the team. At the time, Paul had a contract with the Browns that gave him total and absolute control over all football-related matters, including players' salaries; all personnel decisions, including trades, cuts, signings, drafts, etc.; the location of the training facilities; and even purchases of medical supplies. There was not one aspect of the team Paul did not control.

Modell, who came out of New York City with a background in Madison Avenue and TV advertising, brought with him an enthusiasm for the game and the money connections to see to the financial security of the club. Art had grown up in Brooklyn and hung out at Ebbetts Field as a boy, where he loved to watch the old Brooklyn Dodgers pro football team.

In 1939, Art found a job at the Bethlehem Steel shipyards for 87 cents an hour, attended night courses at NYU, then went into the Air Force in 1943. After the war, Modell got into television production and quickly rose through the ranks, achieving prominence and success. A theatrical agent named Vince Andrews had learned that the Browns were available for purchase. He contacted Art, and six months later the Browns had a new owner.

Unfortunately, the team did not respond. In 1961, Art's first year, the Browns went 8-5-1, finishing third in the East behind the Giants and the Eagles. In 1962, they barely broke .500, with a 7-6-1 mark.

Of course, the other thing I remember about 1962 was the Ernie Davis tragedy, which to this day remains one of the toughest things I've ever witnessed in sports. Paul Brown had made a series of trades that year designed to strengthen the ball club. He sent quarterback Milt Plum, halfback Tom Watkins, and linebacker Dave Lloyd to the Lions in exchange for quarterback Jim Ninowski, halfback Hopalong Cassady, and defensive end Bill Glass.

Paul also picked up halfback Tommy Wilson from the Rams with the idea that the veteran runner would spell Davis as the brilliant Syracuse rookie was learning both the offense and the ways of the NFL. To back Ninowski, Paul traded for Frank Ryan, a Phi Beta Kappa from Rice University who was part of the Wilson deal. And from Pittsburgh, Paul obtained Charley Scales, a bruising fullback known for his blocking who could come in to spell Jim Brown and give the Browns added backfield depth. In all, Paul shipped off 11 players and got eight in return. In the end, he had a more mobile quarterback, a bigger and deeper backfield, and a tougher defense.

However, the biggest addition to the squad following the 1961 season was Ernie Davis. Ernie actually came to the Browns in a trade that Modell and Paul Brown engineered with the Washington Redskins, who were 1-12-1 in '61. The Browns packaged their first-round pick that year, LeRoy Jackson, and sent him along with running back Bobby Mitchell for the 6-foot-2, 205-pound Davis, who was selected No. 1 by the Skins.

In his final year at Syracuse, Davis averaged an unbelievable 7.8 yards per carry. Running alongside Brown, he would give Cleveland an unstoppable backfield tandem that would not only control the games on the ground but also help the passing game as well. With two marquee running backs, defenses could not stack up against Brown and some of the load could be more evenly distributed (in 1961, Jim Brown had carried the ball 305 times).

The idea of Davis teaming up with Brown in the same backfield caused excitement throughout the league and practically on that basis alone (that and the retooling of the team through the other trades), the Browns were predicted to run away with the Eastern Division in 1962.

It didn't work out that way.

Back then, the reigning NFL Champ would annually play a team of college all stars prior to the start of the NFL exhibition season. Davis, of course, was the featured back for the All Stars as they prepared to meet the World Champion Green Bay Packers. During camp, a routine dental exam revealed Davis was suffering from a virulent form of leukemia, an often-fatal blood disease.

One day Ernie was lining up in the backfield at practice. The next day, he was in the hospital, his life in danger. It didn't make sense, and it hit everybody like ten tons of bricks.

Art Modell brought in the top specialists in the country, sparing no expense in an attempt to get Ernie well. I can still remember going into Art's office and seeing him in tears. That's how I got the news about Davis—from a distraught Art himself. For Modell, losing Ernie Davis was much more than losing a gifted football player.

Art had developed a close relationship with the Davis family, and the news hit Modell extremely hard, almost the way it would a member of the family.

Sadly, Ernie Davis never got to play one down in the NFL. He didn't even take one snap in training camp.

That winter, Ernie played in some pickup basketball games with the Browns, but in February 1963, the leukemia came back with full force. Davis struggled courageously for three months. Finally, on May 16 he came to the Browns offices for one last visit. (Morey 35).

He was there to say goodbye. I expressed my regrets and wished him well. We shook hands. There weren't a lot of words, just eye-to-eye contact that said it all. Ernie then went into Modell's office and was there for some time.

I never asked Art what words the two men exchanged that day, but I know they were deep and meaningful. For years after that, Art would often mist up when talking about Ernie. Two days later, on May 18, 1963, Ernie Davis was dead. He was 23.

Ernie Davis' untimely death hit the entire organization hard. I felt a great sense of loss and couldn't imagine what it must have been like for that fine young man to be robbed of not only his love, which was football, but also life itself. It was a gut check for everyone who was part of the Browns organization, the kind of situation that helps put things into perspective and assigns priorities to the myriad events of our lives. The Browns chartered a plane to fly to Elmira, N.Y. to attend the funeral. It was an incredibly moving day, one I will never forget.

Making a Move

It's no secret that Paul Brown and Art Modell did not get along well and by the time the '62 season was over, the need for change was apparent. The players sensed in Modell an ally they felt they didn't have in Paul, and Art hired assistant coach Blanton Collier to become the new head coach of the Browns. Blanton had been with the Browns for nine years and knew the system as well as anybody. He was the perfect choice.

Collier, gentleman that he was, went to Paul Brown for advice before he accepted the offer. Brown advised Collier to take the job.

True, Paul wasn't happy about leaving the team, but he wasn't going to make it difficult for Blanton. Thus, the new coach took over with the deposed master's blessings.

Collier was an easy going, mild-mannered man who had a great football mind. One of the jobs he had under Paul Brown was to analyze film on every player in every game—literally every player's every play. Few men came into a head coaching job with a better idea of personnel than Collier. Few were better prepared. Blanton became the right man at the right time for the right team.

Under Collier, the Browns had immediate success. In 1963, Blanton's first year, the Browns went 10-4, pushing the Giants to the last game of the season before falling short by one game. In 1964, they went 10-3-1, won the Division Crown and also the World Championship. The next year, the Browns repeated as Eastern Division champs, improving their record to 11-3 only to fall to the Packers in the championship game.

Shortly after Collier took over, he and the coaching staff drew up plays that would take advantage of Jim Brown's tremendous power, agility, and speed, particularly his ability to get around the corner to the outside.

Jim responded. Under Collier's system, he found more room to express himself, both on the field and in the locker room. In 1962, Paul Brown's last year, Jim ran for 996 yards, the only time in his career other than his rookie season that he failed to break 1,000 yards. But for the next three years playing in Collier's offensive system, Brown amassed yardage of 1,863 yards, 1,446, and 1,544, averaging almost six yards a carry in that span. He began enjoying himself once again on the football field and taking a much more active role in the clubhouse.

With Blanton, there was no fuss, no great lectures. His philosophy was basically to let the players play. No one appreciated this more than the great Jim Brown.

CHAPTER 4

Jim Brown

THOSE TOUGH, HARD YARDS

Chiseled out of Granite

In December 1999, the Associated Press voted Jim Brown the greatest football player of all time. Really, there was no other choice.

To the best of my knowledge, I'm the only person who saw Jim play every game he ever played—and every play of every game—as a professional football player. This is more than just an oddity and more than a footnote to my life as a professional sports broadcaster.

It's a very big deal. Why? The AP got it right: simply put Jim Brown was *the best* running back of all time. He destroyed defensive lines, made holes where there were no holes, and once in the secondary, with fleet defensive backs to deal with, he simply outran them.

Jim Brown stood 6 feet 2 inches tall and weighed 228 pounds. He had an 18-inch neck and huge shoulders that tapered gracefully to a 32-inch waist. He was, as they say, a specimen, looking like he was chiseled out of granite, with hard, taut muscles that rippled with every step. In civilian clothes, Jim looked lean, more like 190 pounds, something that can be attributed to his fine taste in clothes but also to the graceful way he moved about, as if even the smallest motion was ripe with athletic potential. He could make walking look like an athletic performance.

Jim Brown had unbelievable physical gifts. He ran with the grace of a gazelle, the speed of a jaguar, and the power of a bull. He was an unparalleled combination of a halfback's speed and maneuverability and a fullback's raw, straight-ahead brute strength. To top it off, Jim Brown was as intelligent a man who ever played the game.

"When Jim is in the lineup," Giants coach Allie Sherman once said, "you start out losing 10-0. You've got to figure he'll score one touchdown at least and get them close enough to kick a field goal. He's just the best I've ever seen" (Donley, "Why Jimmy Brown…" 10).

I agree with Allie Sherman. Jim was then and still remains the best running back of all time. Ever. Period.

This is not to demean Bronco Nagurski, Ernie Nevers, Jim Thorpe, Marion Motley, Walter Payton, Gale Sayers, Barry Sanders, Emmitt Smith, or any other great running back you wish to name. Great they were. But Jim Brown was something else, a runner in his own category.

Jim came out of Syracuse, where he played football and lacrosse and was an All-American in both. A tremendous athlete, Jim could have gone on to success at just about anything he tried. He even once got a letter from Yankees manager Casey Stengel, asking him if he'd be interested in trying out for the team. Jim declined. Norman Rothschild, the Syracuse boxing promoter, offered Jim $25,000 to turn pro and fight as a heavyweight. Again, Jim turned it down, but I'm sure if he did, he would have become a champ.

Jim was one of those rare people who can do just about anything. His football coach at Syracuse, the legendary Ben Schwartzwalder, evaluated Jim this way as Jim was about to turn pro: "I've said it before, and I'll say it again. There's nothing Brown can't do in sports. He starred in football, lacrosse, track, and basketball here, and he could have done well in other sports if he had the time. He will probably go into pro football and become one of the all-time greats" (Silverman 9).

He could have done anything, but Jim wanted to play football and that he did. After the 1956 college football season, four other players were taken before Jim Brown in the NFL draft: Paul Hornung, John Brodie, Ron Kramer, and Len Dawson. Cleveland, picking fifth, selected Brown, who was third in the nation in rushing and sixth in total offense.

I have a special feeling for Jim Brown. We were teammates. Even though I performed in the booth and Jim on the field, we were both members of the Cleveland Browns.

Of all the media people in Cleveland, I was closest to Jim, though it took a while to get on those terms. Jim was quiet, even guarded around people. I think Jim came to appreciate my approach to the game. He knew I understood football and I think he appreciated the dedication I brought to my job. That's how Brown played football—with total commitment. That's also how I approached my broadcasts. I attended as many team meetings as I could and stood in at practice every day. I was around that team as much as any player.

I think Jim also came to respect me because I was a man who kept his word. Jim had been burned by the press before, particularly the national media. Guys looking for stories would print quotes out of context or even deliberately misquote him, and the next thing you knew Jim was making headlines, bulletin board material for use by opponents.

That never happened with me. Jim confided many things to me over the course of our nine years together, and never once did I betray that confidence simply to "get the story." Jim respected that. It's the sort of respect when you can look a man in the eyes and see complete and unqualified trust.

We really got close when he started doing a TV show with me. "The Jim Brown Show" aired on Saturday nights in Cleveland, and we taped on Wednesday. I was the announcer. I will never forget what he said to me when we started out doing the show: "Looking at the red eye of the television camera scares me more than facing the LA Rams' front four." Those were the days when the Rams front line was dubbed the Fearsome Foursome.

Jim not only had superb natural ability but he also worked harder than anybody else. He was that rare talent, a superstar with the work ethic of a second stringer having to bust it on *every* play.

His great ability would have enabled him to coast, but his pride and his pursuit of excellence prevented him from doing that. The result was the greatest combination of power, speed, and intelligence anyone had ever seen, or has seen since, in a running back.

Beyond the Numbers

You can talk about all the statistics you want, but for all of the time Jim played, it was a 12-game or 14-game season, not today's 16 games. There's no question that with an extra two to four games a year, Jim would have amassed a career-yards total well out of reach of anyone. The other thing you have to keep in mind when looking at Jim's total yardage is circumstance. He got the toughest yards when everyone in the stadium knew he would get the ball. Few people fully realize what a difficult accomplishment that is.

In the late stages of a game, with the Browns ahead by seven with five minutes to play, Jim got the ball again and again, simple as that. Some 84,000 people in Cleveland's Municipal Stadium knew he would get the ball. More importantly, 11 men on the other side of the ball knew it. They knew this and still couldn't stop him. He would hammer out four yards, bang the line for five, hit it again for three more, then—wearing down the defensive line—he'd slip through for seven.

Whatever was needed, Jim Brown usually found a way to get it. If he got hit at or behind the line, he would spin out of that first tackle, pick up steam, and somehow get a few yards out of nothing. If he found just the slightest hint of an opening, he was through it in a fraction of a second, his appearance no more than a rumor to frustrated defensive linemen.

Jim Brown had a signature way of getting up after being tackled. After he was brought down, usually gang tackled, he would get out of the pile and slowly walk back to the huddle, walking gingerly, as if he were out of gas or maybe hurt. He walked as if he were Walter Brennan carrying a safe on his back. Jim would creak his way back to the huddle, and the opposing defenses would think they had him. The fans wondered about his health. Was he out of breath? Was he hurt? You couldn't imagine he'd be back for one more play.

But the Browns would huddle up, and Jim would take his place behind Milt Plum, Jim Ninowski, or Frank Ryan. On the next play, Jim would explode into the line with an energy that no one else on the field seemed to have late in the game. That's when he controlled the clock and the game. People remember the long, spectacular runs. I remember those tough, hard yards, and the fact that he got them when the team needed them most.

In his rookie year, Jim Brown gained 942 yards on 202 carries for a 4.7 average. He was just starting to learn the offense and reading the defenses. Sophomore jinx? Jim never heard of it. He began 1958 with 171 yards on opening day against the Rams. By season's end, Jim had set what was then the NFL record of 1,527 yards in a season (257 carries, 5.9 average).

One game that sticks out in 1958 was the tenth game of the year at New York. Oddly enough, for Jim it was a dud. The Giants held Jim to 12 yards in 11 carries. Sam Huff, Rosey Grier, Andy Robustelli and the rest of the Giants' defense were all over him. It was just one of those games where it seemed that on every play, the Giants had called the absolute right defense to shut down the offensive play. That's the game that probably cemented Huff's reputation, particularly as Jim's nemesis. That's also when the critics started in on Paul Brown, that he was running Jim into the ground with overwork. That became a theme for the remainder of Paul's career with the Browns, especially every time the team had a setback or Jim had a subpar game—he had overworked his great fullback.

But what struck me about the 12-yard clunker against the Giants was how Jim rebounded in the last two games: 138 yards against the Eagles in game 11 and 148 yards against the Giants, the same team that shut him down two weeks earlier.

"I never thought I was being overworked," Brown said during that off-season. "In fact, I wouldn't mind carrying the ball even more. After all, that's what they're paying me to do" ("Why They Can't..." 10).

He got his wish. Jim ran for 290 times and 1,329 yards in '59. In 1960, he practically "loafed" by comparative standards, running for "only" 215 times for 1,257 yards. He thus became the first man ever to lead the league in rushing for four consecutive years. Former coach Earle "Greasy" Neale called Jim the best running back in the history of pro football, and Neale had seen them all.

Still, the criticism of Paul Brown persisted. People kept saying Jim Brown would wear down, but year after year Jim led the league in rushing. Critics pointed out that over those four years, Brown carried the ball on almost 40 percent of the Browns' offensive plays.

Paul Brown's explanation? The "big gun" theory: "When you have the big gun, you shoot it."

Jim was tough and intelligent. Even though he led the league in rushing as a rookie, Jim knew he was still learning.

"Actually, I wasn't a finished runner in my rookie year," Jim said. "I used to run with my head down, but I found that I was missing plenty of opportunities to break away. Now I run with my head up. Sometimes the hole isn't where it's supposed to be, and I can veer off and head for where the hole actually develops."

Running on Courage

Part of Jim Brown's intelligence was knowing when to hold his peace and also when to hammer. One of the most memorable games I called involving Jim Brown came at Yankee Stadium, on October 13, 1963. It was a game that not only illustrated his tremendous versatility as a runner but also testified to his courage.

The Browns had won their first four games that year and now were facing their bitter rivals, the Giants, on the road. The Giants got off to a 7-0 lead early in the game. The crowd was really into it. The Browns took the ensuing kick out to the 21, then marched 79 yards with Jim carrying on almost every play. Finally, from the Giants' one, Jim got the ball from Frank Ryan. The Giants' goal-line defense led by John LoVetere stacked up the offensive line pretty good. No problem. Brown scored by leaping over the top.

But an odd thing happened during that drive. Jim would come back to the huddle rubbing his eyes. He spent the rest of the game trying to find relief from some irritation in his eyes.

Late in the second half, with the Browns trailing 17-14, Jim scored again. Ryan called "85 flare screen" in the huddle. Frank dropped back while Jim ran a flare 15 yards to his left (Riger 31). Ryan delivered him the ball with a nice, soft toss.

The play worked as designed. As Jim cut inside with the ball, two blockers took care of Tom Scott on the outside. Sam Huff was waiting ten yards deep, and as Jim came up, he gave Sam a slight juke inside, then swerved outside, faking Huff right out of his shoes.

Jim then put it into high gear. Erich Barnes dove and came up hugging air and Jim was off. He went straight down the left sideline with that tremendous speed, leaving the defense in his dust. The play went for 72 yards and gave the Browns a lead they never relinquished.

Later, Brown scored his third TD on a 32-yard run in which he completely reversed his field and snake-hipped his way around several befuddled Giant defenders.

This run illustrates Jim's gifts as a runner.

Early in the game, Collier had Brown lined up in his normal "6 position," just behind the offside tackle. However, Huff picked this up and began shooting over center and into the Browns backfield before Jim could get to the strong side. At the start of the second half, Jim asked Frank Ryan what he thought about Jim lining up not in the "6" but in the "2 position," directly behind the center. Ryan liked it. The two were the only ones who knew about the change. With Jim running from a 2 spot, he would be two steps closer to the hole, and if Huff shot center, he'd be at least one step behind, even if he came in unmolested (32).

The tiny adjustment made a huge difference. On Jim's third TD run, he ran from the 2 spot, from which he'd have three options —over center, off tackle, or outside. He chose outside because that's where the opening was. One of the linemen put a great block on Andy Robustelli and halfback Ernie Green took out linebacker Jerry Hillebrand. If Jim had continued outside, he would have picked up the first down easy before the defense caught up with him. But Jim wanted to score and he took a calculated risk. He cut sharply to his right and ran 30 yards straight across the field. This lateral move left the defense going the wrong way. Jim opened up full throttle and scored.

Jim was always a ferocious runner, but this day he seemed more fired up than ever. He had displayed his amazing versatility, scoring on a 1-yard plunge, a 72-yard screen, and a 32-yard dash. The Browns won, 35-24.

The Giants, especially linebacker Sam Huff, always played Brown hard. The Giants, in fact, often gave Huff instructions that he was to hit Brown on every play, regardless of whether or not Jim carried the ball. After the game, I went into the clubhouse and noticed that Jim's eyes were all puffed up and red. He didn't say anything about it to anyone. He just let it pass, even though all the media were around him in front of his locker room wondering about it. They let it pass, too. It was clear that Jim didn't want to talk about it, and no one felt comfortable bringing it up. That's just how it was with Jim Brown. You gave the man his space.

The following Wednesday night, when we were taping his TV show, he leaned over and said to me: "You know what happened with my eyes?"

"No, Jim, but like everybody else I've been wondering about it."

"Whenever we got down into the infield part of the stadium, the Giants were throwing dirt into my eyes. Everything was blurry. They were trying to get me mad enough to get me into a fight and out of the game. I wouldn't fall for it."

Jim paused. His eyes narrowed and the expression on his face hardened.

"But I tell you what, Ken. If it ever happens again, I'll get whoever did it. Right then and there. I guarantee it. That person will never think about doing it again. Nor will anyone else."

The Giants' Tom Scott, a man who liked to take liberties with opposing ballplayers, once nailed Brown with a late hit. Jim said nothing, but later in the game, he took a pitchout on the left side and Scott tried to make the tackle. Tried, I say. Jim lowered his head and just barreled him over. Scott had to be helped off the field.

Following a 7-0 start in 1963, the Browns faltered and they ended up at 10-4 to finish behind the first-place Giants by one game. In the NFL Championship game, the Giants faced the Chicago Bears (Chicago 14, New York 10). I broadcast that title game, with Bill Osmanski, former Holy Cross and Bears great, working as my color analyst.

The Giants-Bears title game was broadcast on closed circuit TV throughout Chicago at selected locations, including the cavernous McCormick Place and a downtown theater. In those days, games were subject to local blackout.

Osmanski had prepared a massive amount of material for use during the broadcast, but then a funny thing happened. The crowd at McCormick Place was making so much noise they couldn't hear the broadcasters. So my producer Marvin Halpern requested that I just handle it like I was a public address announcer at the stadium, and that's just what I did. They'd run a play, and I'd say something like, "Wade the ball carrier. Huff makes the stop. Second down, 7" or "Tittle complete to Morrison for seven yards. O'Bradovich makes the tackle. First and ten." Poor Bill was left there with all his notes and nothing to say.

Sadly, 1963 was marked by one of the most tragic events in the history of our country. On November 22, 1963, at 12:31 p.m. Dallas time, President John F. Kennedy was assassinated while riding in a motorcade through Dealey Plaza. We were all shocked, of course, by the news from Dallas. We wondered if Commissioner Pete Rozelle would call off the NFL games that weekend, but he ordered the games to be played. Football was the game Jack Kennedy loved to play, and Rozelle thought it would be better this way.

Like everyone else who was around at the time, I remembered precisely where I was. I had just left the WDOK studios on my way to watch the Browns practice at League Park. I turned on the radio and heard the announcement that the president's motorcade had been fired upon in Dallas. They didn't say if the president was hit because they didn't know. But when I got to League Park, everyone was huddled on the field, listening to a portable radio and the word came through. President Kennedy had been murdered.

Of course, we all followed the tragic events of that weekend on television. The Browns played the game at home on Sunday, but it wasn't televised. The entire nation was transfixed, glued to their screens by the unfolding drama. I'll never forget that Sunday.

The locker room, usually a noisy place, was somber. At one point while the guys were getting suited up for the game, Jim Ninowski, always a kidder, burst into the clubhouse, breathless.

"Did you hear?" Jim cried excitedly. "Somebody just shot Oswald!" The guys got on him.

"Geez, Jim. Not now. Will you stop kidding around like that."

"No. No. It's true." And so it was. The murder of Lee Harvey Oswald by Jack Ruby was an anti-climax. We were all numb at that point and this execution of Oswald by Ruby, the first-ever murder on live national TV, added to the feeling of unreality.

Later, the Browns beat Dallas to move into a three-way tie for first with New York and the Steelers, but I'll tell you, the game seemed completely insignificant. I've never been in a winning locker room quite like that one. There was no celebrating, horsing around, laughter, or that sort of thing. Guys were quiet. They just came in, got undressed, talked quietly, and went home.

Then the season resumed, but the team lost some key games down the stretch. Defenses were still puzzled, though, on how to stop Jim Brown. The answer was simple: "You don't."

Stopping Brown could give a defender 15 minutes of fame. In a game on November 10, 1963, Steelers linebacker Bob Schmitz blitzed with the Browns backed up near their own goal line. As Frank Ryan pitched the ball to Jim, Schmitz came racing through. Halfback Ernie Green didn't pick him up, leaving Jim exposed. Normally, Jim could shake the tackle, but Schmitz hit him just right, and Jim went down, like a mere mortal. Caught in the end zone, the play went for a safety and ironically provided the margin of victory in a 9-7 Steelers' win.

The next day, the papers were full of Schmitz's play. He was named NFL Lineman of the Week, practically on the strength of that one play. That's what it meant to bring Jim Brown down alone.

Opposing defenses tried to key on Jim, but for the most part it didn't work. There were guys around the league who would go out of their way to "get Jimmy Brown," but Jim never missed a game in his entire nine-year career from 1957 to 1965. That's one of the most amazing facts from a long list in Jim's career, especially given the number of times he carried the ball and the physical beating he would take in a game.

Jim only had to leave a game once because of injury. That was the last game of the 1959 season against, you guessed it, the Giants. Andy Robustelli stood Jim up and nailed him with a direct hit. It was hard to hit Jim that way, given his combination of speed, power, balance, strength, and shiftiness.

Anyway, Robustelli nailed him, and Sam Huff came along to finish the job. Jim woozily got to his feet and he had to be taken out with a concussion. It was the only time I can ever remember Jim being visibly shaken. Later in the game, Paul Brown sent Jim back in, and he took some criticism from the writers for that. But that was Jim: he insisted he was ready to get back in the lineup. For him, it was both a matter of pride and making a statement to the Giants defense that "You can't stop me."

Jim and Paul Brown didn't get along well, but they shared a deep and mutual respect. They respected each other as men, even if they could agree to disagree on issues pertaining to football. Jim thought Paul Brown's style of offense was too conservative for his style of running.

For his part, Paul Brown wanted to make use of Brown's special talents within the framework of the deliberate type of game plan the coach favored. Blanton Collier saw more possibilities for Jim, which is easier for a new man to do because he wants to put his own stamp on things. Both Paul and Blanton had a valid approach in their use of Jim Brown. Both philosophies were justified because both philosophies worked.

Strictly Business

Jim and I were not only teammates but also business partners. It was a billiard parlor—okay, a pool hall—but a very nice one, what people today would call "upscale." It was located off the campus of Kent State University in Ohio. We called it All-Pro Golden Cue. Some other members of the Browns were also in the venture, but Jim was the biggest name and biggest draw.

On opening night, the great Willie Mosconi came in representing Brunswick Equipment Company. We had 18 Brunswick tables in the establishment. Because I was the best pool player in the ownership group, I played Mosconi in a 150-point game of straight pool. Let me put it politely: I finished second.

Willie then put on a display of some trick shots and ended up with the one where a handkerchief is put over the balls. He called on Jim Brown to make the shot. Jim was not a pool player and later told me he was nervous about having to make the shot. But Willie set up the balls and told him what to do. Jim listened intently, then did it. He pulled the cue back, shot, and all of those pool balls went flying into pockets. The stoic running back almost came unglued with excitement.

Jim told me later: "I was nervous because when you're an athlete, you're supposed to do everything right. That shot just amazed me."

Jim showed his finesse in making that shot, but football, of course, is a game that feeds on violence—as a defender, you not only want to stop the guy with the ball, you want to really punish him. That's the attitude. All the guys understand that and not only expect it, they *respect* it. In this regard, Jim could take a hit as well as anybody. In return, he was a punishing runner, and he often left defensive players lying on the ground.

That's what football players mean when they talk about "getting physical." It's code for "the need to intimidate and punish." If there was ever one man in football who couldn't be intimidated, it was Jim Brown.

Another great story goes back to the 1959 season, when the Colts and Browns hooked up for the first time since Weeb Ewbank left as Paul Brown's assistant to take over the head coaching job of the Colts. It wasn't a friendly parting, and there was a lot of anticipation going into the game.

It was a big game for both clubs, not just because of the Ewbank-Brown sideshow. The game was also billed as a showdown of sorts between Colts quarterback Johnny Unitas and Jim, the league's two reigning superstars.

The Colts studied films of Jim Brown and worked in practice on how he could be stopped. The Colts' great defensive tackle, Gene "Big Daddy" Lipscomb, got up in one of the meetings and started thumping his gigantic chest:

"Don't you worry none about that cat. Big, strong Daddy's gonna take care of him. Don't worry, because I've been waiting a long time to get my hands on that cat. Big, strong Daddy will take care of him" (Nutter 90).

Big Daddy was a prototypical defensive lineman who stood 6 feet 7 and weighed 290 pounds. He also had enormous arms which, when spread out in a wingspan, made it extremely difficult for runners to get by him. He played on a great line that included Gino Marchetti, Art Donovan, and Don Joyce.

Weeb Ewbank described Big Daddy's defensive technique this way: "On a running play, he sorts out everyone he runs into and keeps the guy with the ball." Big Daddy would use his size to drive the offensive lineman back on his heels a couple of yards, then use that brief instant of time to observe how the play was developing. On a pass, Big Daddy would put on a ferocious bull rush. On a run, he'd be after the ball carrier. He created such a jam in the line that often he'd disrupt the play. He wouldn't get the tackle, but he'd force the back to make a different cut, usually running into Marchetti, Donovan, or Joyce.

Before the Browns-Colts showdown, Ewbank told the reporters, "Just stop that big guy Brown, and we'll win."

Easier said than done. All Jim did was score five touchdowns to spark a 38-31 win. Jim had almost 200 yards against Big Daddy, Marchetti, and company.

Jim's first touchdown was unforgettable. He took a pitchout from quarterback Milt Plum. Five defenders had shots at him, but Jim either juked around them or they just bounced off him. He ran with a burst of explosive power, and once he got past the line, no one could bring him down one-on-one. The play went for 70 yards. Following that, Jim scored on a 17-yard draw play then three times from inside the five.

Big Daddy could be seen walking off the field, shaking his head in disbelief.

"I don't hit that cat as often as I'd like to," Big Daddy said. "And even when I do hit him, sometimes he don't stay hit" ("Why They Can't..." 10).

The death of Big Daddy between the 1962 and 1963 seasons (May 10, 1963, just eight days before Ernie Davis died) of a heroin overdose shook the football world, and I know it bothered Jim Brown. Big Daddy used to see Jim as a threat, a challenge that both men enjoyed.

Gene "Big Daddy" Lipscomb had a tough life. When he was 11, his mother was stabbed 47 times and died on a street corner. At 16, he got off the streets and joined the Marines, where he drew his first athletic attention as a shot putter (Morey 34). He came into pro football hungry and played that way. His death and Ernie Davis' death, occurring as they did just days apart, left the NFL reeling.

"Act Like You've Been There Before"

One of the greatest tributes ever paid to Jim came from his rival and nemesis from the Giants: "If it hadn't been for Jim Brown, nobody would have ever heard of Sam Huff," said Huff of his fabled rival.

Huff was an interesting man. Robert Lee Huff came to the Giants out of Edna, West Virginia, a small coal-mining town in the northern part of the state. For a reason now lost in the obscurity of time, a grammar school teacher nicknamed him "Sambino." The nickname stuck, and schoolmates shortened it to Sam.

Football had been Sam's ticket out of the mines, where his brother and father worked. He wasn't particularly big, standing at just over 6 feet 1 and weighing about 225. But he tackled as hard as anybody and used his guile to where it was almost like having a defensive coordinator right there on the field. He starred at linebacker for four years at West Virginia University in Morgantown, and the Giants drafted him No. 3.

He was a perceptive ball player, one who made few wrong moves, and he enjoyed many "interesting afternoons" tangling with Jim Brown. Put these two types of players on the field opposing each other and you have the formula for a series of epic encounters. The fans loved it and so did the league.

In one game in the early 60s, Sam stopped Jim the first three times he got the ball for no gain, a one-yard gain, and a one-yard loss—three carries, no yards. Each time, as Jim would get up slowly from the pile, Huff would lean over and say, "Jim, you didn't look so good on that."

Jim said nothing. Later in the game, Jim broke a run by running right through Huff and breaking the tackle. He scored. On the next Browns offensive series, Jim walked by Huff.

"I look OK now?"

Sam just smiled.

Look at films of Jim Brown scoring a touchdown. He did it with understatement, with class. When Jim scored, he wouldn't celebrate, dance, or engage in any of the histrionics that are now so commonplace in today's NFL. He had a great quote about why he was never demonstrative when scoring, something he used to tell the other Browns ball carriers:

"Act like you've been there before."

That says it all. A man who has "been there before" doesn't need to call attention to himself or show off.

Today, on just about every play in a football game, there's someone doing a dance or showboating, to the point where it's gotten completely out of hand. What started as celebrating has now turned into taunting. You see it a lot in the NBA also. In fact, it came to the point where the NFL has had to step in and threaten sanctions against certain demonstrations, such as the awful "throat-slash" gesture that had become popular in 1998 and 1999. Just before Thanksgiving weekend in 1999, the NFL had to threaten fines and penalties for the throat-slash taunt. It's just a terrible thing to allow, and to the NFL's credit, it did something.

When I was broadcasting in the NFL, this kind of act would have been unthinkable. First, if any player did something like this, the coaching staff would step on him hard. I mean, just try to imagine Paul Brown or Vince Lombardi tolerating the throat-slash gesture. Second, if the coaches didn't see it, the other players would do their own policing. Believe me, the "hot dog" would be cut down several pegs right then and there, by his teammates.

Football and Beyond

When Jim retired at the end of the 1965 season, he had run for 12,312 yards on 2,359 carries for an amazing 5.2 yards per carry. He scored 106 rushing TDs, won two MVP awards (1958 and 1965), and led the league in rushing eight of his nine years. In 1971, Jim was elected to the Pro Football Hall of Fame. His retirement caught everyone by surprise.

When Jim talked about walking away from the game, no one took him seriously. Magazines would run stories titled, "Jimmy Brown —Why He Can't Quit." Then, on April 12, 1966, Jim made a stunning announcement from a London, England, sound stage, where he was starring in "The Dirty Dozen" for 20th Century Fox.

He announced he was quitting football. Initially, he had planned on playing through the end of his contract, which expired after the 1966 season. Jim had discussed this with Art Modell. He liked the way LeRoy Kelly was developing as a runner and thought that ten years in the league would be enough. So after the 1965 season was over, we all counted on having Jim for one more year. That's why there was surprise in Jim's announcement—it wasn't *that* he was quitting but *when*.

"I'm getting older (he was 30 at the time) and when I'm through running, I don't want to be a walking mess of scars … Football isn't my life," he said about his decision to retire. "Football is a very short career, a very small part of my life that does not take on the greatest importance. It's been very good to me, and you know it has given me a lot of things. Financially, it's been tremendous. I think the education I had—at high school and at Syracuse and being in the Army for a while—I think this is very important to me. So, consequently, football plays a part of my life, but it is not the most important part. I am looking forward to the business world and to various other things that can be more important" (Saunders 68).

It was an honest man speaking the truth.

I think three things prompted Jim to push up his retirement. First, he wanted to concentrate on his acting. Second, he had accomplished all that he had set out to do on a football field. And third, Jim was looking beyond football for a wider meaning in his life. Jim took his acting seriously, and he had made a big impression in Hollywood.

"We were very happy with him," recalls Bill Howard, casting director in Jim's first film, "Rio Conchos," in which he played a U.S. Calvary sergeant. "Old timers couldn't believe their eyes. There's a certain naturalness about Jim. He photographed with a certain dignity. He never blew a line or muffed a scene. We never had to do one over because of him. He was letter perfect" (80). When the film had its Cleveland premiere, I emceed the gala event.

It is now 2000, 35 years since Jim Brown retired. He has spent much of that time working on behalf of African Americans on a program that I believe is right. He feels that the only way for black people to better themselves is through economics, as all other ethnic and racial groups have done.

Jim preaches the philosophy of self-reliance—that the best way up from the bottom or near the bottom is not to wait for a handout but to become proactive. This means making good decisions, working on self-improvement, and assuming self-responsibility. He teaches the skills of the entrepreneur and talks about the need for a good work ethic. It is not an easy road, and it is not in my capacity to explain how Jim's program works. I just know that it does. I think it is the right road, and I admire Jim for having the courage and the selflessness to give so much of himself to help others.

As early as 1964, Jim founded the Negro Industrial Economic Union, an association that set up programs for job placement and low-interest business loans. There were chapters in Cleveland, Los Angeles, and Boston.

In 1965, Jim Brown became an investor and vice president in Main Bout Inc., an organization that promoted heavyweight champion Cassius Clay. Main Bout promoted Clay's fight with George Chuvalo in Toronto, right around the time Clay was changing his name to Muhammed Ali and declaring he didn't want to fight in Vietnam or join the military service. Jim even did television color commentary for the Chuvalo-Ernie Terrell WBA heavyweight title fight.

Brown took some serious flak from his association with Ali, who was just about to discard the name of Cassius Clay. It was Ali, not Clay, who set the country on its ear with his strident Black Muslim views and what were seen by many as his anti-patriotic views. Brown defended his interest in Clay/Ali and Main Bout as strictly a business venture. It had nothing to do with the Black Muslim movement, he said.

"I have never been pressured to join the Black Muslim movement. Not by Clay, Herbert Muhammad, or anybody else. I have my religion and they have theirs. I don't believe in the things Clay does and he doesn't ask me to. I don't ask him to go along with my beliefs, and our relationship has been on a strictly business basis.

"We all have the right to feel and act as we want. I spent four years in the ROTC while at Syracuse, and I was commissioned a second lieutenant. I put in my tour of duty at Ft. Benning, Georgia. And went on to complete four years in the active reserve, coming out a captain. I feel my military activities speak for me on the subject of the draft and service to my country" (69, 74).

Jim brought 15 other African American pro football players into Main Bout as theater exhibitors, giving them a chance to make money, including Ernie Green, Cookie Gilchrist, and Johnny Brown. That's the kind of person Jim Brown is.

Jim had many friendships with athletes in other sports, including Ali and Wilt Chamberlain, who died so tragically in 1999. Jim was once asked to name the man he thought was the greatest athlete in sports.

"Wilt Chamberlain," he replied. He then told a story of a party one night in Los Angeles. After the party, Wilt challenged Jim to a race in the street. Jim described Chamberlain's huge stride and how surprisingly fast Wilt could move. Then he started to embellish on Chamberlain's speed. He made Wilt sound like a combination of Jessie Owens, Maury Wills, and Bob Hayes, three pretty fast runners. He then got that twinkle in his eyes.

"But Jim," the writer asked, "if Wilt is so fast, how on earth did you manage to beat him?"

"I beat him off the mark," Jim said with a grin.

Right around the time Jim retired, a sportswriter once asked him why he quit football and was spending his time working toward correcting racial injustice. He answered this way:

"Because I'm a man, and I have to be a man before anything else. I have to be true to myself. I don't want to become financially successful by losing my self-respect. I have to live with myself."

I haven't seen Jim since the championship game at the end of the 1965 season. He was in Cleveland for an event in 1992, where my son Casey is a successful TV and radio sportscaster. He told Casey, who in the early to mid 1960s worked at the Browns training camp as a youngster, "Say hello to your dad for me."

I took that hello with the graciousness with which it was given and I say in return here on the printed page: "Hello, friend Jim."

I like him very much, and not just because he could run with the football. I liked him as a man who played football, but also as a man.

CHAPTER 5

The Browns Get Back on Top

PARROT FEVER AND A MAN NAMED VINCE

Asymptotic Values

Besides the production of Jim Brown both on and off the field, another reason for the success of the Browns under Blanton Collier was the emergence of quarterback Frank Ryan as a leader. Frank's performance helped put the Browns over the top. Ryan developed consistency in 1963 and especially in '64, the one thing that had eluded him in his career up to that point. Under Ryan's direction, the Browns' offense found its pace.

Frank Ryan was one of the most amazing men I have ever met in sports. He had a genius IQ. He studied pure mathematics in college at Rice University, where he wrote a dissertation titled, "A Characterization of the Set of Asymptotic Values of a Holomorphic Function in the Unit Disc." Deep stuff, I mean to tell you, far beyond the intellectual means of a humble sportscaster who had trouble balancing the checkbook.

Mickey Herskowitz, sports editor of the *Houston Post*, once asked Frank to explain what his thesis meant in layman's terms. Ryan scribbled out something on a piece of paper and handed it to Herskowitz. It read:

"It concerns a set of complex numbers which arises as limit values of a certain type (holomorphic) of function designed in the unit disc when the independent variable is restricted to an arc which tends to the boundary."

Mickey stared at the paper and said, "Thanks a lot. That certainly is simple enough" (Hand 23).

Ryan was a college professor, played chess, strummed the guitar, looked a little like actor Jimmy Stewart, and had a great, bone-dry sense of humor.

Frank had a frustrating early career. In college at Rice, he was second string behind King Hill. With the Rams from 1958 to 1961, Frank again rode the bench behind guys like Zeke Bratkowski, Billy Wade, and Buddy Humphrey, waiting for a chance that never came. When he came over to the Browns in '62, he was again a backup, this time to Jim Ninowski. Frank had actually wanted to be traded to the Steelers, where his good friend Buddy Dial was a star wideout. When word came that he had been traded not to Pittsburgh but to Cleveland, his wife Joan said Frank just sat there in his chair, stunned, with his head in his hands. But she reminded him that this could be his big break. That's what it turned out to be.

Looking back on his first year with the Browns, Frank once told a writer, "What bothered me was the fact that Ninowski got 75 percent of the work in camp, and I got about 25 percent. (Paul) Brown had traded away Milt Plum (for Ninowski), and I guess he had to make it look good. Probably if Jim and I had a war right there, he would have beat me, fair and square. But I was still bitter from my days with the Rams" (Cartwright 81).

As it turned out, Ninowski got injured late in the '62 season, and Paul Brown put Ryan in at QB. Frank did a good job with his audition, and when Blanton came in 1963, that wasn't lost on him. He announced Ryan would be No. 1. Blanton said he didn't want a quarterback controversy. Blanton had watched Ryan closely in the games he started in '62 and liked what he saw: a man who was cool under pressure. Collier said Ryan could be the kind of quarterback the team needed to keep defenses honest and to complement the Browns' tremendous running game. Frank scrambled a little too much for Blanton's preference, but the coach liked Ryan's makeup.

Part of the problem of the Browns from 1956, the year after Otto Graham retired, to 1963 and Collier's appointment, was instability at quarterback. The Browns had used seven quarterbacks in that time—George Ratterman, Vito "Babe" Parilli, Tommy O'Connell, John Borton, Len Dawson, Milt Plum, and Jim Ninowski. That's why Paul Brown reacquired Ninowski in 1962, because he felt Plum wasn't the man to lead the Browns' aerial attack. Collier solved this problem by tapping Frank Ryan as the No. 1 quarterback.

"Blanton," Ryan once said, "was the first coach to give me something concrete. The others just accepted the fact that I could throw a football, but Blanton reduced throwing to a procedure, a series of basic steps, so when things went bad, I could check and find out why—was I holding the ball too long? Not watching the right spot? Not looking quickly enough to my secondary target?"

That approach was perfect for an analytical man like Frank Ryan.

"I remember going to (coach) Bob Waterfield my last year with the Rams," Ryan continued, "and telling him about a problem—a thing of getting tense while I was waiting back in the pass pocket. The more time I had to throw, the more nervous I got. Blanton would have an answer. He would have told me to concentrate on my key. The point is, he gave me specific answers and I'm a man who needs specific answers, even if they are wrong. I need something to think about. Otherwise, I flounder" (81).

Frank had a great sense of humor, and again, it was just what the team needed. Jim Brown could be an intimidating man and could get into quiet, serious moods, and the team needed another leader who could offset that, augment that really, and loosen the team up when required.

One time in 1964, Frank got into Lou Groza's equipment bag and secretly put a dead seagull in Lou's kicking shoe (30). On the flight from Cleveland to St. Louis, Frank made a big deal about walking around the cabin and telling everyone a story of people getting violently ill, even dying, from what he called "parrot fever." He said it was some kind of disease from birds. He played it up real good and later in the locker room, when Lou got his cleats out, he discovered the bird. With Ryan's story of "parrot fever" still fresh in his mind, Groza jumped back a mile. He told the clubhouse boy to get him some disinfectant, and Lou spent the next two hours treating the shoes.

Frank wasn't there when Lou found the bird, and it's lucky he wasn't, because Lou was hopping mad. But all the guys got a huge laugh, afterward joined by Lou Groza. It had the effect of loosening up the whole club.

Ryan's pranks were always in good taste. He loved a gag, but he wasn't one of those guys who always has to be "on." Actually, Frank provided leadership from the quarterback's spot as much through his reserved demeanor as through his love of a practical joke. It was an interesting study of one man's personality contrasts.

During the team's annual open house and photo day in 1963, Frank pulled one of his best gags. He graciously posed for all the typical quarterback shots that photographers took in those days—running back crossed step, ball cocked, and looking down field; or arm poised to throw, that sort of thing. Everything was great except that in all the photos, Frank had posed as a left-handed QB (Hand 21). Sports editors across the country were baffled when they saw the *left-handed* Frank Ryan, and you have to believe that many photographers got chewed out by the sports desk for not picking up on the stunt. Some papers actually ran photos flopped, showing Frank right handed. Of course, there was one minor problem: Frank's number 12 would come out in reverse.

On the field, Frank Ryan again presented a study in contrasts. He had the disciplined analytical skills that were a prerequisite to his calling as a mathematician, skills he put to great use on the football field. Conversely, he could improvise and respond to a particular game situation with spontaneity and flair.

His biggest flaw as a quarterback was inconsistency. Frank could be brilliant one game and erratic the next. Sometimes, he'd manifest this Jekyll-Hyde tendency in the same game. He'd be on target for one quarter and come out the next looking as if he had never thrown a football. Collier was the perfect coach for a man like this. Ryan knew Blanton wouldn't pull him for throwing a couple of bad passes or having a couple of bad games, something that happened when Frank was with the Rams.

Frank's best season for the Browns came in 1964, when he quarterbacked the team to the World Championship. In the game that clinched the Eastern Division crown against the Giants, Frank completed 12 of 13 passes for 202 yards and five touchdowns.

The following June, Ryan completed course work for his doctorate in mathematics at Rice. Soon after, he was a professor teaching junior and senior math classes at his alma mater. Frank was often compared to another egghead quarterback of the time, Charlie Johnson of the St. Louis Cardinals. They were both Texans, both had great years in '64, and like Ryan, Johnson earned his Ph.D. the following June (20).

One sportswriter once observed that Ryan was easy to follow but hard to understand. Well, one man who did was Blanton Collier, and because of it, the Cleveland Browns became football's World Champs.

Another key figure on that '64 Browns team was veteran defensive tackle Dick Modzelewski, who came over that year from the Giants. Dick knew what it was like to be a winner and play in big games, having appeared in the previous three title contests—all losses (to the Packers in '61 and '62 and to the Bears in '63). The losses left Dick with a burning desire to win a world title. Some of that rubbed off on his new teammates. Modzelewski became a stabilizing influence, especially when injuries hit.

In the season's opener, defensive tackle Frank Parker blew out his knee in the first half and was lost for the season. It was a big loss, as the team needed Frank's 6-foot-5, 270-pound frame to put heat on opposing quarterbacks and clog up the line. Then in game four, defensive tackle Bob Gain broke his leg. The line needed shoring up and Dick filled in admirably, anchoring the defensive line, playing lots of minutes, and providing a huge dose of veteran leadership. When the team felt down, Dick was there to lift them up.

For example, following the 1964 season's 13th game, a 28-19 loss to the St. Louis Cardinals, the Browns were at their lowest point of the year. They had gone into the game coming off a loss to the Packers, and their lead in the Eastern Division had been shaved to a razor-thin half-game. The press and the fans began to harbor doubts and wondered out loud if the Browns would once again fall short down the stretch, as they did the year before. Dick provided the answer. After the Cardinals game, Dick made a locker room speech I wish someone had preserved on tape.

He got emotional, speaking from the gut about being so close the previous three years with the Giants. He then said he knew talent, and this team had the talent to go all the way. Modzelewski then told the guys to forget this loss and concentrate on the next game, the season's finale against New York. It was just what they needed to hear.

The following week the Browns decimated Dick's former team-mates and now bitter rivals the Giants, 52-20. It was a sweet win for Dick and a huge victory for the team. In the locker room after the game, many players cited Modzelewski's rousing speech following the St. Louis defeat. The shellacking of the Giants gave the Browns their first division crown since 1957.

The '64 team was a veteran outfit that fit in beautifully with Blanton Collier's approach, but one rookie had a huge impact. He was 23-year-old Paul Warfield. Paul, who had 9.7 speed in the 100, came out of Ohio State. He was a local kid from Warren, just down the road from Cleveland. At 6 feet 1, 180 pounds, he wasn't that big, but he was fearless about going over the middle for a catch, risking the "BIG" hit.

Warfield had 52 catches for 926 yards and nine scores. It was the most catches by a Browns receiver since Mac Speedie caught 62 balls in 1952.

Another important though unheralded component of the offense was halfback Ernie Green. To complement Brown's massive offensive totals, in 1964 Green rushed for almost 500 yards on 109 carries and caught 25 passes for 283 yards. He was a good blocker who provided enough offense to keep defenses honest and prevent them from keying exclusively on Brown.

Title Town

In the title game against the Colts, Baltimore came into Cleveland actually favored on the road. The Colts had led the league in both offense and defense. The team set franchise records for points scored, games won, and tickets sold. They were led by second-year coach Don Shula and quarterback Johnny Unitas. Shula, just 34 years old, had played under Paul Brown and was making his mark as one of the fine young coaches in football. He was a tough coach, a taskmaster, and he reflected a lot of Paul Brown in his no-nonsense approach to the game.

"Football—the game and the practice for the game—is a serious business with me," Shula said. "I expect a full effort from everyone all the time. Although I was a defensive coach for the Lions when I came here (to Baltimore in 1963), I sat down with Charlie Winner, who has always done a good job with the Baltimore defense, and we took the best qualities of each of our defensive systems and blended them together" (Riger 7).

On paper, the prognosticators gave the championship-game edge to the Colts, an excellent team in all phases of the game. They were 12-2 and had avoided major injuries all year. Unitas, the league's MVP that year, had thrown for 19 TDs and had only six interceptions. Opponents had little success in finding soft spots in the Colts, either on offense or defense.

Unitas had rebounded well that year from a couple of what were for him subpar seasons. Of course, a "bad" Johnny Unitas year would be plenty good for most quarterbacks in the league. But in 1964, Johnny came to camp like a man on a mission, and he remained that way all year.

After Shula took over the Colts in 1963, Unitas became more of a field general. He wasn't shy about getting on his receivers if they didn't run the correct route or made some other mental mistake. He also hounded his offensive line for more support.

"The guys forget to concentrate on what they do," Unitas said. "They get up there and blow an assignment. This guy will blow one. Next play somebody else will blow one. Instead of everybody just dropping dead on one play, they take turns. Consequently, I'm on my rear end all day. What're you going to do? I talk to 'em. I holler at 'em I tell 'em, 'Damn, pay attention to what you're doing.' It runs right off the top of their heads" (Olderman 80).

Once, one of the Colts' running backs had been repeatedly complaining about his injuries. As the Colts huddled up for a play, Unitas' eyes locked eyes with those of his "injured" runner.

"You okay?" John asked. "If not, get your butt out and send me someone I can use."

Shula, who had been the defensive coordinator the previous three years in Detroit, came in and basically told Johnny that he (Shula) would handle the preparations, but he'd let Johnny run the game.

That's just what Unitas did . . . using psychology and asserting leadership: "I'm tired of patting 'em on the butt. Tired of begging them to do this and that. That's for the birds. I got to go out and do what's necessary, like blocking. The man next to me should do the same thing. There's no priority for anybody. Ten other guys go along with the quarterback. He's only as good as the men standing in front of him. If they don't give me time to do my job, forget it" (80).

John got the time and to go along with the revamped line, Shula had inherited a fine receiving corps to complement Unitas— the great Raymond Berry, Jimmy Orr, Willie Richardson, and John Mackey.

Berry, a Hall of Famer who virtually defined the role of wide receiver, presented opposing coaches great difficulty. If you keyed on him, it opened up the other fine Colts receivers.

Berry came out of Paris, Texas, a skinny young man whose life was turned around when he went to the movies as a boy and saw a film called "Crazylegs," about the Los Angeles Rams' end Elroy Hirsch. Berry kept going back to see that film, and after maybe the tenth showing, knew he wanted to be like Crazylegs. Berry wore contact lenses and had cleats put on only one of his football shoes (the other he had a ripple sole) because one leg was shorter than the other, but no one was more adept at running precision routes or more sure-handed in catching the football. In addition, no one practiced harder or worked longer on perfecting routes than Raymond Berry.

Ray also knew the game of football. In fact, some 20 years after the 1964 title game, Berry became coach of the New England Patriots and led them to their first Super Bowl appearance in 1985.

Berry was Unitas' "go-to" guy, especially on third down. In 1964, the 10-year veteran from Southern Methodist became the all-time leading receiver in football history. His 43 catches pushed his career total to 506, ahead of Don Hutson (488) and Billy Howton (503).

John Mackey presented opposing defenses with a different problem: how to stop a big, powerful, fast man who could run right over as well as outrun you. Mackey, a second-year tight end from Syracuse, was one of the first tight ends to become a big part of a team's offense. Berry was one of Mackey's biggest fans, and he took him in as a kind of protege.

"John Mackey is just so powerful they better not give him any room," Berry said during Mackey's rookie year, "because if they do, he's gone! There is no way to describe what he will do for our ball club. Common sense will tell you when you have that kind of man on the end it has got to help the two outside receivers" (Riger 6).

Defensively, the Colts were anchored by defensive lineman Gino Marchetti, who would be playing the last game of his career in the championship game; linebackers Bill Pellington and Steve Stonebreaker; defensive end Ordell Braase; and defensive backs Bob Boyd and Lenny Lyles.

Yes, the Colts had a great team on paper, but the 1964 championship game was not played on paper. It was played on Dec. 27 on the hard turf of cold, windblown Municipal Stadium in front of 79,544 fans.

The Browns had a superb week of preparation in the seven days leading up to the title game. In practice that week, the coaches implemented a defensive scheme with two key elements:

1. Play the Colts' receivers tight and not give them any room.
2. Pressure Unitas.

It worked beautifully. Unitas had trouble the whole game trying to spot his receivers. Whenever he dropped back to look downfield, he saw Browns defensive backs harassing his receivers. On almost every play, his primary receiver was covered. That forced Johnny to take a second look, but by that time the defensive linemen were moving in on him. The great Colts quarterback spent much of the scoreless first half running out of the pocket for his life, eating dirt, or throwing prematurely and on the run. He completed some passes but could not put together a drive. Thus, the potent Colts aerial attack became a non-factor.

Two Games for the Price of One

The championship was an odd game, actually more like two games in one—the scoreless first half and the laugher of a second half.

The first "game" ended in a 0-0 tie. It was a conservatively played half, both teams feeling each other out, playing cautiously and probing for softness or weakness. I was calling the game for the nation on CBS along with Baltimore's superb play-by-play man Chuck Thompson and rookie announcer Frank Gifford.

One play from the first half stands out. The Colts had set up a perfect screen pass, with Unitas lofting the ball softly to dangerous running back Lenny Moore. Moore had several blockers in front, and it appeared certain the play would break for big yardage, maybe even a touchdown. However, just as Moore started to accelerate to head down field, linebacker Galen Fiss shot through three would-be blockers and knifed into Moore's legs, dropping the All Pro half-back for a loss. Instead of a long gain and maybe even a score, the Colts were faced third and long. It was a bold, audacious play, one that turned the game around.

Moore was an explosive running back out of Penn State who was equally gifted at catching balls from Unitas out of the backfield. Lenny posed all sorts of problems for opposing defenses.

Paul Brown used to say that Lenny Moore would earn his salary even if he didn't touch a football the entire game. It was so hard to cover Moore because you didn't know what he was going to do. Therefore, he opened everything up for the offense and consequently defenses had to play "soft" or else get burned by his blazing speed.

When Fiss knifed through the Colts' defense to take down Moore, the game turned. You could sense it. The defense received a shot of confidence and kept the Colts' offense on its heels. Bernie Parrish, Walter Beach, Larry Benz, Ross Fichtner, Fiss, Vince Costello, Modzelewski, Bill Glass, Jim Kanicki, and Paul Wiggin took charge. They disrupted Unitas, Moore, Berry, Orr, and the rest of the offense for the remainder of the game. Out of synch—that's the kind of offense the Colts took into the second half. On the other hand, the Browns were just finding their offensive rhythm.

The second "game"—quarters three and four—featured an old-fashioned country whippin': Browns 27, Colts 0. Ryan and wide receiver Gary Collins teamed up for three TDs, and Lou Groza added two field goals and three extra points. Ryan didn't throw all that often—he finished the game 11-for-18—but with the three TD scores having secured the game, all he had to do was hand the ball off to Jim Brown and Ernie Green to grind out yards, obtain first downs, and eat up precious time. When you have a lead like that and you find Jim Brown lined up behind you in the backfield, you can feel pretty good about things.

Offensively, the only game plan the Browns needed came down to something that Collins told me the week before during practice. I'm sure he told Ryan the same thing. Gary walked up to me and said, "Ken, I can beat (Colts secondary man Bob) Boyd all day."

Collins was a big man, 6 feet 4 and 215 pounds, an All-American out of the University of Maryland. He came up to the Browns in 1962 and became a regular the next season, when he caught 43 passes for 674 yards and 13 touchdowns. Oddly enough, given the fact that he was the offensive star in the title game, his statistical performance was down in 1964—35 catches, 544 yards, 8 TDs.

But one of those catches was enormous. It came at home against the Cardinals in the second game of the year. The Browns faced a 4th-and-19 on the St. Louis 45 with about a minute left. Ryan launched a high, rainbow pass—today it's called a Hail Mary—to the end zone. Using his height to great advantage, Gary leaped up and came down with the ball with two defenders all over him. The Browns tied the game, and that tie eventually produced the team's half-game margin of victory over the Cardinals for the Eastern Division crown, the Browns finishing at 10-3-1 to the Cardinals' 9-3-2.

In the second half of the championship game, Collins did just what he told Ryan he could do—beat Boyd. He burned Boyd for touchdowns of 18, 42, and 51 yards. One of those grabs was a highlight-reel grab with Boyd draped all over him; not only did Collins beat Boyd to the ball, he somehow eluded the tackle to ramble in for the score. In all, Collins caught five balls for 130 yards. The three TD receptions set a title game record and earned Gary the game's MVP Award. The Browns finished the game with a 339-181 edge in total yards over the Colts, and Cleveland went wild with its new title.

The Browns' locker room was dizzy with excitement. It was their first world title in ten years. There was the usual screaming, hijinx, champagne spraying and all of that.

All the more reason to notice Jim Brown.

This was Jim's first (and only) time as a World Champ, and he sat there quietly with a satisfied look on his face, drinking it all in, and I don't mean the champagne.

In our postgame interview, I asked him how he felt.

"It feels good, Ken. We had a good week of practice, and I just had the feeling by the way the defense was playing in the first half, we'd probably score some points and lose them. We beat a tough football team out there today, and I'm proud of this team accomplishment."

That was it—no wild exhortations or gloating, no taunting, just a few appreciative words and a large helping of dignity and class. Jim had finally achieved the one remaining goal in his football career—a world title.

"Act like you've been there before," he would say.

Jim, you were right.

A Man Named Vince

Though the Browns repeated as Eastern Division champs in 1965, it wasn't quite as strong a team. Paul Warfield, who as a rookie in '64 set the league on fire, broke his collarbone in the 1965 College All-Star game and never fully recovered. Ryan had an off year at quarterback, haunted by his old bugaboo, inconsistency. From game to game, you didn't know what to expect from Frank.

The team went 11-3, but it was a deceptive 11-3. Coach Bill Parcells has a great saying about won-lost records: "You are what your record says you are." I believe that, but nonetheless the 11-3 Browns were the exception that proves the rule. They were a "soft" 11-3—two of the losses were routs: 49-13 to the Cardinals and 42-7 to the lowly Rams. The Rams' loss came after the team had clinched the title, in the year's penultimate game. I remember Blanton Collier expressing his concern that the letdown might affect the team.

"No good, Kenny, no good. I don't like it," Blanton said in his deliberate way, shaking his head. "This kind of game leaves a taste in your mouth that's hard to wash out. I've seen this sort of thing before. You think you can just forget it, shake it off, but you can't. That's why I'm concerned."

"How do you try, though, to put this behind a team?" I asked him.

"You get at it in practice," Blanton replied. "You look at the films, determine what went wrong, and work hard to fix it. Still, you just know this sort of thing can linger. But that's my job as head coach. To get these guys prepared to win."

In the season's finale, the Browns just managed to slip by the Cardinals, 27-24. I could see Blanton and the coaching staff were still concerned.

Going into 1965, most of the pre-season magazines predicted another title. Ryan, who graced the cover on many football magazines coming off a career year, seemed ready to blossom into a full-fledged star. In the backfield, they still had the great Jim Brown.

You could talk about Warfield's injury, Ryan's inconsistency (119-for-243 for 1,751 yards and a completion rate of 49 percent), the aging of the team (e.g., Modzelewski 35, Fiss 35, Costello 34). You could look at team figures like No. 7 in total offense, No. 11 in rushing attempts, No. 12 in passing yardage, and No. 13 in pass defense. But you had to go beyond that—some of the passion wasn't there, the raging fire in the gut.

Once again I was working the championship game broadcast nationwide for CBS and around the globe through the Armed Forces Network. I worked with the great Ray Scott, Green Bay's announcer, and Frank Gifford. It's only natural to get nervous before a game like that, going out before the world, but I had learned to channel that sense of anxiety and anticipation into my performance.

The most difficult time for me was always right before the broadcast went on live, but when the camera's red light came on I got into my "zone." The butterflies flew away, as they always ultimately do, and the nervous anticipation gave way to the single-minded focus it takes to call a football game on network TV. To this day, I'm flattered when fans remember my football work and say that I made it all look so easy.

The weather that week had been fine, but on game day a misting rain developed overnight that quickly turned to snow and ice in the morning. This would have an effect on later developments.

Commissioner Pete Rozelle asked his supervisor of officials, Mark Duncan, to inspect the field. The field itself was covered with hay for protection, but on the sidelines snow was piling up. Worried about the snow on the sidelines, Duncan commandeered a cab out to the Brown County Veterans' War Memorial Association Arena, where he tried to borrow the blue dye that they use to mark the hockey blue lines. Duncan wanted to use it on the sidelines to cover the snow, but they didn't have any extra dye on hand.

Duncan then ordered up a helicopter, which he had hover about 25 feet above the stands to blow off snow from the seats. Frank Gifford and I got into the stadium at 9 a.m. to tape the "billboards" (those are the brief commercial announcements you read at the top and bottom of the show). We discovered that some of the CBS equipment had been stored in Vince Lombardi's private sauna bath, which Jerry Izenberg, one of the country's top sportswriters, likened to "making wine in the church basement."

Vince was gracious about it, however. In fact, on game day, no one was more affable or upbeat than Lombardi. During the week, Vince could terrorize his players to get them ready, but on game day he was friendly, open, and laughing.

Vince was like Paul Brown: he left nothing to chance. During the week preparing for the title game with the Browns, Vince had his players wear different numbers to confuse any spies who might be in the stands for the workouts. The final practice before the game lasted one hour and 15 minutes. He worked the Packers hard, and I mean hard.

"An hour to work," Vince said later in the coaches' room, "and 15 minutes to get the lead out of their tails."

But on the day of the game, it was a different story.

"Hey, Paul…Paul Hornung," he'd say. "Are you ready to have the greatest game of your life today? Man, you looked great this week. And you, Mr. Starr, you were superb out there yesterday, just superb." Vince would go around the locker room to each guy, giving him a big build up and making each man feel as if he could run through a wall.

Still, Vince didn't know how to answer when he was asked in his pre-game press conference if he could tell whether the team was ready.

"You look at them all week," Vince said, scratching his head, "and you listen to them and you say to yourself they are hopeless. Then they go out and beat somebody's brains in. Other weeks it's the reverse. You cannot put the human mind in a pigeon hole" (Izenberg 44).

Vince had the only IBM computer set up in football at the time. By today's standards, of course, it was a primitive machine. Your hand-held calculator probably has more memory than Vince's IBM, but back then it was considered very high tech. Vince had the IBM system set up so he could feed in a stack of punched cards and learn the Browns' tendencies in certain situations. For example, he could find out what the Browns actually called during the year on third and long, on second and 3, and the like. He had all this information on charts.

A writer asked Lombardi about the machine. "The machine is great, but it can't coach," Vince said of his computer. "Football is still blocking and tackling."

How would the Packers try to stop Jim Brown? Perhaps Jerry Kramer had the best answer.

"You pick up Willie Davis and throw him at him."

At noon on game day, the field buzzed with guys handling snow shovels and pushing snow blowers. The players could work out only in the middle of the field, room for not much more than throwing the ball around and stretching. The snow then turned to ice before settling into a bone-chilling rain.

Vince surveyed the messy field, smiled, and boomed for all his players to hear, "My, what an excellent day to win a football game."

Vince Lombardi was a native New Yorker, a Fordham graduate who was a 180-pound guard, part of Fordham's "Seven Blocks of Granite" line. He was too small for professional football, so he bounced around in the semipros, making $50 each Sunday by playing for the Wilmington, Delaware, Clippers in the American Association. For the rest of the week, he taught Latin and chemistry at Saint Cecilia's High School in New Jersey. Vince later served as an assistant coach at Army under Col. Earle "Red" Blaik. He broke into the NFL when the Giants' Wellington Mara offered him a job as offensive coordinator under Jim Lee Howell.

Vince had found his calling in coaching. It was like putting a camera in Stanley Kubrick's hand. Vince was an NFL head coach for ten years, all but his final year (1969 Redskins) with the Green Bay Packers. Lombardi *was* the Packers. Writer Harold Rosenthal once described him not as a coach but as "a Mongol warlord."

Lombardi finished with a career winning percentage of .728 in the regular season and an amazing .900 in postseason play. No coach who coached as long ever had a better overall winning percentage than Lombardi's .740 mark.

There are many great Vince Lombardi stories. Like all myths, some prove to be true, some not.

One of my favorite Lombardi stories, this one true, involves the time a young man, very polished and executive-looking in his crisp Brooks Brothers suit, walked into Vince's office in Green Bay in January 1964. He introduced himself as Jim Ringo's agent. Ringo was Lombardi's All-Pro center.

"Ringo?" Vince said. "Oh, sure. I can't talk with you right now, though. Can you wait outside for a few minutes? I have a very important phone call."

The agent left the office. Finally, several minutes later, Vince's secretary told him he could go back in to see Coach Lombardi. Vince was behind his desk with a huge grin on his face. This put the anxious agent at ease.

"I'm here to talk to you about Jim Ringo's contract."

"Ringo?" Vince asked, a look of puzzlement on his face. "Why talk to *me* about Jim Ringo?"

"Because he plays for the Green Bay Packers," the agent retorted.

"There must be some mistake," deadpanned Lombardi. "Ringo isn't with our club. He's a member of the Philadelphia Eagles. I'd suggest you contact them" (Rosenthal 160-161).

With the agent cooling his heels outside Vince's office, Lombardi had picked up the phone and traded his star center to the Eagles.

Here's one Lombardi myth that's not true. Most people believe he coined the saying, "Winning isn't everything. It's the only thing!" Actually, that was a line uttered by John Wayne, who played a football coach in the film "Trouble Along the Way."

But he did say to his players: "No one is ever hurt. Hurt is in your mind." He used that approach to get his Packers to play fearless football.

Deep Depth

The 1965 Packers had what Baltimore Orioles manager Earl Weaver used to call "deep depth," with stars on both sides of the ball. On offense quarterback Bart Starr spearheaded the Packer offense. Starr was a man who could run Vince Lombardi's schemes to perfection. Starr wasn't flashy or showy; he was a methodical, technically sound quarterback who executed flawlessly, rarely beat himself with a mental mistake, and knew how to pick apart defenses.

In the backfield, they had fullback Jim Taylor and halfback Paul Hornung. Taylor, No. 5 in the league in rushing in 1965 (734 yards), was a destructive runner who could dish out as much or more punishment than he received. He liked to say that as a runner, he felt he had to make tacklers respect him. How? By hitting them harder than they hit you, each and every play.

Taylor hailed from Baton Rouge, Louisiana, and was known as a talker on the field. If he took a big hit from a defensive player, Jim's way of handling it would be to ask something like: "Is that your best shot? I thought you had more than that." Or he'd get up from the pile and with a small laugh say, "Nothin.' Absolutely nothin'." Taylor preferred to run *over* tacklers rather than around them and got the reputation around the league of being a head hunter. Jim felt this gave him an edge, much the way a pitcher has an edge if batters suspect he's throwing a spitter.

Just as the Packers designed an end sweep for Paul Hornung, they devised a special play for Taylor. On the fullback slant, Taylor would get the ball from Starr and have his choice—hit the hole over tackle, come through center, or—if those two holes weren't there— go to the outside.

Whereas most runners know when they are stopped and let up to conserve energy, Jim wouldn't stop churning his legs. He'd squirm and fight until he was put on the ground and the whistle blew. He'd do this even if he had been stacked up by five guys in a gang tackle, where resistance was useless.

Taylor always said the toughest game of his career was the 1962 championship game against the Giants in New York, a game in which the Packers methodically turned back the Giants 16-7 on Jerry Kramer's three field goals and Jim's seven-yard touchdown run.

In the December 30 game, Jim set a championship game record by lugging the ball 31 times (good for 85 yards) on a rock-hard frozen field. I called the game for CBS, and I mean to tell you that Jim took a fierce pounding that day. The temperature at kickoff was 17 degrees and in the single digits by the fourth quarter. Throughout the game, a brutal 30-mph wind whipped through Yankee Stadium.

After the game, Taylor was the last to get dressed. He had a two-inch gash in his right elbow, a nasty bruise under the left eye, and a deep contusion of the hip. His body was covered with bruises and scratches, and he kept putting a towel to his mouth to absorb the blood from his tongue, which he had bitten.

On the first-quarter play where he hurt his hip, Jim had to leave the game. There was doubt if he would make it back, but in the second quarter, there he was, running the ball and taking more punishment. It was one of the greatest displays of courage I've ever seen on a football field.

Hornung, who missed four games in 1965 because of injury, added an element of unpredictability to the Packers' attack because he was so versatile. He had a so-so year in 1965, but Paul was known as a money player, a guy who came through in the biggest games.

Hornung was drafted No. 1 out of Notre Dame fresh off his Heisman Trophy season in which he played quarterback, halfback, fullback, and kicker. Irish coach Terry Brennan called Hornung "the greatest ever," and there was an ensuing avalanche of publicity and hype proclaiming Hornung's greatness. There were also Hollywood talent scouts waving contracts in front of the young running back with the matinee idol looks.

The woeful 1957 Packers drafted Paul, but coach Lisle Blackbourn couldn't make up his mind on how to employ the versatile Hornung. As a result, Hornung's play suffered, and the fans grew restless. They grumbled that the Packers were playing Hornung only to justify their investment—an unheard of three-year contract that totaled almost $50,000. Some of the writers and other "experts" sized up Paul this way: not fast enough to be a halfback, not enough of an arm to be a quarterback, and not powerful enough to be a fullback.

Hornung chafed under Blackbourn's indecision and conservative play calling. He once recalled his lowest moment from that dismal first year.

"When Blackbourn sent me in at quarterback in 1957, I was under strict orders to call only a few plays—rollout right or left, option-run right or left, or a quarterback sneak. In a game against the Chicago Bears, Bill George saw me coming in off the bench and yelled to his teammates: 'Look who's here—rollout right or left, option right or left, and quarterback sneak'" ("Paul Hornung Gets…" 13). The Bears, and the rest of the league apparently, enjoyed a good laugh. Hornung quietly fumed and some in the league took delight in seeing the "pretty boy" get his comeuppance.

The 1958 season was as much of a bust as '57. Ray McLean was brought in to turn Green Bay around, but they went 1-10-1. That's when the Packers gave the head coaching job to a little known but highly respected assistant of the New York Giants, a man by the name of Vince Lombardi.

Vince became Paul Hornung's patron saint. He immediately determined that Hornung's talents had been underutilized and that if the Packers were to become winners, Paul Hornung had to be a key component.

Taking a page out of Paul Brown's book, Lombardi locked himself up in his office in Green Bay and watched all of the game film from the prior season. He had a special reel of film made of every single time Hornung touched the ball in the 1958 season. Vince became convinced Hornung could be best utilized as a left halfback, and then made an audacious announcement to the press: the Packers' attack would be built around that position. It was a football first and the birth of the famed Packer Sweep.

In 1959, the team improved to 7-5. In 1960, they went 8-4 to win the Division Crown. They lost a heartbreaker in the title game, 17-13 to the Philadelphia Eagles led by QB Norm Van Brocklin. In that game, the Packers drove the ball to the Eagles' 22-yard line with under ten seconds to play. On the game's last play, Starr completed a pass to Taylor, who ran inside the Eagle ten before Chuck

Bednarik brought him down, eight yards from a world champion-ship.

The Packers had learned how to win and proved that by becoming World Champs in '61 and '62. They were going for a third title in 1965 as they met the World Champion Cleveland Browns.

The Packers also had one of the best offensive lines in football in tackles Bob Skowron and Forrest Gregg, guards Jerry Kramer and Fuzzy Thurston, and Ken Bowman at center. For its time, it was a big line, averaging 6 feet 3 and weighing 240 pounds. Today, they would be considered practically midgets.

The secondary featured Willie Wood, Bob Jeter, Dave Hart, Tom Brown, and the incomparable Herb Adderly. Adderly didn't give up one touchdown the entire regular season. The line backing corps was as good as it was mean—Lee Roy Caffey and Dave Robinson on the outside flanking the imposing Ray Nitschke in the middle.

Nitschke was, as they say, a piece of work. Orphaned as a young teenager, Ray was left to grow up on his own and grew up on the wild side. He later matured and learned to channel his rough edges into his play on the football field.

Ray had a theory—you have to enjoy hitting to play middle linebacker, actually relish it. The more punishing a hit you could lay on a ball carrier, the better you felt. A big hit would not only stop the play but also send a message.

"You have to make them remember," Nitschke said during the week leading up to the championship game. "If you do, the next time they come, they are going to be a little shy about it. The whole premise is to make them think about the next play" (Izenberg 44).

Snow and Ice

After a week of practice, the Browns flew to Wisconsin and checked into the Holiday Inn in Appleton, 30 miles south of Green Bay. In fact, the choice of hotels and the weather would play into the events on the field later that day.

On the day of the 1965 title game at Curley Lambeau Field (actually, January 2, 1966), the snow and ice had accumulated in the greater Green Bay region. The Browns players were slipping and sliding in the hotel parking lot as they boarded the team bus, and the bus got caught up in the weather. The traffic moved at a crawl, and it took the team bus more than an hour and a half to make the trip to the stadium. In fact, this sounds unbelievable, but the Browns were close to not showing up on time for the title game. They arrived about 30 minutes before the scheduled start time. That sort of thing simply could not happen today, when the NFL's contingency plans have contingency plans.

As was typical for the championship game in those days, the game was played in a frostbiting, damp cold. The final score: Packers 23, Browns 12. The Packers' dominance can be seen not in the score but in an amazing statistic from that game: in the entire fourth quarter, the Browns only managed to get their hands on the ball five times, and one of those was a punt.

Actually, the game mirrored the 1964 championship in that it was a close first half and a mismatch in the second.

The Packers opened the scoring in the first quarter on a 47-yard TD pass from Bart Starr to Carroll Dale. Dale was being covered step-for-step by Walter Beach, but Beach slipped on the wet turf when Dale made his cut to the ball. He caught the pass and went in unmolested for the score. The Browns answered with their own passing score, Ryan-to-Collins. The Packers got a taste of their own medicine on the play. Just as Beach had slipped against Dale, Adderly went down covering Collins. It was the first (and only) touchdown Adderly gave up all year.

It looked as if the Browns had tied up the game. All they had to do was go through the motions and kick the extra point. Routine, right? Not on this day, especially on that muddy turf. Placeholder Bobby Franklin had trouble holding the ball on the point-after snap and fumbled. The fumble resulted in the unlikely scene of Lou Groza attempting a pass, which failed. The teams exchanged two pairs of field goals (the Browns actually led, 9-7, after the first quarter) and they left the field at halftime with the Packers in front, 13-12.

The second half turned a one-point game into a rout, mainly because of the Packers' ground game.

Hornung and Taylor ran wild, shooting past the Browns' defensive line virtually at will, picking up first downs and controlling both the ball and the clock. They basically kept the Browns' offense off the field. When the Browns did get the ball, the Packers shut down Jim Brown, gang tackling the Browns' star on just about every play. Forced to go to the pass, Ryan found himself under a heavy rush with no one to throw to.

It was a discouraging day, but in the CBS broadcasting booth, of course, I could not let my disappointment show. I'm proud of the fact that viewers that day couldn't tell of my rooting interest in Cleveland. That game was the last time Jim Brown ever carried the football in the NFL. It also marked the last time I did a Browns game as Voice of the Browns.

We bowed out together.

CHAPTER 6

The Indians

PART OF THE TRIBE

Speaking of the Game

When I first became a broadcaster of professional sports with the Browns in 1952 and later with the Indians in 1954, I would come home periodically to North Quincy and I would visit with my friends, the fellows I grew up with. I remember one time the Indians played the Red Sox at Fenway in '55, and of course as visiting broadcaster, I came into town for the series.

After one of the games I sat at an outdoor cafe on Boylston Street near the ballpark. My friends Robbie Williams, Larry Watt, and Dick Gallagher and a couple of other fellows were there. They were old friends, good people, and you know what? I felt very uncomfortable. I felt that if I spoke about my *new* friends—Bob Feller, Bob Lemon, Mike Garcia, Herb Score, Larry Doby, Al Rosen, and the like—they would think I was name-dropping, just trying to impress them. So I kept my mouth shut.

My point is that I didn't trust my friends enough to share that part of my life with them. I made up my mind that they would think I was acting like a big shot. I should have shared my experiences with them, because as I later came to realize, true friends will not think that way about a guy. In fact, I'm sure now that they would have loved to hear me talk about my Big League experiences.

Later, I enjoyed very much talking about the game and the players in it and what a wonderful bunch of men they were, men like Bobby Doerr, Ted Williams, the DiMaggios, Carl Yastrzemski, and so on. It was all part of dealing with my new life in the big time, I suppose.

Back in those days, announcers weren't the instant experts or hammering critics that you often see today. We didn't have trash-talk radio. The players were my friends. We weren't hired to constantly criticize. Unlike today, broadcasters back then were reporters describing action, not opinion-givers commenting on it. The same held with the print journalists. They reported much more than they editorialized or criticized.

Dick Enberg, a good friend and a superb broadcaster in all the sports he does, said once in radio/TV critic Jim Baker's column in *The Boston Herald:* "The key to announcing is to make a one-sided game interesting," or words to that effect. I disagree with Dick. You can't do that. By the middle of the third quarter, the real fan knows it's over. The key to announcing is to describe the game properly. That's all.

So much has changed. They still call it the National Football League, but now the championship game is called The Super Bowl. Back when I was working in it, from 1952 through 1965, it was the NFL Championship Game. I got to broadcast seven of them. In those days we did them at the home field of one of the two teams.

My NFL championship game broadcasts included:

- The Browns and the Rams in L.A. in 1955 (Cleveland, 38-14),
- The Giants and Bears at Yankee Stadium in 1956 (New York, 47-7),
- The Browns and the Lions in Cleveland in 1957 (Detroit, 59-14)
- The Giants and Packers at Yankee Stadium in 1962 (Green Bay, 16-7)
- The Giants and Bears at Wrigley Field in 1963 (Chicago, 14-10),
- The Browns and the Colts at Cleveland in 1964 (Cleveland, 27-0), and

- The Browns and the Packers in Green Bay in 1965 (Green Bay, 23-12).

I also had the privilege of doing many network games during the regular season for CBS.

The title game was better in those early years. Players got muddy and the fans froze, really froze, but they were real, down-to-earth fans—blue-collar working people who loved their team and who got to see them play for the championship. Now the big playoff games, particularly the Super Bowl, are practically all corporate. The Super Bowl has gone Hollywood, as the expression puts it, ruled as it is by the high rollers and big business. The little guy has been priced out of the year's most important game, and that's a shame.

The Indians and Rising Fortunes

It wasn't long before the job with the Browns mushroomed to Cleveland television, where I became the Voice of the Cleveland Indians. My fortunes rose, and I became well known, also landing work in town as early and late sportscaster for WJW-TV, WEWS-TV, and KYW-TV. For the next dozen or more years, I settled into a very secure and solid position in Cleveland. Over those years, I established myself and it looked like nothing could ever come along that would tempt me to leave.

It was strange in one sense to become "known" in the city. As a guy on TV and on the radio as much as I was, I became locally famous. I found celebrity a curious thing. Complete strangers would have the feeling they knew me based on seeing me or hearing me on the air. It leaves you at a disadvantage in some social situations, but I have to admit I enjoyed being recognized. I also took it as a compliment that they would feel at home with me. I took it as a validation of my approach on the air.

Celebrity also meant that some people had the illusion that they knew you intimately, which of course wasn't true. Broadcasters are in a very real sense performers, and what you see on the TV or hear on the radio is in some ways larger than life. That's just the nature of broadcasting. When we're off the air, we're just like anybody else—people with the same problems, worries, joys, and consolations as other folks. But the audience never sees that part and draws almost all of its conclusions based on the broadcaster's public face.

The vast majority of fans I have met over the years have been good, decent people, thrilled to talk to you but respectful at the same time. Oh, there have been a tiny few exceptions; you know the type. It's the loudmouth in a restaurant who has had too much to drink who wants to razz you about the team, get on you about something you said on the air, or prove that he knows more about the game than you do. With these folks, you just play along for a moment, then find a way to excuse yourself.

I envisioned myself in my role as a broadcaster as a guest being invited into the homes of friends. I tried to behave like a guest would —familiar, friendly, and never overbearing. I wanted people to feel comfortable with me and trust me enough to keep asking me back. That came to define my style behind the microphone—informative and descriptive, upbeat, yet saying what needed to be said, and not being afraid to inject the right amount of pauses and silence.

I tried to report the action, not be a cheerleader or homer. Fans liked that; they knew they could rely on me for an honest description of what was happening. If it was a great play, I called it like a great play. If a guy pulled a rock, I described the error without shying away, making excuses, or for that matter blowing it out of proportion. Over the years, the fans warmed to my style. I found, surprisingly at first, that I had developed a large and loyal following as well. It was flattering and a bit humbling.

When fans would come up to me and want to chat or ask for an autograph, I tried to remember my days as a fan and to picture what it would be like to meet with a famous ball player or sportscaster. I completely understood where the fans were coming from and always tried to accommodate their requests for pictures, autographs, and things like that.

Over the years in Cleveland, I met many tremendous people and had the honor of being around some great moments in sports, not the least of which was the incredible 1954 Indians team that won 111 games.

In 1954, manager Al Lopez and his Tribe managed to loosen the stranglehold that Casey Stengel's Yankees had on the American

League pennant. In fact, from 1949 to 1964, the Yankees only failed twice to win a pennant—in 1954 and in 1959 to the White Sox. Both times, they lost to teams managed by Al Lopez. Ironically, the 1954 Yankees had their best season in the 18 years that stretched from 1943 to 1960. They won 103 games, only to finish eight games out. Ironically, that was Casey Stengel's highest victory total—ever—as a manager.

Lopez had long held the Major League record for games caught (Bob Boone broke it in 1987). Al, who was a big favorite of my dad's, liked to build his teams around pitching. Lopez was a popular, decent man who treated his players with respect and earned the same in return from them.

The '54 Indians were a classic Al Lopez team, propelled as they were by an incredible pitching staff. Bob Lemon (23-7) and Early Wynn (23-11) tied for the league lead in victories. Mike Garcia (19-8) and Art Houtteman (15-7) rounded out the Big Four. 35-year-old Bob Feller got in 19 games, all of them starts, and went 13-3, while rookies Don Mossi and Ray Narleski combined for nine wins and 20 saves. Garcia also led the league in ERA.

At the plate, the Indians were led by center fielder Larry Doby, who took the home run (32) and RBI (126) crowns. Bobby Avila won the batting title at .341, and third baseman Al Rosen hit .300 with 24 home runs and 102 RBIs. First baseman Vic Wertz was a key acquisition during the year. Vic had come over from the Orioles (new to the league in 1954, having moved to Baltimore after a long run with the St. Louis Browns) and solidified the infield while contributing many clutch hits.

The Indians came into the World Series as prohibitive favorites against the New York Giants, but the Giants pulled a stunning four-game sweep. The Series turned around in Game One when Willie Mays made his spectacular over-the-shoulder catch off of Wertz late in the 2-2 game. Wertz drove the ball 450 feet to center off lefty reliever Don Liddle, but somehow Mays caught up with the ball and made the catch with his back turned to the plate.

Knowing the Score

Another noteworthy development in my early years with the Indians was the privilege of meeting one of baseball's great men, Herb Score, who joined the team the following year in '55.

People today remember Herb Score, the broadcaster. But you have to go back a few years—about 45—to remember that Herb Score was once baseball's next GIGANTIC star. No pitcher had caused as much excitement since Lefty Grove broke in with the old Philadelphia A's in the mid 1920s.

Herb Score of the Cleveland Indians was hit in the face on May 7, 1957 by a smoking line drive off the bat of Yankee Gil McDougald. The impact almost killed him, and it put him out of action for the rest of the year. The near-tragedy shocked the baseball world because Score, at the age of 24, was on his way to becoming the most dominant pitcher of his time. His future seemed limitless, and there's no telling what he might have accomplished if he had stayed healthy.

Herb was a born pitcher. His mother Anna once recalled how Herb would throw anything that wasn't bolted down in the house—socks, pencils, food, anything. This included eggs, which to his small hand felt proportionately like a baseball. Same color, too.

Herb came from a broken home and was raised along with his two younger sisters by his mother, with some help from the parish priests. He spent his early childhood in Rosedale, Long Island, and from the time he formed his first conscious thought, Herb Score wanted to be a Major League ballplayer. He dreamed of playing the outfield, but his first coach on the Catholic school team, Father Thomas Kelly, converted him to pitcher. Father Kelly had played shortstop for Fordham and recognized the truly incredible gift that was Score's left arm (Cobbledick 56).

Herb almost lost that dream at the age of 3 when he was run over by a truck. Both legs were crushed just below the pelvis. For a while, it looked like amputation would be necessary, but the toddler pulled through. In fact, this was just the beginning of a troubling trend, as the young Herb was prone to illness and injury – fractured ankle, emergency appendectomy, pneumonia, an acute colon condition, high blood pressure (which kept him out of the military), a separated left shoulder, rheumatic fever (54).

Herb's family broke up when he was still a boy. Herb, his mother, and two sisters moved to Lake Worth, Florida when Herb was 15, but the shy young man had trouble adjusting—until he discovered that in Florida, you could play baseball year round. Sports provided an outlet for his personal frustrations. Herb became a high-scoring forward on one of the state's top high school teams. Baseball, though, became his game.

Various teams scouted him. A Yankees scout took a look, and though he liked Herb's lively arm, didn't like his wildness. The verdict? "Class C, maybe B, is his limit" (57). It was baseball's equivalent of Decca Records telling the Beatles in 1962 that "Guitar groups are out."

However, Cy Slapnicka, an Indians scout whose discoveries included Bob Feller and Hal Trosky, took one look at the young, rawboned kid and saw something. What he saw was Herb strike out 18 batters in a seven-inning game with a blazing fastball.

Slapnicka convinced Anna Score to let Herb sign with the Indians. The Tribe offered him a $60,000 bonus. They took it, although there were higher offers. In fact, Trader Frank Lane, then running the Chicago White Sox, left orders with the White Sox scouting staff to top any other offer, no matter how high.

"Neither my mother nor I felt that we ought to play one club against another," Herb later told *Sport* magazine. "Somehow it didn't seem like the honest thing to do. All the bids, including Cleveland's, represented so much more than we ever thought there was in the world, that a few thousand more or less didn't seem to make a difference" (57).

At the signing, the team had a press conference, and when I met him, Herb seemed like something out of a Norman Rockwell painting: a well-built, though gangly kid, with wavy blonde hair and sparkling blue eyes.

He had a well-scrubbed look, a wholesome, All-American boy image. Of course, none of it was cultivated. That was just Herb being Herb.

Indians pitching coach Mel Harder introduced us: "Herb, this is Ken Coleman. He does our TV broadcasts."

"Nice to meet you, Mr. Coleman."

"Call me Ken."

"Yes, sir."

You couldn't help but like him.

After the signing ceremony, they put Herb in a uniform and brought him out on the field at Municipal Stadium to let him throw a few.

"Al Lopez, manager of the Indians and an old hand at catching, put on a mitt to sample the phenom's stuff. His eyes grew wide as the boy fired a succession of pitches that popped into the mitt with the sound of a giant firecracker going off in a telephone booth. They grew wider, and the Lopez chin dropped to the Lopez chest when Slap (Slapnicka) called, 'All right, Herbert. I guess you're warmed up now. Show him your fastball.'

"'You kiddin' or something?' Lopez said accusingly.

"'I am not,' Slapnicka assured him. 'The kid's just been loosening up. He's had a long train ride and he's kinda stiff'" (57).

Indeed, Herb threw absolute bullets. The ball would look like a white BB coming in on the batter off the young man's gifted left arm. You just couldn't believe the speed Herb could generate.

In the minors, Score struggled in his first few years. The "can't miss" began missing—the plate, that is. Batters feared getting into the box with Herb's combination of blazing fastball and wildness. In 1952 (AAA Indianapolis) and '53 (AA Reading) Herb walked 188 batters in 170 innings. However, when he returned to Triple A in '54, coach Ted Wilks discovered a flaw in his delivery. Score was kicking his right foot too high, causing his head to move too much. Herb worked hard to correct it and reduced his walks to 140 in 251 innings that year. Incidentally, he went 22-5 with 330 strikeouts, averaging almost 12 strikeouts over nine innings pitched.

That record would have been even better if not for a bad cold that turned into pneumonia that robbed Herb of his strength for much of the last month of the season and put him in the hospital the last week.

Indianapolis got into the playoffs that year against the Louisville Colonels, the Triple A farm club of the Boston Red Sox. Herb got permission to come out of the hospital and pitch in the playoff series. He hooked up with Ike Delock in a tremendous 0-0 pitcher's duel. Herb pitched 10 innings, gave up but one hit, and struck out 14. He was lifted for a pinch hitter in the 10th, and the Colonels went on to win the game in the 11th (58).

Word of Herb's exploits began to filter up to Cleveland, and we couldn't wait to see him for ourselves. Herb would not disappoint. Even the most hyperbolic press accounts seemed like an understatement.

When he came up to the Indians in 1955, Score cut down on the walks even further and proved just as tough for Major League hitters. In 1955, at 22 years of age, Score went 16-10, with 245 strikeouts in 227 innings and a 2.85 ERA. He had ballparks buzzing throughout the American League because of his electrifying fast ball.

From Herb's first start, we knew he was a unique talent. Score made his debut in Detroit the day after Opening Day with Hank Foiles, his minor-league teammate, behind the plate. It was a raw April day, and there couldn't have been more than 4,000 fans in Briggs Stadium.

Manager Al Lopez told Herb to go as hard as he could as long as he could. That was before the current methods of pitching, where starters, particularly in the early part of a season, are on rigid pitch counts and are monitored closely.

Herb was visibly nervous. He gave up a run and a couple of hits in the first, then began the second by walking the bases loaded. That's when he recorded his first Major League strikeout, pitcher Frank Lary. He got out of the jam without serious damage.

Finally, in the fourth inning, Herb settled down. His fastball began to crackle, and he started getting his curve over the plate. The Indians got some runs and held on for a 7-3 win. Herb went all the way—in his complete game, he had walked nine and struck out nine. He threw 172 pitches (58, 59). Of course, today, he would have been pulled in the fourth or fifth inning the way his pitch count was going. Fr. Murphy, his high school coach, was in the stands to see Herb win in his debut. It was like something out of a Hollywood movie, with Bing Crosby cast in the role of Fr. Murphy.

It's a funny thing about phenoms. Some make it and some don't. For every 17-year-old Bob Feller there's a Danny Murphy. In 1960, the Cubs signed 17-year-old Murphy from Beverly, Massachusetts for a $100,000 bonus. Under the old Bonus Rule, a bonus baby had to remain with the parent club all year. Murphy went 9-for-75 for a .120 average, and didn't have much of a career beyond that, getting up to the plate just 130 times, racking up a .177 average. Once, Murphy struck out in an exhibition game against the Indians at Hi Corbett Field in Tucson. As he was heading back to the dugout, a leather-lung yelled out from the stands, "That hundred grand won't help you hit the curve, kid."

Herb Score, of course, was one phenom who made it.

In 1956, he defied the sophomore jinx with a vengeance, going 20-9. In 249 innings, he fanned a league-leading 263 batters while lowering his ERA to 2.53. Five of his 16 complete games were shutouts, which also led the league.

Baseball's Next Great Pitcher had arrived, a pronouncement that came from none other than Theodore Samuel Williams of the Boston Red Sox. Boston General Manager Joe Cronin thought so too. With the approval of owner Tom Yawkey, Cronin offered the Indians the unprecedented sum of $1 million in cash for Herb Score's contract. The offer was tendered two weeks before the May 7 game against the Yankees. The Indians turned the offer down.

Baseball's most promising pitcher since Bob Feller started out 1957 in the same fashion as the year before, winning two of his first three games with a 2.00 ERA and, of course, more strikeouts than innings pitched. Three of his first four appearances were complete games, one a shutout. But one swing from McDougald's bat changed all that.

A Moment of Impact

When you look back on it, maybe this was an accident destined to happen. Herb once told me—this was before the McDougald incident—that he seldom saw the ball when it came off the bat, particularly after he threw a fastball. This stemmed from his high leg kick, the exaggerated overhand motion, and the subsequent follow-through, which carried his head down below his knees. By the time he could straighten up, the ball had either been hit or caught by the catcher. When Herb would catch a fan looking on strikes, he often wouldn't know it until he either heard the ump's call or saw the batter walking back toward the dugout.

In fact, in Herb's previous start before the fateful McDougald game against the Yankees, he had a close call. A Senators batter, Roy Sievers I think, scalded a liner through the box. The ball shot through Herb's legs and into centerfield for a base hit. Herb never reacted to the ball, because he hadn't seen it. I mentioned this on the air, how he didn't seem to react until after the ball was by him. It left me feeling a little uneasy.

We asked Herb about this after the game, and he thought nothing of it, because that's how he always pitched. Pitching coaches had experimented with Herb's follow-through so he'd be in position to pick up the ball earlier, but they found that it messed with Score's natural delivery, and he would start walking lots of batters. So he had a choice: sacrifice his control or continue pitching the same way and take his chances. He remained committed to his natural delivery.

Herb decided to take his chances. On May 7, chance caught up to him.

May 7 was a mild evening in Cleveland. Herb had just finished his warm up tosses in the top of the fourth inning. I was calling the game from the broadcasting booth. In the press box at the time—almost at that precise moment, in fact—Hall of Famer Tris Speaker was speaking about Herb: "If nothing happens to this kid, he has got to be one of the great ones" (54). McDougald stepped into the batter's box.

Moments later, the best pitcher of his generation was being carried off the field on a stretcher.

Gil sent a line drive straight through the box. Just as in Herb's previous start against the Senators, he didn't pick up the ball. This time, however, instead of a line drive through the wickets, the ball smacked him flush in the face. After the ball hit him, Herb went down in a heap. It was so serious, a priest was called to administer last rites. It was a sight that just made you heartsick. There was widespread fear, of course, that his career was over.

Herb never lost consciousness. In the clubhouse, he was given emergency first-aid treatment in the trainer's room while they waited for an ambulance. A nervous and very concerned Mike Garcia, one of the Tribe's star pitchers and one of Herb's best friends, popped his head in to check on the young lefthander.

Herb cut the tension by managing a joke.

"Well, Bear," he said. "You can't say I didn't keep my eye on the ball."

McDougald was shaken badly by the play. He announced that if it turned out that Herb's vision was permanently destroyed, he would quit baseball. Gil was only 29 years old at the time of the accident, but he played only three more years. To the end of his playing days in 1960, the play haunted McDougald, and you have to think that the ill-fated moment laid a big claim on the infielder's career.

Al Smith, who was in the lineup for the Indians that day, recalled the frightening moment:

"In May, I was playing third base against the Yankees, and Herb was hit by Gil McDougald's line drive. When Herb threw the ball, he always fell toward the hitter, moving downward. McDougald's drive came right back at him and hit him in the eye. I picked up the ball and there was silence in the stadium. I started running toward Herb, who had collapsed on the mound. They started hollering, 'Throw the ball to first!' I almost threw it in the stands, but I got McDougald out. When I reached the mound, blood was pouring out of Score's nose, mouth, and ears. It was sickening. He looked like a boxer had just demolished him. But he never lost consciousness. He kept asking for Mike Garcia, his good friend" (Peary 371).

Needless to say, Herb was done for the season. Some doctors expressed the opinion that Herb's eye was damaged beyond hope. If he did regain sight, they feared it would not be sound enough for him to continue in baseball.

Herb spent three weeks in a darkened hospital room at Cleveland's Lakeside Hospital with lots of questions and no answers.

That's when you find out about a person. How do they react when things look grim? It's easy to be optimistic and cheerful when you're leading the league in wins and strikeouts and routinely being hailed as baseball's next great star. But what happens when the bottom falls out? Many people, maybe most, fall into despair, disillusionment, and even depression. Herb didn't do that.

Incredibly, he even remained cheerful. Herb held on to a deep, abiding religious faith to get him through. His belief in providence gave him a wonderful inability to give in to despair. For example, when he was in his hospital room recovering from the drive off McDougald's bat, he could find the humor to say, "One thing about being in here—at least I'm not walking anybody."

Herb thought of his injury as God's will. He accepted it as part of a bigger plan, and that's what got him through his ordeal.

Following his hospital stay, Herb rested for a week at his uncle's home in Hagerstown, Maryland. Then he reported back to Cleveland, where he was examined and tested daily. Even several weeks after the injury, Herb could only see everything with a fuzzy haze. He said it was like looking at a film when the projector is badly out of focus.

One other significant outcome of the injury was that it gave Herb time to get married. Originally, Herb had intended to marry his fiancée—Nancy McNamara, a senior at St. Mary's College in South Bend, Indiana—in October at the end of the season. The injury, however, caused the couple to advance the date, and on July 10, Herb and Nancy exchanged vows. They honeymooned for a week, then returned to Cleveland.

Herb spent the rest of the season recovering at home, doing eye exercises to strengthen his damaged vision. In late July, the doctors allowed Herb to resume light workouts. He played pepper and played catch. You would watch him, and he'd seem okay, but then you'd see him reach for a ball that wasn't there. He'd wave at the air as the ball skipped by. He just didn't have focus or enough depth perception to follow the ball. It was tough to witness.

Herb diligently worked to build up his arm strength and his legs, but one troubling fact still haunted him: he couldn't see the catcher clearly enough from 60 feet, six inches. Anyone who saw Herb work out in an empty Municipal Stadium on an off day or when the team was on the road thought it was over. He just wasn't the same.

After the season, Herb continued his eye exercises and spent the winter in Cleveland. He worked for the Indians doing PR, making speeches before civic organizations and youth groups. In the off season, Herb and I resumed playing racquetball. Outside of Doctor Charles Thomas, the eye specialist who cared for Herb and gave him hope that he would play again, I was probably the first person to see Herb's improvement.

I had to take it easy on him when we first started playing again. He couldn't really see the ball all that well. You could tell by his reactions; they were tentative. Then we went out one day and he beat me. A couple days later, he beat me again. The next time we played, I decided to really bear down. Herb came out on top once again. I never felt that good about getting beat, because it was apparent he was picking up the ball. Herb told me that all of a sudden around that time, his vision clarified. It was as if someone had twisted the lens of that projector to make the picture come into focus again.

Dr. Thomas confirmed the improvement. He explained that sometimes with eye injuries, the eye needs time to heal itself. Mechanically, everything looked fine inside the eye, and by the time February rolled around, Herb was acing his eye tests. Herb's explanation? The power of prayer.

On February 5, Herb and Nancy Score packed their car and left their two-bedroom apartment in Edgewood Towers in the Cleveland suburb of Lakewood for the 2,200-mile drive to the Indians' spring training camp in Tucson. We broke for spring training camp on the same day with the buoyant hope that Herb Score was back.

Making the Grade

By the time spring training rolled around in 1958, Herb seemed fully recovered. At the beginning of camp that year in Tucson, Arizona, he was throwing the ball as hard as he ever threw the ball, maybe harder. His speed was awesome. Watching him warm up on the side, you could hear the ball whiz by with an audible hissing sound.

The sibilant Score fastball, the blur of a ball, was there in all its untouchable glory.

In fact, Herb faced and passed three tests early that spring.

1. The Batting Cage.

He had arrived early and spent his time in the hitting cage going up against Iron Mike, the pitching machine. That was the first big test. You certainly can't hit a ball if you can't see it. Against Iron Mike's mechanical arm, Herb sprayed line drives all over Hi Corbett field.

2. Facing Live Hitters.

The second test came when the roster players showed up. Rocky Colavito was another early bird to camp. Rocky, a fine outfielder and hitter, had been Score's roommate and Herb's best friend on the team.

"Grab a bat and let's see as if you're as lousy a hitter as ever," Herb needled Rocky one day.

"You sure you want to?" asked Rocky. "I mean, do you think it's all right? You sure you're ready?"

"I'm ready," Herb said in utter seriousness.

Colavito stepped in, and it was clear he was trying to pull everything down the line in left. Rocky was adjusting his swing just so he wouldn't send anything back up through the middle. Score stopped throwing.

"Look, Rock, you're not swinging naturally. You're trying to avoid hitting one back through the box. Forget it. I'll take care of myself. If I don't, if you hit me in the teeth with a line drive, you get a cigar" (Cobbledick 54).

3. Game Action

The third test came in the Grapefruit League exhibition games. It was one thing to throw batting practice to a teammate. How would it go with opposing batters digging in? You had to think many batters were going to try to send it back through the middle, just to rattle Herb or test him. How would Herb react to a line drive hit at or near him?

In a game against the Chicago Cubs, we found out. John Goryl lined a ball up the middle. It took a quick, angular bounce, then skimmed off the grass back to the box like a stone skimming water, picking up speed as it did. Herb calmly picked the ball out of the air in front of his face with the glove hand and tossed to first for the out (54).

Herb Score was back.

And that's what people either forget or simply don't know. That early in 1958's spring training, Score was throwing the ball as well as he ever had. His eyes were good and his blazing fastball was faster than ever. No one looked better.

Over the years, the myth has grown up around his eye injury. The myth holds that Herb was never the same pitcher again after the McDougald line drive. That myth has been accepted as fact. Let me now correct the record and put to rest one of baseball's accepted (but untrue) myths.

In spring training of 1958, he was the same Herb Score. What happened subsequently to Score wasn't the lingering effect of McDougald's line drive but rather an errant foot in a pick-up basketball game. This story has never been told until now. It's the real reason for Herb's ultimate decline as a star pitcher.

A Fateful Day on the Court

It never rained in Tucson. I mean it *never* rained in Tucson. But as fate would have it, this one day in the spring of 1958, it rained. It's funny how little things like this figure into the big picture of life. If it hadn't rained, I'm convinced things would have turned out far differently for Herb Score.

Because of the rain, the Indians canceled practice. With some time to kill, Herb invited me to go to a local gym to shoot some baskets. We went and shot around, having a lot of fun. Later, however, Herb got into an intense game of one-on-one with another guy. The competitive juices took over, and they really got into it. They played it like it was Game Seven of the NBA Finals. Then on one play, everything changed. Herb shot and missed. His opponent, a big man, crashed the boards and went up for a rebound. He came down and landed directly on Score's foot.

The man's weight pinned Score's foot, but Herb's body kept moving forward with its natural momentum. As he went forward with his foot pinned the ankle popped and Herb went down. Herb had suffered a severely sprained ankle. That ended the game, of course, and I helped Herb hobble into the car.

The drive back to camp was a long one, let me tell you. Here I was with the ace of the staff, a man eager to bounce back from the injury-ruined 1957 but now a man holding his throbbing ankle. It started to balloon up real bad. I felt sick. I felt bad for Herb, of course, but also for the team. I could see any realistic chances of a pennant slip away in the back seat of that car.

"I did it real good this time, Ken," he said quietly. Even for a man as used to setbacks as Herb Score, it was a bitter blow. Yet I must say that Herb handled even that with his usual optimism. He didn't moan or complain; he accepted what had happened.

Back at camp, Herb iced his ankle down and made up a story about slipping in the shower. He did not want it in the papers that he had hurt himself playing basketball. I was the only other person to see what happened that day on the court. Herb and I agreed that the story would go no further, to keep it out of the papers. And to this day, some 42 years later, the story still hadn't been told.

Herb, in his rush and anxiety to recover from the ankle injury, hurt his arm. Instead of taking time off for the ankle to fully heal, he tried to come back too quickly. Favoring the ankle put a strain on his pitching arm, which led to a sore arm. Herb got into only 12 games in 1958, with just five of those appearances coming as starts. He finished with 41 innings pitched, an ERA approaching four, and a 2-3 record. Although he showed the occasional flash of brilliance, such as when he pitched a shutout in recording his only complete game of the year, clearly he wasn't throwing properly. What people feared after McDougald's line drive hit him in the face had come true as the result of a freak injury suffered in a completely meaningless game of pick-up basketball.

For all intents and purposes, Herb's career was over. He pitched with Cleveland through 1959 and with the White Sox until 1962, but was never the same again—18-26 over the last five years of his career. That afternoon on the basketball court in Tucson produced one of baseball's great tragedies: depriving the game, the fans, and this man from putting up the dazzling numbers that surely would have followed had he remained healthy.

The silver lining in all this was that it drove Herb Score into the broadcasting booth. I guess that was the "bigger plan" that Herb always believed in. He became a gifted sports announcer, and when I left the Indians after signing a personal service contract with Art Modell of the Cleveland Browns in 1964, Herb Score replaced me. I can't tell you how glad I was for Herb the day he got the No. 1 job. He's still No. 1 in my book.

Don't Knock the Rock

Perhaps no one on the team felt worse about Herb Score than Rocky Colavito. Rocky and Herb had been teammates and roommates in the minors. In fact, 1958 was a year of contrasts for the two friends. Herb hurt his arm in spring training and had a horrible year. On the other hand, Rocky came into his own and was named Indians' Man of the Year by the baseball writers. Rocky hit .303, blasted 41 home runs, and drove in 113 runs in playing 143 of the Tribe's 154 games. He even made one pitching appearance, going three innings in relief without giving up a run.

Each year, the Cleveland baseball writers had what they called their "Ribs and Roasts" dinner in January. They would present their awards from the previous season, also including some good-natured needling. The writers wrote a tribute to Rocky in the form of a song, sung to the tune of "Swanee:"

> *Rocky, when you're cloutin' hear 'em shoutin'*
> *We love you, Rocky.*
> *The way you smash that ball*
> *It gets the fans all hip-hoorayin, hear 'em sayin'*
> *Rocky, how we love ya' how we love ya'*
> *We're here to shout it.*
> *They named the right guy Man of the Year.*
> *Let's give the Rock a mighty cheer* (Kalman 17).

Rocky was a good-looking, affable man from the Bronx, New York. He had the dark, swarthy appearance of a movie star and the swagger to match. He began his career with the Indians and instantly the home town fell in love with its new right fielder.

Colavito could hit for average and power, and no one had a better arm in the outfield. He had an absolute howitzer for a throwing arm. Rocky brought optimism and an energetic style of play that captured the fancy of the fans and the press. For Bobby Soxers, he became a poster boy. For young boys, he was the guy they pretended to be when they were up there in a backyard game of pickup. For young men, he was the guy they wanted to be in the eyes of the girls. For the club, he was a box office sensation.

Rocky played with an enthusiasm that was contagious. Such was the love of the town for Rocky Colavito that when he was traded to the Tigers in April 1960, attendance dropped from 1,497,976 in 1959 to 950,985 the following year, Rocky's first out of Cleveland. The downward trend continued, bottoming out at 562,567 in 1963.

I've never seen such a reaction to a trade as when "Trader" Frank Lane announced the Colavito deal. It was bedlam. The only thing from my broadcasting days that came remotely close was when the Red Sox shipped fan-favorite Ken Harrelson to the Indians in the spring of 1969 for pitcher Sonny Siebert and catcher Joe Azcue.

The Colavito-Kuenn deal was made on April 17, 1960, two days before the start of the season. The deal shocked the Rock and sent the town of Cleveland into an uproar. Frank Lane was hung in effigy. People cancelled their season tickets. There were protests in front of the ballpark. Outraged fans picketed the front office.

Harvey Kuenn had led the American League in hitting with a .353 mark in 1959, but fans were nonetheless furious. Lane had traded their untouchable, handsome, charismatic star. The media treated it like an announcement of the next World War. The columnists and writers did their best and sometimes worst to fan the flames.

Lane defended the trade. He thought the team had enough pitching and power without Colavito, who had led the league in home runs in 1959. He made a throw-away comment that came back to haunt him. He pointed out that Kuenn could run, hit, and throw, while all Rocky could do was hit home runs. That remark enraged Cleveland fans. It made it sound like Rocky was just some one-dimensional stiff who could do nothing but slug the long ball. In fact, Rocky was a great all-around ballplayer whose only weakness was slowness afoot.

Tiger fans loved the trade. Kuenn was never that popular in Detroit, playing as he did in the shadow of superstar Al Kaline. For example, the next day the Detroit Free Press ran a banner headline: "42 HOME RUNS FOR 135 SINGLES!" That pretty much summed it up.

When the Tigers came to Cleveland for their first series in 1960, the game got top billing. There was a feverish tone in town similar to the atmosphere you get for a big football game. The fans cheered Rocky's every move, even though he struck out four times, popped up, and hit into a doubleplay.

"That was the only time in my whole pro career I ever struck out four times," Rocky said after the game. "I'd done it only one time in the sandlots" (Cope 54).

As it turned out, Kuenn was with us for only the one year. Harvey's average dropped from .353 to .308, with nine home runs with just 54 RBIs. All in all, considering the enormous pressure of coming in and replacing Rocky Colavito, it was a good year. But it just wasn't good enough, and all year Tribe fans gave Harvey a rough ride. Following the 1960 season, the Indians sent Kuenn to the San Francisco Giants for pitcher Johnny Antonelli and outfielder Willie Kirkland. That trade seemed as inevitable as the Colavito trade had seemed unlikely.

Colavito was a friendly man, full of life and nervous energy. He wore nothing but the best clothes and drove a black Cadillac and a white Thunderbird. He had a decent five years in Detroit. His best season came in 1961, when he hit 45 home runs, drove in 140 runs, and batted .290. The Tigers went 101-61 that year and even at that finished a full eight games behind the powerhouse '61 Yankees with the Maris-Mantle tandem and Whitey Ford going 25-4.

Rocky finally made it back to Cleveland in 1965 in a complicated three-way trade involving the Indians, A's, and White Sox, the kind you don't see any more in baseball.

The Indians sent pitcher Tommy John, catcher John Romano, and outfielder Tommy Agee to the White Sox. The A's got outfielders Jim Landis and Mike Hershberger and pitcher Fred Talbot from Chicago. The Indians picked up Rocky from the A's plus catcher Camillo Carreon from the White Sox.

The Indians were a mediocre ball club through the mid-60s; from 1961 to 65 they could be counted on to finish around .500 each year—sometimes a little below, sometimes a little above. They never seriously challenged for a pennant. Part of that was managerial instability. After Jimmy Dykes was fired at the end of the 1961 season, the Indians brought in Mel McGaha, who at 35 was the youngest manager in the majors. The idea was that McGaha would bring discipline and stability to the club for years to come, but he lasted only a season. Birdie Tebbetts replaced Mel in 1963.

McGaha came in and tried to be the disciplinarian. He stressed fundamentals and banned card playing in the clubhouse. In spring training, he'd fine players for missing the bus. During the season, he enforced curfews and pulled bed checks on the road, something that hadn't been done in years. He would bark out orders and personally supervise all workouts. For example, he'd rhetorically ask pitchers: "Did you do enough running?" If a player made a mental error, he'd threaten them with laps around the park.

The get-tough approach didn't work, and the Indians finished at 80-82, good for sixth place, 16 games behind the Yankees. Under Tebbetts, the team's performance wasn't that much better.

Monster Mash

We really did not have a great team or even a good one in the early to mid 1960s, but we were better than the Red Sox, who I still continued to follow. But I do vividly remember Birdie Tebbetts telling the team when we would go into Boston in those years, "You guys had better be ahead, because if you're not, The Big Guy will come in around the fifth or sixth inning, and if he does, that's it."

"The Big Guy" Birdie referred to was Dick Radatz, probably the most overpowering reliever ever to pitch. Dick was called The Monster, and the man who gave him that nickname was Mickey Mantle. Radatz faced Mantle 63 times in his career and struck him out 47 times. Mantle got one hit off Radatz, and it was a home run. When Mick crossed the plate, he hollered out to the mound, which was not his style at all.

"I finally got you, Monster," Mick yelled, laughing. Radatz nodded back. The nickname stuck.

It's interesting—Radatz came to Cleveland from Boston in 1966, the same year I made the same trip, except in the reverse direction. There's a remarkable story about Radatz and his Boston manager at the time, Johnny Pesky.

In 1963, Johnny had used Dick in seven straight games. Now at that time, Radatz was living in Milton, Massachusetts, not far from Fenway Park, and Pesky ordered Dick to stay home so that he wouldn't be tempted to use him for an eighth consecutive time. Dick did as he was told, and watched the game on TV for three innings but then got itchy. He couldn't stay away, so he drove to the ballpark, put on his uniform, and walked into the dugout.

"What are you doing here?" Pesky asked. "Go down to the other end of the dugout."

Pesky felt that if he sent Dick to the far end, he wouldn't think of using him. The "out of sight, out of mind" theory.

Radatz moved down to the far end of the bench and stayed there. The game was close and in the seventh inning, Radatz looked at Pesky. Pesky looked back. Dick gave Johnny a little Cheshire-cat smile. The next thing you knew, Radatz was in the game, which went into the 14th inning. Dick pitched eight innings of brilliant relief and got the win. It's never happened before or since that I know of—the winning pitcher starting the game by sitting at home watching the game on TV.

After the game, Pesky called Radatz into his office.

"If you show up tomorrow, it will cost you $1,000," the manager said.

"But Johnny," Dick said in his deep, husky voice, "I'm only making $11,000."

"One thousand if I see your face tomorrow," Pesky repeated. "You don't even know the way to Fenway Park for tomorrow's game."

The next day, Dick went to Cape Cod.

But that's the type of guy The Monster was and remains to this day—always there when he's needed. That's been true off the field as well. Radatz has done much work for others in need, particularly for the Jimmy Fund of the Dana-Farber Cancer Institute in Boston and also the Major League alumni association, helping former players who have fallen on tough times. Dick made a lot of saves, both in and out of baseball, and I'm proud to know him.

So that's the way my career went through the 1965 season and in the early days of January 1966. I felt incredibly lucky all that time to be making my living broadcasting professional sports, to get paid good money for covering guys like Otto Graham, Jim Brown, Herb Score, Rocky Colavito, and Bob Feller.

It had been a succession of stops that beginning in the late 1940s had led me closer and closer—and finally into—Major League broadcasting (football and baseball). But it also led me farther and farther away, or so it seemed, from my hometown of Boston.

Besides, I was happy with my career in Cleveland. I had done Browns football and Indians baseball, did the 6 and 11 p.m. TV sports, broadcast Ohio State football, hosted a TV show called "Cleveland Browns' Quarterback Club," did daily sportscasts (12:10

p.m. and 5:50 p.m.) on WHK, and was kept busy with other TV and radio work and speaking engagements. I couldn't imagine anything that could get me to leave the situation I had built up for myself in Ohio.

And as I realize now, that's exactly when fate comes knocking on your door: just when you least expect it.

CHAPTER 7

Mention My Name
Back in Boston

A RETURN TO THE HUB

Going Home

In 1963, General Manager Gabe Paul of the Indians surprised me with a request I didn't understand. He asked me to give up Browns football. For ten years, I had been doing both Browns and Indians games. Now for some reason, Gabe wanted me to concentrate exclusively on baseball. Gabe basically gave me an ultimatum. He said I had to give up the Browns in order to continue with the Indians.

I had a decision to make, and Art Modell made it easier than it otherwise would have been. I signed a personal-services contract with Art to continue as Voice of the Browns.

Art, always a sharp businessman, saw Gabe's request as an opportunity. In addition to sweetening my deal with the Browns, Art also included in the deal other TV shows, including a bowling show and golf tournaments. The financial arrangements were generous, and they enabled me to leave the Indians while actually making more money. That's the kind of guy Art Modell is. Sure, he was trying to "lock me up" for himself, but he did so in a way that completely supported my aspirations and my situation. Given the amount of money Art was offering along with the added exposure, it became a no-brainer.

I must say that Gabe Paul was great about the whole thing. Gabe said that while he was sorry to see me leave as Voice of the Indians, he understood why I accepted Art Modell's offer. We parted on friendly terms.

In fact, I was at the Wigwam, the pressroom at Cleveland's Municipal Stadium in the winter of 1966 having lunch with broadcaster Herb Score and Gabe. Rosemary O'Connor of the Tribe's PR staff came in the room and casually mentioned that the wire just ran a piece on Curt Gowdy. Curt was leaving his long-time broadcasting job as Voice of the Boston Red Sox to go full time with NBC. Gowdy was and still is a broadcasting legend. Curt—a solid, competent broadcaster, really one of the best of all time—was a Boston fixture (Curt has since gone on to broadcast more major events than anyone else in sports broadcasting history).

The news of Gowdy's departure came as a great surprise. As soon as I heard it, a light went on inside my head. That's a cliché but that's exactly how it felt—one of those "Eureka!" moments. I've never had a moment quite like that one. I was instantly clear on what I had to do. I got up from the table and made it to the nearest phone. As quickly as my fingers could spin the numbers on the rotary dial, I called the Red Sox offices on Jersey Street in Boston.

At Fenway Park, Helen Robinson answered. Helen's an amazing woman. She's been the switchboard operator at Fenway for six decades and is still going strong. I asked for Sox General Manager Dick O'Connell. Dick came on the line, and I told him I was interested in the job. He said he was pleased to hear that and told me he'd get back to me.

It's probably best I rushed right away to that telephone; I was thinking with my heart more than my head. If I had thought about it logically and abstractly, I probably would have talked myself out of it, rationalized a great deal about my comfy set-up in Cleveland, and gone on eating my lunch.

Here I was in Cleveland, well established with a nice home, strong community ties, a TV sports show, a radio show, six times named best Ohio sportscaster, and recipient of 14 awards from

AFTRA for broadcasting excellence. I was entrenched, almost a local institution. I was set. "Secure" might be a better word. But security is an illusion. The only security in life comes from attitude; it doesn't come from what you have but from who you are.

I knew in my heart that if I didn't make a push for the Boston job, I'd regret it for the rest of my life.

About a week later, I got a call from O'Connell. He invited me to meet with him and Harold Clancy, the boss of the old *Boston Herald Traveler* and head of WHDH Radio and TV. The night before, my wife Ellen and I flew to Boston. I remember saying to Ellen:

"If all things are equal (I meant financially, what with five children to support), I *must* take this job. It's something I've always wanted, going back to my childhood days."

Ellen agreed. When the choice is between home and anything else, you go home if you possibly can.

I met with O'Connell and Clancy at the WHDH studios on Morrissey Boulevard in Dorchester. It didn't take long. They made me an offer of almost twice what I was making in Cleveland. I was almost bowled over, though I didn't show it. You never should in these types of negotiations, although I never had a problem expressing my deep appreciation, which I did to O'Connell and Clancy.

They were very clear on one point, however. They insisted that if I took the job, I was to do what *they* wanted when it came to other work. Gowdy had been doing a lot of outside work; they didn't want that to happen with me, which was fine. My only request was that I would not be involved in doing both the 6 and 11 o'clock sports reports on television during the off season, which I had been doing for 12 years in Cleveland. When they agreed to that, I knew we had a deal.

We agreed to meet the next day to finalize the deal. Ellen and I took a drive down to a part of Wollaston Beach where we occasionally stopped when I was courting her. We discussed the situation. There wasn't much to discuss, really. From a financial standpoint, I would probably have to accept this deal if it were in Lame Deer, New Mexico. But this was home, the place I grew up. This was the ocean, fried clams, and lobster. This was family and friends.

And mostly, it was Fenway Park and the Boston Red Sox. Ellen felt the same way.

We were absolutely thrilled.

I called Dick O'Connell and officially accepted the offer. I could almost "hear" Dick's smile over the phone. I was the man they wanted, he said, and believe me, that felt great. Art Modell, always a class act, released me from my contract. He wanted what was in my best interest when he could have acted selfishly and stood in the way of the Boston job. He congratulated me and said the Browns would miss me. I told him the feeling was mutual.

I would miss the Browns, but if the whole truth is told, I was probably ready for a move after the 1965 season. Football was changing. Jim Brown had announced his retirement. There were also the first rumblings of labor unrest. Bills Coach Lou Saban, coming off an AFL title, quit to take the head coaching job at the University of Maryland. One of the reasons he cited were the huge bonus packages then being given out to rookies (e.g., Joe Namath getting $400,000 from the Jets; Donny Anderson signing with the Packers for $600,000; Tommy Nobis getting $600,000 from Atlanta).

A number of players were grumbling about working conditions and were going public about it, guys like Ernie Ladd and Earl Faison in San Diego, Nick Buoniconti of the Patriots, Gail Cogdill of the Lions, and Andy Stynchula of the Giants.

Stynchula did the unthinkable—he played out his option, forcing the Giants to trade him to Baltimore. There was even talk that Jimmy Hoffa was interested in organizing the players. In fact, it was this unrest that helped lead to the merger of the AFL and NFL, setting up the Super Bowl in 1967 (following the 1966 season). In and of themselves, these changes didn't bother me, but when taken in the context of the Red Sox offer, it made it just that much easier to say goodbye to the Browns.

When I took the Red Sox job, it was to do baseball only in what is perhaps the greatest sports town in America. My signing made the front pages of the Boston papers. The team had a full-blown press conference at Fenway Park. My brother Bill was there and the press took a picture of the two of us looking out at Fenway Park. It was a great moment to share with family. The Red Sox and press made it into a big deal, but I can honestly say my hat size remained the same.

We ended up living in Cohasset on the South Shore because of former Indians pitcher Dick Donovan, my high school classmate and teammate. When I was a senior at North Quincy High in 1943, Dick was a sophomore. We also played countless hours of sandlot ball together. A whole bunch of us would play all day, starting in the morning around 9 a.m. and going until noon, when we'd break for lunch. Following that, we'd resume and go all afternoon. Incidentally, Dick's older brother Mickey was a fine ballplayer too.

Dick was one of those kids who grew up late. Donovan was maybe 5 feet 6, a small, almost fragile boy. But even then I had a feeling about him as a ballplayer. He played shortstop while I pitched. He wasn't very fast, but he had a sense of the game. He batted left and could hit the ball a long way.

Dick Donovan eventually did what all the rest of us at O'Neill Field only fantasized about: he made it to the Major Leagues. When I came back from the war, Dick was under contract as a pitcher for the Boston Braves. Dick kicked around for a few years in the minors before he made it.

In fact, he not only made it, he made it big. He was in the starting rotation for the American League champion Chicago White Sox in 1959, coming back from an appendectomy operation. He also had a couple of outings in the World Series that year against the Dodgers. In fact, he started Game Three in the Coliseum, which was the first World Series game ever played west of St. Louis. That sounds unbelievable to hear it now. It was also played before the largest crowd in baseball history—92,294.

Dick had gone into the seventh inning with a two-hit shutout. It was an odd game. The White Sox got a bunch of hits and had all sorts of runners on, but they couldn't deliver the runners. In the bottom of the seventh in a 0-0 game, with one on and two outs, Dick lost his control. He walked Norm Larker, then Gil Hodges. With the bases loaded, Al Lopez came to the mound and took the ball from Donovan.

Dick, fierce competitor that he was, didn't want to leave the game and was not happy about being lifted. Lopez brought in reliever Gerry Staley and Walt Alston countered with pinch hitter Carl Furillo. Furillo hit a ground ball to Luis Aparicio's left. The ball hopped over Luis' glove for a base hit and two runs. The final score of the game was 3-1 Dodgers, with this line score:

CHICAGO...........1-12-0
LOS ANGELES.....3- 5-0

Dick's start in Game Three stands out in my mind for another reason. The Cleveland Browns had played the Chicago Cardinals on a Sunday afternoon in Chicago and at the Chicago airport, the whole team was watching the World Series. There I am, a professional broadcaster for one of the powerhouse teams in football, looking up at the little box showing the pictures. And there is Dick, the small kid who played behind me at shortstop in high school, pitching brilliantly against Don Drysdale and matching him with goose eggs through six innings. The moment had a surreal quality about it.

Dick appeared in two more games in the '59 Series, both in relief. In fact, he got the save in the 1-0 White Sox victory over Sandy Koufax in Game Five.

Dick had a fine career. In 1961, he led the American League in ERA (2.40) with Washington. He won 20 games for the Indians in 1962. He also hit 15 home runs (tied with Lefty Grove), which was a great total for a pitcher. He finished with career totals of 122 wins, 99 losses, and a 3.67 ERA.

Dick and his wife Pat had a home in Cohasset in 1962. Whenever the Indians visited Boston, I stayed with my mother, Frances. One Saturday that summer, Dick invited me to his home for a cookout. Mom insisted that I go, and I went with Herb Score, the man who later replaced me as Indians' broadcaster.

It was a beautiful afternoon in late August, and Dick drove us around the town. I never knew Cohasset before. I loved it, and I remember going back to Cleveland and saying to Ellen: "I don't picture us ever moving back to Boston, but if we ever do, I've found the town we'll live in. It's beautiful."

And so it was that four years later, as newly named broadcaster for the Boston Red Sox, we moved to Cohasset, a lovely home 23 miles from Fenway Park and two miles from Nantasket Beach. Friends, neighbors, and colleagues in Cleveland threw a surprise party for Ellen and me at Lakewood Country Club. Many of the Browns football players were there, as well as the team's coach, Blanton Collier. It was hard to say goodbye, but that paled in comparison to the dream I was about to fulfill of being the announcer for my team, the Red Sox.

"Mercy!"

In spring 1966, I joined the Red Sox in Winter Haven, Florida, for spring training. The men in the booth with me were terrific. Mel Parnell, our TV color man, was a great Boston lefthander in his playing days and truly a Southern gentleman. Al Walker, our engineer, was from Methuen and one of the most thoughtful, conscientious, hard-working, and decent men I've ever known.

And then there was broadcast partner Ned Martin. Ned's strengths were his superb, understated vocabulary, his literate insights, his intelligence, and his sense of the rhythm of the game of baseball. He understood the game in all its aspects, and that was his greatest asset, that along with a resonant, energetic voice.

Ned had a couple of signature lines that fans just loved to hear. When someone would do something extraordinary on the field, Ned would say "Mercy!" A frozen rope that a batter would line into the outfield would be described as "Rip City." Ned would call Al Walker "Demon Engineer Al Walker" in tribute to Al's dedication, and that's how a generation of Boston baseball fans came to identify Al.

Ned was also adept at rising to the occasion. He could make a big moment in a game sound appropriately dramatic. In a laugher, Ned somehow found a way to keep people tuned in.

I remember a writer once telling me in Cleveland that he hated blow-out games.

"That's got to be murder on your guys in the booth."

"Yes," I replied. "It's tough to keep your concentration. But let me ask you, do you hear it in the announcer's voice?"

"Sometimes," he replied. "It's like they're not calling a real game, but a replica of a game."

"A replica of a game." That's an interesting phrase to describe what happens when an announcer's just going through the motions. Sometimes it happens, but I can honestly say that in all the years I did games with Ned—thousands of games—I never saw him do this once. I guess you have to be a seasoned broadcaster to realize how special that is.

In fact, there was only one ticklish matter in my coming to Boston and taking the No. 1 job with the Red Sox. Ironically, it involved Ned. I knew that Ned wanted the top job, and understandably so. He had been covering the team since 1961. When I accepted the Red Sox offer, I was a little worried about how Ned would react and take to me.

Today I can look back on those feelings and laugh, because if I had known Ned then the way I do now, I wouldn't have been concerned at all. Because, you see, besides being one of the all-time great broadcasters, Ned was even better as a person. He fought with the Marines during World War II, seeing some tough action on Iwo Jima. If that's not character and bravery, I don't know what is. True to form, Ned never talked much about that experience. He was quiet and modest about his accomplishments and his life, a true gentleman all the way.

Once I got the Boston job, I wrote Ned a letter. I wrote that I definitely was a guy who didn't have people work *for* me. My partners on the air worked *with* me, and I worked with them. From that time on, Ned and I developed an excellent relationship on the air and off, a relationship that remains true to this day. He's one of my closest, dearest friends, and I think he stands as one of the best baseball broadcasters ever. I put him up there with Red Barber, Vin Scully, Mel Allen, and Jon Miller.

"I'm Here to be Me"

A writer asked me at my first press conference in Boston about the pressure of "replacing" Curt Gowdy. There was a forest of microphones recording my every word, film cameras whirring, tape recorders in motion. It was a touchy question, because if I answered it one way, it could come off as presumptuous and sound like bragging. If answered the other way, it would sound like I lacked confidence.

I answered this way: "Nobody replaces a man like Curt Gowdy. I'm not here to replace him or become the new Curt Gowdy. I'm just here to do the best job I can, as Ken Coleman. I'm here to be me. If I do that, I hope the fans will respect that and respond to it. I've done Big League baseball for ten years, so I'm comfortable with my style, and I think the fans will be too. You may follow a Curt Gowdy, but you don't replace him."

Unlike how I felt those many years ago going from Worcester to Cleveland in 1952, I had no more fear or self-doubt. I was ready. Unfortunately, the 1966 Red Sox were not.

The 1966 Red Sox were very much like the Cleveland Browns, which is another way of saying that they won about once a week. Seriously, they wound up winning 72 games and losing 90 that year. Most of the wins came in the second half.

Hall of Famer Billy Herman, who was a great Cubs second baseman in his day, was the manager. Billy liked talking about his golf game more than he did about his baseball team. He was fired in September, and Pete Runnels managed the last 16 games of a season in which the Sox finished ninth in a 10-team league.

But during the second half of 1966, there were indications that next year might be better. A young pitcher named Jim Lonborg won 10 games and was rapidly maturing on the mound. Jose Santiago came over from the Kansas City Athletics and pitched fine baseball in the starting rotation. Carl Yastrzemski, Rico Petrocelli, Tony Conigliaro, Joe Foy, and rookie first baseman George Scott were all young and getting better by the day.

Scott had won the Triple Crown the year before at Double A in Pittsfield, Massachusetts, working under manager Eddie Popowski. This earned him a look in the '66 camp, and he had such a good spring that Herman could not leave him off the team. George tore up the league in the first half of the season, hitting 18 home runs by the All-Star break. For his exploits, George was named starting first baseman for the American League All Stars.

I used to sit on the team bus with Scott and enjoyed his company very much. A big man from Greenville, Mississippi, he used to kid me about the fact that he went to Coleman High School. We are all gifted in some things in life and not so in others. We all have talents and abilities. For example, some people are what they call "street smart," while others are book smart. Some can fix cars, some can't. Some can paint pictures, some can write well. George Scott could play first base. He is, without a doubt, one of the greatest defensive first basemen of all time.

TV Versus Radio

As Voice of the Red Sox on radio and TV, I headed a three-man crew that alternated between booths. And the question often occurs to fans: which did I prefer, TV or radio? Also, what is the difference in terms of doing play by play for each? Personally, I preferred doing both radio and television, and alternating between the two during the game. That's the set-up I had with the Red Sox for my first seven years with the club.

The reason I liked it better than just doing strictly radio or strictly TV is that it keeps you sharper over the long haul. In that situation, I think a broadcaster has a tendency to do a little better job because he's less likely to fall into a rut. Doing radio and TV keeps you fresher, because each requires a different approach in terms of play-by-play broadcasting.

There was much more radio involved. Typically, the Red Sox would broadcast every game of the 162-game schedule on radio and between 50 and 60 on television. In 1967, for example, we did 56 TV games. That was the perfect mix as far as I was concerned.

When we were doing a TV game, I would broadcast the first three innings on television, the middle three on the radio, and the final three on TV. Ned Martin would do just the opposite: 3-3-3 on radio-TV-radio. The third man in the booth, Mel Parnell in the middle 1960s, would do nine innings of color on TV only. Ned had a postgame television show, while I did pregame radio and TV shows. Al Walker, our engineer on radio, served in effect as our producer. He was the guy who kept us on the air, who gave us our cues and handled the technical side of things. When we were doing just radio, Ned and I shared the game. I called the first three and the last three, with Ned the three in the middle.

One thing a broadcaster must be alert for when switching from radio to television in doing a play by play is to "put on the brakes." By that I mean you have to cut your descriptions to the bone for TV. I think one of the problems with televised baseball today is that

TV broadcasters talk too much. Radio as a medium and TV as a medium are completely different and should be treated as such.

You watch tapes of some of the old games, and you'll see what I mean. Not long ago, I had a chance to catch a rebroadcast of one of the 1969 World Series games between the Mets and the Orioles. The game had been aired on NBC and featured Curt Gowdy and Lindsey Nelson with the play-by-play. It was immediately apparent how Curt and Lindsey let the pictures tell the story. It was so refreshing to hear—or not to hear, to be more precise. Contrast this to today, where you get two or sometimes three guys in the booth each trying to out-talk the other. I always thought of television as putting captions underneath pictures.

Almost all of the broadcasters I know say they prefer doing baseball on radio. Baseball is a radio game. Listeners rely on you to paint a word picture so they can "see" it in their heads. That's why they call radio "the theater of the mind." And the radio audience is often much bigger than television. For example, on a weekend, people are on the move—they're in cars going somewhere, at the beach, around a picnic table, outside working in the yard. They're not sitting in a living room when it's sunny and pleasant outside.

I think radio audiences are much more attentive than TV audiences, because they bring their imaginations into play. When listening to a radio description, they must provide the mental image. The radio announcer sees the live action first-hand and describes it. The fan listening in takes that description and "peoples" it according to his imagination. You might say, for example:

"Runners on first and second for the Yankees. Martinez looks in at Varitek for the sign, now finds one he likes. Pedro comes to the belt and checks the runners. He pauses. He pitches. Jeter sends a hard ground ball to short. Nomar to his left, makes a nice pick up, steps on the bag and throws to Stanley at first. Double play! The Red Sox are out of the inning!"

Each listener sees Martinez pause in a different way. Some will have him check the runners two times. Some will have him look over once. Garciaparra's grab of the ground ball will appear differently to each person listening. It's that job of creation that makes listening to the radio fun. The listeners are literally creating something out of your words.

The media critic Marshall McCluhan used to make the distinction between "hot" and "cool" media based on the degree of audience involvement required. Radio is a "hot" medium because the audience is more involved. TV is "cool" because the audience is much more passive. They just sit there and stare at the screen.

For a broadcaster, radio is simply more fun to do. You have more to do and get a greater chance to exercise your vocabulary, knowledge, and creativity. Everything that happens on the field must be described, and it's all done on an improvisational basis.

Some broadcasters have the talent and the knack to improvise much better than others. Ned Martin was a master at it. So were Vin Scully and Ernie Harwell. Today, I think Jon Miller and his partner Joe Morgan are probably the best. Jon, who does network television for ESPN baseball broadcasts, is the exception to the rule— he's a TV broadcaster who doesn't try to overwhelm the images with his talking. He lets the pictures largely speak for themselves.

On television, if you're broadcasting correctly, your words should never dominate, or even equal, the pictures. What a TV broadcaster says should supplement and not override what the viewers see. As I said, the job of the TV broadcaster is simply to put captions under pictures.

If a TV announcer were to try to broadcast a game as if he were on the radio, people would say, "What is that idiot doing?" For example, you don't do this on TV play-by-play:

"Morehead goes to the resin bag, now tugs at the bill of his cap. He stares now at his outfield, now he squares up on the rubber, looking for a sign from Tillman. Morehead goes into his windup, rears back, and comes in directly overhand. The fastball catches the outside corner to run the count to 0-2. He gets the ball back from Tillman and slaps it into his glove. Now he toes the rubber..."

If you did that on a TV broadcast, the viewer would say, "Why is he telling me all this?"

Sunday Morning Coming Down

Every day I spent at the ballpark was a great thrill for me, but my favorite day was Sunday, especially at Fenway Park. Sunday is a day made for baseball. The Day of Rest fits the Game of Rest like a well-broken-in fielder's glove, brown and oiled into cozy familiarity. The weekend chores are done, the Saturday night dinners and parties are over, work is still one day away for the fans, and the Sabbath eases slowly from morning into early afternoon to the ringing sound of batting practice.

I guess that's how I see heaven—as a sunny Sunday in Fenway Park in mid June, at about 11 in the morning, with Ted Williams in the cage taking BP. The park is empty, except for a sprinkling of stadium workers, who take a moment and sneak a look to the field. Players mill around the cage, waiting their turn, though they'd be content to watch all day as long as Ted stayed in there. The BP pitcher throws Popsicles, melons, roses, and lollipops, which The Kid returns with a cadence of rifle shots. The echo of the white horsehide meeting the nut-brown ash rings throughout the park and if it were a color, it would have to be translucent gold. If it were a food, it would have to be honey. The white spheres rise on a line up into the blue Boston sky, landing with a rattle in the deep right field stands. That's heaven.

To me, a baseball game played on a fair Sunday afternoon is delightfully contained in its proper time and element. Weeknight games, on the other hand, often get over past 10 p.m. By the time you get to your car and on the road, it's 11, 11:30. Then add the time it takes to get home. You're thinking of getting up for work the next morning. Your mind jumps around like someone's aiming a remote control device at your head, changing channels too quickly.

Sunday showcases baseball the way the right setting sets off a diamond.

Baseball is a game that doesn't engage you viscerally, the way hockey does. It doesn't overwhelm you the way football does, which, by the way, also loves its Sundays. Baseball lacks the constant running and pace of basketball. That's why to properly enjoy baseball, you need to clear off the mental desk.

If you can come to the contest willing to suspend your worries for three hours, baseball can take you out of yourself and help you lose your problems, if just for that time. If you can do this, nine innings becomes a soothing vacation. If you can't, nine innings becomes a restless ordeal.

This colored my approach to broadcasting. I tried not only to describe the action but also remain true to the pace of the game. I'd never try to artificially pump up my accounts.

I think I was able to induce a relaxed manner into my accounts of the game, something that helped me with players when I had to do interviews. I quickly got the reputation of someone who was fair and affable. Players didn't mind going on the air with me. They sometimes let their guard down and gave me more information than I would have otherwise obtained by taking a more hard-lined or aggressive approach.

For example, I remember doing a dugout interview one day with Brooks Robinson, Baltimore's great third baseman, at Fenway Park. I asked him: "You played a lot of baseball here in Boston. What is your most memorable moment?"

His answer was very interesting, I thought, and somewhat typical of Brooks Robinson, because it wasn't about some exploit of his:

"My biggest moment at Fenway Park was the final game we played here in the 1960 season, when Ted Williams came to bat against Jack Fisher and hit a home run in what turned out to be his last at bat in the majors.

"I'm playing third base. I'm just a young ballplayer in the league, a kid, really. Unbelievably, Ted puts one out into the Red Sox bullpen in right field. So here comes this legend pounding around second. He's over 40 years old. He's a great big guy, not the Splendid Splinter any more at this point in his career. When he trotted on by me, I said, 'Nice going, Ted.' He gave me, well, not quite a little bit of a wink, but a friendly glance. And he went on. I never had a bigger thrill in Fenway Park, and it was one of the great moments of my entire career."

A broadcaster always wants to have the excitement come through his voice when the moment warrants it and not let the boredom show when the game is a stinker. The best at this today, in my opinion, are Jon Miller and Vin Scully. Among the best all time, again in my view, were Red Barber, Ned Martin, and Mel Allen.

How About That!

Allen had the most incredible broadcasting voice; his "pipes" were simply amazing. Writer Curt Smith, who was chief speech writer for President George Bush and who authored the definitive book on baseball broadcasting titled *Voices of the Game*, once wrote of Mel, "A florist must have decorated his voice." Lindsey Nelson called Allen the best ever. I have to agree. The Voice virtually owned the World Series, because from 1949 to 1964, the Yankees were only out of it twice. And before 1966, the World Series was broadcast by the local teams' Voices. In all, Mel announced a record 20 World Series. That's how he developed a national following.

Speaking of Mel's famous voice, the great broadcaster Jim Woods once said, "It was a historic, astounding fit. Ignore his voice and Mel still did it all—the specifics, the clarity of detail, and love of language. Add it, and, well, even Dodgers and Giants fans listened in spite of themselves."

Mel would speak of pitchers who had "sundered a batsman." Batters would "call forth good." He used to think of the radio audience as "one solitary fan, who I imagined sitting a few feet away from me. In my mind, that one guy was my audience. I was talking to him" (Smith 52).

Tom Gallery, who was NBC's sports director during the height of Allen's success in the 1950s, recalled that "Mel was perfect for the big event. There was something about him, something in his presence, that brought a special drama to the moment" (53).

People were shocked when the Yankees fired Mel after the 1964 season—fans, players, and his broadcasting colleagues couldn't believe the Yankees would let him go. Red Barber said, "He gave the Yankees his life, and they broke his heart."

Almost 30 years after the fact, Allen's face would turn red and get flushed with anger and hurt at recalling his exit from the Yankees: "The Yankees never even held a press conference to announce my leaving. They left people to believe whatever they wanted, and people believed the worst. The lies that started were horrible, that I was a lush or beat relatives or had a breakdown or stroke or was numb from taking medications for my voice" (54).

Sports Illustrated put it this way: "Allen became a victim of rumors. He was supposed to be a drunkard, a drug user, but he couldn't fight them. It was as if he had leprosy" (54).

Fittingly, Mel made a triumphant return to baseball in 1977 when he became the narrator of "This Week in Baseball," which became the highest-rated sports show. *SI* wrote in a 1985 profile that The Voice was "back where he belongs, an old campaigner, a keeper of tradition. For years, he was a forgotten man, but it has all come back to him in abundance. The taste must be sweet" (54).

I know it was for me. When Mel came back with "This Week," I felt a tremendous sense of satisfaction. It was as if a wrong had been righted. It's not always or maybe even often that life works out that way, but sometimes it does, and when it does, it's "sweet" indeed.

Mel went into the Baseball Hall of Fame in 1978 along with Red Barber. How about that!

8

A Miracle in Boston

THE IMPOSSIBLE DREAM

Transformation

I'm often asked to identify the biggest thrill of my career. There have been many of them. I've done network play-by-play for World Series and NFL Championship games, broadcasting games to the entire country. I've been on hand for some of the most memorable moments in baseball history, for example, Rocky Colavito hitting four home runs in one game, Pete Rose's 3,000[th] hit, and the night Roger Clemens struck out 20 batters for the first time in baseball history. I was in the booth to call the games of the 1954 Indians and The Big Red Machine at its zenith. I also had the thrill of calling both Carl Yastrzemski's 400th home run and 3,000[th] hit.

But despite all of the great things I have been a part of in my long career as a sports broadcaster, I have no problem or hesitancy identifying *THE* single thrill that stands out among all the rest. That would be the improbable championship of the 1967 Boston Red Sox. That season has gone on in baseball lore to be known as The Impossible Dream.

If you grew up in New England and were interested in baseball, chances are you were and still are a zealous Red Sox fan. You might have known the old timers who could remember that the

Sox were baseball's first dynasty, when they won six world championships by 1918 (that includes the 1904 default of John McGraw's New York Giants, who, rather than risk humiliation by being defeated by Boston's upstart American League team, conceded the title).

The Red Sox didn't win their next American League pennant until 1946, a powerhouse team that had two 20-game winners in Tex Hughson and Dave "Boo" Ferris, the peerless doubleplay tandem of Johnny Pesky and Bobby Doerr, the underrated Dom DiMaggio in center, and of course, Teddy Ballgame in left.

The Sox came close to a pennant a few more times in the late 40s and early 50s, but by the late 50s, the Red Sox had declined, finishing in the second division eight straight years from 1959 through 1966.

Then came 1967, when what couldn't happen did.

Wherever I go on speaking engagements, public appearances, or just run into people on the street, invariably I get asked about what it was like in 1967, when a 100-to-1 longshot cashed in on one of the most unlikely championships in sports history. I should know how to answer that because I was there for literally every single pitch, from the top of the first inning in the Grapefruit League opener (March 10 on the road in Sarasota, Florida.) to the final out in Game Seven of the World Series (October 12 at home in Boston).

The true answer to the question, of course, is, "You had to be there." And many of them were, following the team as it went through the roller coaster ride of the closest pennant race in baseball history.

To fully understand why 1967 became what it has become, you have to go back to the eight years of futility preceding it. There were some great individual performances by such players as third baseman Frank Malzone, outfielder Carl Yastrzemski, and pitchers like Bill Monbouquette, Earl Wilson, and Dick Radatz, but too many of Boston's players were second-line talents.

Some players who showed enormous promise never really fulfilled it. Cases in point would be two players who starred as rookies in 1961 only to flop in '62: second baseman Chuck Schilling and pitcher Don Schwall.

Schilling broke in with the Red Sox in 1961 after two years in the minors in which he hit .314 and .340. He had a great first year. His average wasn't gaudy, .259 from the lead-off spot, but he had more hits that season than Roger Maris (61 home runs) or Mickey Mantle (54 home runs). Schilling did everything well—he got on base a lot, drove in key runs, sacrificed and moved the runners along, and always seemed to be in the right position on the field. In fact, defensively at second base Chuck was spectacular, setting an all-time record for fielding at the keystone corner.

Second base had been a problem ever since the great Bobby Doerr ended his 14-year career when he retired in 1951, but after Chuck Schilling's promising debut in 1961, the Sox looked set at second base for the next 14 years. However, in 1962 Chuck started the season 0-for-26. Just when he was starting to hit, he broke his wrist. He struggled to hit .230, and soon after he was relegated to the bench.

Schwall was named Rookie of the Year in 1961 with a 15-7 mark, but in 1962 he slumped to 9-15 with his ERA rising from 3.22 to 4.94. The next year, he was traded to Pittsburgh for slugger Dick Stuart.

Lu Clinton, Jim Pagliaroni, Jim Gosger, Bob Tillman, Dave Morehead, Tracy Stallard, Jerry Stephenson and so many others seemed to possess all the tools necessary to succeed in the Big Leagues but couldn't put it together. Clinton was a star for the second half of the 1962 season. Morehead was a star for one game, when he pitched a no-hitter at Fenway in 1965. Stallard achieved fame for one pitch —he gave up the 61st home run hit by Roger Maris in 1961.

There were some great young arms in the early to mid-60s who never made it at all, except for a token appearance or two. These included pitchers like Gloucester's Bill McLeod (who went a perfect 18-0 for Double A Pittsfield in 1965), Hal Kolstad, Stew MacDonald, Pete Smith, Pete Magrini, Bill Spanswick, Pete Charton, and Dave Gray.

Some bonus babies were signed for huge money but never paid off in dividends for the Sox or their fans. Bobby Guindon of Brookline, right outside of Boston, was a local hitting star at Boston English High School. The Red Sox outbid almost every other club in baseball to sign Guindon for a reported $125,000, only to find out too late that he couldn't hit a curveball. Bobby got a total of eight at-bats in the Majors, all in 1964. He got one hit, a double. For $125,000, it was one of the most expensive doubles in history.

Bill "Rudy" Schlesinger and Pete Jernigan were two other bright hitting prospects in the mid-60s, again signed for big money. Schlesinger made his one and only plate appearance on May 4, 1965, and was never heard from again. Jernigan signed with the Sox in April 1960 after starring in four sports in high school. He was a hitting sensation at Alpine in the Sophomore League, where he hit .342. The following year at Waterloo in the Midwest League, Pete batted .382. He was with the Sox in spring training that year and impressed everybody, but never got into one Major League game—not in 1961 or any other year.

Attendance at Fenway Park plummeted, reaching a low point on September 28, 1965, when 461 lonely souls filed into Fenway for a game against the Angels. That's unimaginable now, a gate that low, but that gives you an idea of how badly baseball in Boston had declined. There were even rumors that Tom Yawkey was looking to sell the team, and that the buyers would move the Sox elsewhere.

In 1966, my first year as Voice of the Red Sox, the Red Sox finished ninth in a ten-team league, one-half game ahead of the New York Yankees. At first glance it looked like more of the same—a bleak performance by an uninspired team before indifferent fans. However, underneath the surface, some strong currents of hope were flowing and starting to ripple up to the top.

For one thing, Boston played some of the best baseball in the league during the season's second half. In fact, from the end of July to season's end, they had the best record in baseball (which shows just how miserable they were in the first half).

The positive feelings going into 1967 intensified when the team named firebrand Dick Williams as its new manager. Williams had been managing the club's Triple A club in Toronto. In 1963 and '64, Williams was a journeyman on the Red Sox finishing up a long baseball career in a utility role. He experienced the Red Sox at a time when the team had a reputation of being the Country Club of baseball. They were underperformers on the field, and overdoing it off the field—late hours, carousing, that sort of thing.

Williams, a product of the Dodger system, took notes on what he saw during his two years as a player in Boston. What disturbed him the most was the complacency: not enough fire for winning.

When he became manager, Williams vowed that the Country Club days were over in Boston. From the beginning of his tenure as Sox manager, Williams made it clear who was boss. He didn't manage—he dictated. He let everyone know that one person and one person only ran the show in Boston, a man by the name of Dick Williams. All others who said or acted otherwise were pretenders to the throne and would soon be defeated. Williams said he wouldn't make the mistake of trying to make his players happy. He was going to run the club *his* way, take it or leave it.

Dick had the reputation of being tough, brash, aggressive, authoritarian, hard nosed ... and a winner. He was the perfect choice at the exact correct time for precisely the right team. The planets were lining up in the heavens.

When asked at his inaugural press conference to name a goal, he said he was interested in just one thing: winning. Dick also pledged to do whatever was necessary to accomplish that, spare no one or nothing. Some of the jaded Boston press thought of Williams' declaration as a blustery wind that would soon die down once the season began. There were even snickers when Manager Williams had the audacity to announce that the woeful Sox would win more than they would lose. They hadn't done that since the 50s. Many others, though, thought what I did: this wasn't a blustery wind. It was a blast of fresh air.

Some of the snickers stopped when Dick demoted Carl Yastrzemski as team captain. The Red Sox, he said, would not have a player serve as captain.

"There will be no captains on the Red Sox this year," Williams said in announcing the move. "As of right now, they no longer have a captain. They don't need a captain. They have a manager. That's what Mr. Yawkey is paying me to do—lead this team."

One thing was certain: the Red Sox were not going to be the same in 1967. Indeed, by the time the season was over, the Sox had won a championship. Boston baseball, threatened by years of poor play on the field and at the gate, experienced a rebirth. The dying franchise came to life and hasn't looked back since.

Bye Bye, Berde

In 1967, Carl Yastrzemski put together what is perhaps the finest all-around individual baseball season a man has ever had. Yaz won the Triple Crown (the last man to do so) and down the stretch made play after amazing play in the field—brilliant catches, impossible throws to catch opposing runners on the bases, playing the Green Monster like it was a Stradivarius and he was the master violinist.

But his season didn't come out of the blue. In fact, by the time spring training rolled around that year, Yaz had already paid some painful dues. No one worked harder than Yaz that year to prepare for the upcoming season.

The year before, in 1966, Yaz had hit only .278 with 16 home runs. Carl, an intensely competitive man who burned with a desire to win, was determined to change that. He contacted Gene Berde, the physical activities director at the Colonial Statler Hilton Inn and Resort in Wakefield, Massachusetts. Berde had been the Hungarian Olympic coach from 1928 to 1956. Berde invited Yaz down to the Colonial for a meeting.

The first thing Berde had Yaz do was jump rope. After no more than a minute or two, Yaz was too tired to continue.

"I don't know," Berde said in his thick accent and shaking his head, coming off like a Hungarian Don Rickles. "You the big athlete. I see your picture in the papers and everything and you can't jump rope for half a minute. In Hungary, you are nothing" (Sisti 75).

With that, Berde, a man who was 40 years older than Yaz, took up the jump rope and jumped vigorously for five minutes. The gesture punctured Yaz's pride and awoke in him a fiery determination. Carl responded with a fanatic devotion to his workouts. By the time spring training rolled around, Yaz was in the best shape of his life— he had much greater strength and endurance and had hardened his body tissue into nothing but muscle.

Berde recalled working with the budding superstar:

"After about a half-minute of exercise, he almost died. I was very surprised. Yaz had a good body, but he was weak and lazy. How could he be an athlete? But he saw the difference. I don't think anybody ever talked to him like that. It got him a little bit in the head. After all, what do baseball players do? Someone throws the ball, you hit and run. 'Okay,' I said, 'run.' I took him into a corridor about 60 yards long. 'Run,' I said. Yaz was pooped after two trips. Then he picked up the weights to show me he was strong. 'You don't need that,' I told him. 'You're a strong boy. You don't need heavy muscles. Not enough elastic. Too slow. Flabby waist. We build your legs and lungs.' Yaz was always getting tired and didn't have enough resistance. He watched me exercise and I did everything better than him. Then he listened to me" (75).

Yaz dove into his workouts with the zeal of a convert. By the time his winter sessions were over, he was in remarkable physical condition. Yaz stayed in top shape all year and had a season for the ages.

The other star was pitcher Lonborg, who learned to come inside, knocking batters off the plate. Jim went on to win the Cy Young Award, leading the league in strikeouts. Gentleman Jim became the loop's most feared pitcher. In 273 innings, Jim gave up just 228 hits, walked 83 and struck out 246 in compiling a 22-9, 3.16 mark. He also led the league in hit batsmen.

There were outstanding contributions from many unlikely members of the team:

- Weak-armed Jose Tartabull throwing out the swift Ken Berry at the plate in a key late August game,
- Bill Landis getting Eddie Matthews on strikes in a big game in Detroit, and
- Lee Stange throwing a three-hit shutout to quiet the hot Twins in late July at steaming Fenway.

There were unexpected heroics from Jerry Adair and Dalton Jones, who filled in so well when Rico Petrocelli broke his wrist and missed four weeks. George Thomas, Ken Harrelson, and Tartabull took up the slack when Tony Conigliaro went down in August. Mike Andrews and Joe Foy, still youngsters, held their own in the infield. George Scott hit over .300 with power and provided air-tight defense at first.

The pitching staff, largely undistinguished outside of Lonborg, kept the team in games all season long. Pitching coach Sal Maglie and Manager Williams held the staff together with glue, spit, rubber bands, and paper clips, and somehow found the right mix. Guys like Gary Bell, Stange, Jose Santiago, Darrell Brandon, Dave Morehead, Gary Waslewski, and Jerry Stephenson shared starting duties in a rotation by committee. The relief corps featured John Wyatt, who had a 2.60 ERA in 60 games, backed by rookie lefthander Sparky Lyle.

Truly, this was a team effort. Yes, there were tremendous individual efforts, but for the first time in many years, the Red Sox lived and died as a unit. No more "25 guys, 25 cabs." They all got aboard the same bus, one that would take them on a baseball Magical Mystery Tour (it was, after all, 1967—the Summer of Love).

That's why I identify 1967, particularly the pulsating second half of the year, as my greatest thrill in sports. In Boston, the championship season ended a long drought. All of New England, most of the country, and even some of the world got caught up in baseball.

Writer Dan Valenti points out that The Impossible Dream featured one of the most powerful plots in all of literature, the plot from Exodus in the Old Testament. In this plot, people who live in a comfortable homeland are driven out. They spend a long time in a hostile desert, then find the Promised Land in the end. You couldn't script it any better.

Prior to 1967, not one member of the team had ever been part of a .500 ball club in Boston. Winning was a new experience, and it was fun. I witnessed the exuberance of the ballplayers. I can still see a spontaneous celebration erupting in the Red Sox clubhouse after yet another key home victory, this one in July against the Angels.

Tony Conigliaro stood up on his stool and thundered: "We cannot be beat." I can see Yaz, standing in the doorway, and greeting every member of the team as they filed down the runway and into the clubhouse. I can see Joe Foy screaming in delight and Mike Andrews dancing with Reggie Smith. I see Yaz, now seated in front of his locker in his underwear, stirring a mixture of ice cream and soda in a paper cup, pretending it's champagne.

Guys couldn't wait to get to the park. Nothing could dampen their enthusiasm—not slumps, not fatigue, not even Uncle Sam. Jim Lonborg spent some time in Atlanta in July pulling Army duty

The young buck, on the job in 1947 at WJDA in my hometown of Quincy, Massachusetts.

In 1951, I was behind the WJDA microphone to broadcast the Tech Tournament at the Boston Garden. I'm flanked here by Joe Tobin, left, one of the station owners, and Munroe Maclean, coach at Quincy High School.

Flying high in Ohio in the early '50s.

Deep in thought in the Cleveland Browns' TV booth at Municipal Stadium, early 1960s.

My first speaking date in Ohio, August 1952, in Warren. The Browns' training camp was under way, and so was I.

Interviewing THE MAN, Paul Brown, in the early 1950s.

On the set of my Red Sox pregame show, circa 1966-67. Returning to Boston was a dream come true.

(Ken Coleman's private collection)

Coming back to Boston also meant the joy of getting involved with the Jimmy Fund. Here I am with Red Sox outfielder Don Demeter in 1966, accepting a check from some boys representing youth baseball.

(Ken Coleman's private collection)

Interviewing Jim Brown at the premier of his first movie, *Rio Conchos*. Jim got great reviews for his acting. That's Jim's wife in the middle, finding my line of questioning amusing.

(Ken Coleman's private collection)

Carl Yastrzemski explains the winning feeling.

(Boston Red Sox)

(Boston Red Sox)

In the early 1970s, I teamed in the broadcast booth with ex-Red Sox shortstop and manager Johnny Pesky.

"Hi, neighbor. Have a 'Gansett." I could pour a beer into a glass with the best of them.

(Ken Coleman's private collection)

In 1975, I moved to the TV booth of the Cincinnati Reds. This was a broadcast team worthy of the Big Red Machine. Seated from left are Joe Nuxhall and Marty Brennaman. Standing beside me in the snazzy Reds sports jacket is Woody Woodward.

(Ken Coleman's private collection)

In 1974 at the Fenway batting cage with Bob Uecker, a lifetime .200 hitter but a .400 broadcaster. My jacket and Ueck's pants are quite a match, don't you think?

(Ken Coleman's private collection)

After Jon Miller left to take the job as Voice of the Orioles, Joe Castiglione became my partner in the radio booth. I greatly enjoyed working with Joe.

(Ken Coleman's private collection)

(Boston Red Sox)

The Jimmy Fund still remains a big part of my life and work. Here, Dwight Evans and I meet with a fine and courageous young man.

(Ken Coleman's private collection)

Yours truly and The Mick.

(Ken Coleman's private collection)

Shaking hands with President Ronald Reagan in the Oval Office.

Holy Cow!
Sharing cannolis
with The Scooter
himself.

(Ken Coleman's private collection)

Sharing the stage with Curt Gowdy was always an honor. When I came to Boston in 1966, I knew I wouldn't "replace" Gowdy. You don't "replace" a man like Curt.

(Ken Coleman's private collection)

Ken and Zim, two baseball Buddahs.

(Pat Germani)

Earl Weaver takes a puff while I put a question to him in Baltimore, 1989, my final year as a major league baseball broadcaster. His answer was, "Kenny, a three-run homer."

Here I am with Muhammad Ali, mixing it up in Hernando, Florida. We were in town for the opening of Ted Williams' Hitters Museum.

Working in the broadcasting booth at Shea Stadium during the World Series with color man and analyst Sparky Anderson.

The way I'll always want to be remembered—behind the microphone, calling a game.

(can you imagine that happening today to some star pitcher?). He stayed in shape by working out with the Braves. He then flew back to make his next two starts.

What was 1967 like? The season always reminded me of that moment in "The Wizard of Oz," when the film turns from black and white to color.

What was 1967 like? For the briefest moment, even the most intractable problems seemed soluble. Let me illustrate this with an example. We went into Detroit during the peak of the hot summer, not long after awful race rioting had scarred the city. There were National Guard troops, tanks, machine guns, buildings burned down, violence, just all sorts of bad things. It looked like some banana republic under martial rule. It looked nothing like America.

Someone asked Joe Foy, a black man who had grown up on the mean streets in the Bronx, about the race riots. The writer was probably looking for a few inflammatory quotes, but Foy had a remarkable answer. He replied that being involved in the pennant race made it easier for him to deal with the pain of the racial turmoil. Foy went on in a most articulate way to talk about race relations in America, and then he turned it back on the team.

"Look, I'm on a team. There's not X number of blacks and Y number of whites," Foy said, tugging at his road-gray flannel jersey with the word "BOSTON" spelled out in blue felt block lettering across the chest to emphasize the point. "It doesn't say BLACK and it doesn't say WHITE. It says BOSTON. When we take that field, we all got this same uniform on. Man, that's how it's supposed to be. You're white, I'm black. Why should that be a big deal? That's what this team is like. Black, white—were pulling together."

What happened to the Red Sox in 1967 made me and so many others feel alive, energized, and full of life. It wasn't as if all those other problems weren't there, and big problems they were. It's just that they were counterbalanced by something good, something innocent, something fun and joyous.

Seen now from the perspective of the new millenium and the Year 2000, I can compress all of the events of that entire baseball year into one moment in time. All of the great plays and moments of that year, all of the wonderful people, are contained in this one mythical moment.

This is a moment that utilized a great bunch of young men in baseball uniforms as a springboard to achieve something that no one thought could be done. In that sense, I still think of The Impossible Dream in the present tense—part of an eternal present, the experience of life in the moment, a moment that never goes away.

Now I'd like to give my impression of that season. I want to begin with an interview I did with Carl Yastrzemski. It provides a unique perspective on 1967 from the man who almost single-handedly made the Dream come true.

"All of a Sudden, It Started to Happen"

KEN COLEMAN: Was the off season between 1966 and 1967 different for you? I know for the first time you went to Gene Berde, the physical therapist at the Colonial Resort in Wakefield.

CARL YASTRZEMSKI: Yes, it was. I really didn't have the opportunity to work out before during the off season, because I would spend the wintertime finishing up work on my degree at Merrimack College. So I was never in top shape when spring training came around. I don't mean I was out of shape, just not in super top shape. But during the off season before '67, Gene worked with me all winter, and it really paid off. He drove me hard. As a result, I had a good spring training.

I noticed right away that I had more power. The ball was going another 30 or 40 feet. That's when I decided to become a pull hitter, and at that time, we really didn't have that many home run hitters on the Red Sox. I felt I could help the ball club more by being a power hitter than by just hitting for average, so I made the transition in hitting style. It bothered me mentally for about the first month of the season. That's when (coach) Bobby Doerr sat down with me. We talked. We tried to figure it out. That's when we came up with the idea of raising my hands up high.

KEN: You're referring to the morning of May 14, 1967, when you and Bobby went out to the park early before a doubleheader with the Tigers at Fenway. You and Bobby decided to make the adjustment in your swing, with the hands held high. What happened that day?

YAZ: As I said, 1967 was a year of transition for me as a hitter. Up to that time, I was a gap hitter to left center and right center, and I hit for average. I was almost like a Wade Boggs, except I pulled the ball a little more. Early in the '67 season, after I had made the transition to being a power hitter, a lot of my balls were dying in the outfield. They didn't have the takeoff they should have had. They were hopping to the fence or getting caught on the warning track when they should have been in the bullpen. Being six feet tall and 180 pounds, I decided to raise my hands real high to get more lift on the ball. That was the only way I could generate extra lift other than to turn my swing into an exaggerated uppercut, which I think would have been disastrous.

When Bobby and I went to the park that morning, we talked about it. We stayed out there about an hour and a half working on it. After I had made the adjustment of the hands, I was hitting the ball in the bleachers in batting practice. I said to Bobby, "I'm going to stay with it. I don't know if I can get to the ball in the game, because in batting practice, they're only throwing the ball 80 miles an hour. In the game it's going to be 90 miles an hour. But I'm going to try it." In that doubleheader, I hit two home runs against the Tigers. That turned me around. I was confident and stayed with that stance the rest of the year.

KEN: Carl, there was a situation in Chicago when you wanted to do some extra hitting, but Eddie Stanky thwarted your efforts. Do you remember that?

YAZ: Yes. In 1967, I was really killing the White Sox. That's when Stanky came up with that statement, "All Star from the neck down." One day I stayed at Comiskey Park after a game because I wanted to hit. Eddie countered that by having Ken Berry take some extra hitting before me. He had Berry hitting and hitting and hitting and hitting and hitting. So I just waited and waited and waited and waited and waited. Finally, when Berry got through, I thought we would finally get on the field. So what does Stanky do? He goes in the clubhouse and comes back out and says, "You can't have the field." And he brings a dog out. And he's walking his dog all over the field! And we waited some more. We waited about an hour and a half. Finally, Eddie realized we weren't going to leave, so he said, "Okay, you can have the field now."

Of course, Eddie was a character. He was the first base coach in the '67 All-Star Game in Anaheim. I think I was on base four or five times in a row, and every time I came down to him, he put his arms around me and talked to me like I was his long-lost son. So I couldn't figure this guy out.

That '67 White Sox team had great pitching but no offense. I was pretty good friends with Gary Peters (one of Chicago's best pitchers that year). One time, Gary hit me in the shoulder. The next time I came up, he hit me in the neck. After being hit the second time, I was going to go out and fight Peters. Now Gary's six feet four and weighs 220. Bobby Doerr was going to fight him he was so mad. But Peters told me after the game, "We're ordered to do it. Anytime we are ahead in the game, the pitchers are ordered to try and hit you and get you out of the game."

KEN: You joined the Red Sox in 1961. You had the tough job of replacing Ted Williams, and from 1961 to 1966 the team did not fare well. Was the fact that the team was in a pennant race in '67 a real factor in the kind of year you had?

YAZ: Those first years with the Red Sox were very depressing. We'd get 700,000 fans a year. If you got 8,000 fans for a Friday night game you were lucky. And a lot of them were very boisterous in voicing their negative opinions (LAUGHS), and you could understand that. But in '67, we had some new kids. We were five or six games out early in the season, hung tough, then had that road trip in July when we won ten in a row. We made a move and something changed. When we went to play a ball club, instead of expecting to lose a series, we were expecting to walk in and say, "Hey, why can't we beat these guys three out of four instead?" All of a sudden, it started to happen.

KEN: From my perspective in the broadcasting booth, it became apparent that the Red Sox really jelled as a team.

YAZ: True. Everyone participated in the effort, and we went through some tough times together. Probably the toughest was when Tony Conigliaro got hit (August 18). We suffered a tremendous blow in losing Tony, who was just coming into his own not only as a hitter but also as a defensive outfielder. With Reggie Smith in center and Tony in right, it was a tremendous defensive outfield. We all could run, catch, and throw. Then we lost Tony. When he got hit, I remember my reaction driving home that night. I said, "That's it. We don't have a chance at the pennant." Then all of a sudden, Jose Tartabull comes in and he plays like Superman for the last six weeks of the season.

KEN: It seemed as if everyone picked up the slack after Tony went down.

YAZ: It was amazing, maybe the most amazing thing I've seen in my years in baseball. We pick up Jim Landis and he hits a home run to win a game for us (a 7-5 win over the Washington Senators on August 24) and a couple days later we release him. George Thomas made some key starts in right, and then we picked up Ken Harrelson. It worked out. You can't explain it. It was just an unspoken thing that went on in the clubhouse, like when Tony went down, we all looked each other in the eye and said, "You can count on me." Jerry Adair, coming through in the clutch. People were getting on, and it got to the point where they couldn't pitch around me. People like Jerry Adair and Dalton Jones were always on base. They had to pitch to me because so many times I would come up with guys on first and third, first and second. I just got into one of those grooves. I didn't even know I had won the Triple Crown until the next day when I read about it in the papers after the last game of the season.

My only thought down the stretch was, "Pennant, pennant. We've got to win one for Mr. Yawkey." That's the way the whole ball club felt. We kept driving and pushing. Nobody was going to stop us, and nothing was going to turn us back. Everybody pulled together. Somebody would make a good play—I'm not talking about a big hit but about a defensive play—and the bench and the club-house would react as if he had just hit a home run in the bottom of the ninth with two outs to win a game.

KEN: What would you say about your relationship with Dick Williams?

YAZ: Everybody thought I had a problem with Dick Williams. I never had a personal problem with him. I was the only guy on the ball club with no curfew. I was the only guy who had a single room on the road. Dick never bothered me. But I had problems with the way he treated other ballplayers. I thought he should have reprimanded them in private. I thought he should have taken a ballplayer in his office and shut the door. I didn't like it when he went to the press with that stuff, like saying, "Talking to George Scott is like talking to a block of cement." I think that kind of thing is embarrassing and degrading to a ballplayer. I think it hurt more than helped a ballplayer's performance.

That being said, I will agree that in 1967, Dick probably did what he had to do. We had some young ballplayers who had come up with him from Toronto and knew him and his methods. But Dick had to turn around an entire attitude that had infected the team from all the years of losing. He was hard but without any doubt, he was the right guy in '67. I think the club needed his style. You can't take it away from him—he won the pennant. How he did it, with his methods, you have to give Dick 100 percent credit.

KEN: On the last two days of the season, you had all of your relatives in at your house and you stayed at the Colonial (resort hotel in Wakefield). Would you tell us what that time was like?

YAZ: I had about 30 relatives in, so there was no room at home for me to sleep. I went over to the Colonial both nights. On Saturday night I went to dinner, then went to bed early, around ten o'clock. I stayed in bed but I couldn't fall asleep. Finally, about two in the morning, I got up, went out, and walked—and kept walking. I think I walked to Route 128, 10 to 15 miles. By the time I got back, it was dawn. I had breakfast. When I got to the ballpark, it was about 9 a.m. I felt very relaxed. I rested on the clubhouse floor and took a nap for about three hours. I got up at about noon and felt super.

But those two nights I didn't sleep a wink. It was from the adrenaline flowing so hard. Here was a chance. Here was an opportunity. You remember a couple of days before, we were really out of it. If the other teams had won some games on Thursday and Friday, we would have had no chance. But all of a sudden, we learned they got beat. Now we had new life. I can remember when we got beat by Cleveland on Wednesday, everybody was talking about packing up and going home. All of a sudden on Saturday morning, we were back in the pennant race. We had a chance. We had to beat Minnesota twice, and that's what we did.

KEN: That season really turned the Boston franchise around.

YAZ: I think that 1967 not only turned on the fans, but I think it turned the whole Red Sox organization around. I think we became winners instead of losers. We expected to go out and win instead of lose. The thinking changed. We became winners. The attitude in the clubhouse was unbelievable. When you look back and compare our talent—that is, who we had on the field the last six weeks of the season—with the other contenders, you wonder how we won. We should have finished ten games out of first place that year. That's why they call it The Impossible Dream, I guess.

"This Will Not Happen Again!"

As Yaz said, that's why they call it the Impossible Dream. He also hit upon a key point in that interview, namely, how Dick Williams came in and turned the attitude around. Sure he could be a tyrant, but as Yaz indicated, that's exactly what the ball club needed.

In that regard, when you look for ultimate explanations for why the team went on to have the success it did that year, I think you have to look at what happened in spring training. In fact, one of the most underrated and forgotten aspects of Boston's tremendous turnaround in 1967 was the tone Williams established during spring training at Winter Haven, Florida. It was a tone that reverberated the entire year.

The first thing that jumps out is an incident that occurred on Monday, February 27. I mention it because it establishes just how quickly Dick Williams assumed control of the team. The Red Sox had officially opened camp two days earlier with pitchers and catchers reporting. Williams and the coaching staff greeted the 24 pitchers and four catchers, Dick made a speech, and the Sox went through a brief workout.

On the Monday in question, Dennis Bennett and Bob Sadowski, two borderline pitchers, showed up 25 minutes late for practice. In years past, the writers were saying later, this would have been ignored.

"Herman," the *Boston Globe's* Cliff Keane said, referring to previous manager Billy Herman, "wouldn't have noticed. He would have been out working on his (golf) game."

Not this time. We all got to see—and hear—Dick Williams in action.

It seems that the two roommates didn't get up on time because of a late night out the evening before. The pitchers finally showed up in the locker room. Williams saw them and rushed out of his office to confront the two pitchers. They told the skipper that the motel switchboard failed to wake them on time. The rookie manager didn't say a word. He spun on his heels and rushed into his office adjacent to the locker room.

Williams called the motel and left orders that all players, no exceptions, should be awakened each morning at 7 a.m., three hours before practice. Williams had just chopped an hour from the teams' sleep time. Williams then shouted for Bennett and Sadowski.

The two bleary-eyed pitchers made it warily into the manager's office. Williams left the door open and in a voice that could be heard ringing throughout the clubhouse shouted, "THIS WILL NOT HAPPEN AGAIN!"

With that, he dismissed the pitchers. The players sat in front of their lockers in stunned silence. Later on, I'll tell you, the Red Sox ran through as crisp a workout as you'd ever want to see.

After the workout ended on that late February day, Williams met with the press. He wouldn't talk about the Bennett-Sadowski incident; that was over as far as he was concerned. But he did make use of the time with the media to light another fire, this one under talented first baseman George Scott, a man who would be Dick's work-in-progress the entire year.

Great Scott

Williams, knowing how avidly George read the papers look-ing for any mention of his name in a story, said he planned to let Tony Horton battle Scott for the starting job at first base. Williams did that to plant a little bit of uncertainty in Scott's mind.

Sure enough, the next day, there was George, sitting in front of his locker with the papers, shaking his head.

"Horton? Pushing me? How can he do that? I was the starting first baseman in the All-Star game."

Later in the camp, Williams made his famous "cement-head" remark in referring to George. I'm not sure if it was a calculated remark or one that just slipped out in a moment of frustration stem-ming from these two men's inability to communicate with each other. In any case, Williams and Scott became a daily sideshow, as fasci-nating as it was unpredictable.

Williams never let up on Scott for a second. A writer asked Dick if Scott was any better at laying off low balls, referring to the big slugger's tendency to go after pitches in the dirt, something that ate him up in the second half of 1966.

"Yes," Williams shot back icily. "He's improved slightly. At least now he waits until they come up to his shins."

During the spring, Williams used Scott in the outfield while starting Horton at first in a few games. Again, he did it to get Scott's attention as much as anything else. Before one such game, George checked out the lineup card in the dugout and saw his name pen-cilled in with the abbreviation "rf" next to it. He started to mumble and complain.

"Right field, bull——. I ain't no (expletive deleted) right fielder." Scott then expressed the theory that Williams was playing favorites with Horton, who played for Dick the previous two sea-sons in Toronto. Scott went to third base coach Eddie Popowski, his former minor league manager at double A in Pittsfield, and told him, "Pop, this is going to ruin my hitting."

"How can playing right field ruin your hitting?" Pop replied. "The man (Williams) is trying to get you some swings."

"Big deal," Scott answered. "I can get my swings in the cage."

"Yes, George, but it's not the same as in a game."

"I'm telling you, Pop. I don't need it."

"But he's the manager," Popowski answered.

When told of Scott's outburst, Williams said, "I hear Mr. Scott doesn't like right field. Well, if he doesn't want to play, that's OK with me." Dick then took out an organizational roster that included players in the minor leaguers. He ticked off the names of a bunch of other outfielders. He said he was sure he could find someone on the list who would be willing to play right field if George wasn't up to it.

Just before the game began, Scott and Williams locked horns.

"I'm not a right fielder," George said.

"You are today," the manager replied.

"Hell, I ain't never played…" George started again, but was abruptly cut off.

"You are today," Williams repeated, this time more brusquely. Dick then walked away, leaving Scott standing there with his hands on his hips, mouth open, shaking his head. End of discussion. When the Red Sox took the field, big number 5 George Scott could be seen trotting out to right, head down. To George's credit, he played hard out there. In fact, almost too hard.

A few days later in a game on March 23, Scott literally ran himself out of the outfield experiment in a game against the Dodgers. There were two outs in the top of the sixth. John Kennedy lined a drive to right center. Right fielder Scott first broke the wrong way. He recovered and put on a burst of speed trying to get to the ball. Running full tilt, Scott ran into the wall face first. He staggered, then collapsed like a heavyweight fighter decked by a punch. Trainer Buddy LeRoux rushed out and revived Scott with smelling salts. Scott was taken to Winter Haven Hospital as a precautionary measure.

Later, Williams came about as close as he could to admitting the experiment of Scott as an outfielder was a mistake.

"I want George's bat in the lineup, but I don't want him running into fences. Scotty's outfield activities will be curtailed."

That was Dick's version of an apology.

In point of fact, Williams saw worlds of potential in George Scott and wanted to do all he could to help bring it out. He succeeded. In 1967, Scott hit .303, with 19 home runs, and 82 RBIs, while playing a brilliant first base.

No Let-up in Sight

Dick didn't let up for one second. Later in the spring, when speculating on the team he would take north, Williams said it was "subject to change at any time." He didn't want anyone to feel too secure or start coasting.

The next day, the writers asked him again about the roster. Dick held up a sheet of paper with players' names written on it.

"See that? Notice anything about it?" Dick asked, rhetorically. "Not one guy's name on here is in pen. It's all in pencil. Now see this?" he said holding up a yellow No. 2 pencil and pointing to the top. "That's an eraser."

He then vowed that he would take "only healthy pitchers. No pitcher with a sore arm is going to make this ball club. Nobody." That kind of statement tends to get people well real soon.

We just looked on in amazement as Williams went through his single-minded pursuit of excellence. The players may not have liked it and you could hear some grumbling, but no one disputed that the Sox came out of camp looking more prepared than they had in any number of years. The old timers went back to the early 50s and Joe McCarthy's teams of the late 40s to find a suitable comparison.

The team started doing things that hadn't been seen in Boston in years, things such as executing the hit-and-run, stealing bases, squeezing home runners from third. The players were getting very aggressive on the bases, going from first to third on singles, always looking to take an extra base or force a play somewhere.

You could see them slowly taking on the personality of their manager. Williams never chewed a guy out for hustling and trying hard to make a play, even if he got thrown out. As long as the guy was being aggressive and trying to make something happen in a positive way, he loved it. But he couldn't stomach indifference or lackadaisical play. He also hated mental mistakes.

He hammered that message home all spring long. In a Grape-fruit League game on March 11, the Red Sox blew a 4-0 lead to the White Sox, a game that featured poor Boston base running.

One play stood out. Tony Horton, moving from first to sec-ond on a play, rounded the second base bag and strayed too far. Quick-thinking White Sox center fielder Ken Berry threw behind Horton to shortstop Ron Hansen and picked him off second, catch-ing Tony dead in his tracks. In the dugout, Williams seethed.

"Geeez! Stay awake out there!" he shouted. Moments later, when Horton came to the bench, he gave Tony a very salty lecture about the finer points of base running. It might have been that George Scott, right then and there, dropped any notion of Tony Horton being Dick Williams' pet. By the time Dick was done, the paint was peeling off the dugout walls.

After, in his postgame remarks to the press, Williams boomed, "Those mistakes are not going to be tolerated when the season starts. If they continue we'll start hitting the wallet."

Even when there was a break in the Grapefruit schedule, Wil-liams didn't let up. On an off day April 3, Williams had the team on the field for a grueling daylong workout in the fundamentals—cutoff plays, pickoffs, bunting, and rundowns. On another off day on April 7, he held an intrasquad game, much to the players' dis-may.

One last incident should be mentioned that shows how Dick set a tone that would carry over into the regular season. This one again involved Dennis Bennett.

It was in late camp, about the time when everyone was getting edgy. The players want the long spring to end. They're eager for the season to begin and for the games to start counting. The game on April 4 against the Pirates shaped up as a pitcher's duel, with the contest scoreless going into the eighth. Darrell Brandon had gone seven impressive shutout innings, and Williams brought Bennett in for the eighth. With two out, two on, the lefty gave up a triple to rookie George Spriggs. During the play, Bennett just stood on the mound. He didn't run to back up third or home, as a pitcher should on a play like that.

Williams shouted some heated words to the mound. Bennett just glared back in, icicles and darts flashing from the left handed pitcher's eyes. That was enough for Williams. The manager rose from the bench and sprinted out to the mound. In front of the entire ballpark, Dick chewed out Bennett, telling him that no one on any ball club he managed would ever pull a stunt like that and not hear about it. He also told Bennett, and in effect the rest of the club, that he would tolerate no open insubordination. As Bennett found out, Dick wasn't kidding about hitting the wallet. Dick fined him.

By the time camp ended, the team was ready. The young, aggressive Red Sox had poured themselves into the mold that Williams had fashioned. Williams, as ever, played it coy and clever right up to Opening Day. When the press asked him for the Opening Day lineup, he answered "George Thomas" for each position.

"First base, George Thomas. Second, George Thomas. Short, George Thomas…" and so on.

The team closed camp on Sunday April 9 and flew into Boston for the home opener against the White Sox.

Magic was afoot.

"On the Threshold…"

For the record, the Red Sox beat the White Sox on Opening Day on a cold, blustery April 12th afternoon. Some 8,234 hardy souls were on hand to witness the 5-4 win.

Did I say there was a difference in the 1967 Red Sox? Before the season was six innings old, the Red Sox had three stolen bases. Even the winning run came in as the result of hustle. Jose Tartabull beat out an infield hit, stole second, and scored when Chicago shortstop Ron Hansen threw away a grounder hit by Carl Yastrzemski.

The Red Sox won crisply and fans enjoyed the look of the team. Just two days later, destiny put its undeniable stamp on the Cardiac Kids when young lefty Billy Rohr came within one pitch of doing what nobody in baseball history had ever done: pitch a no-hitter in his first Major League appearance.

In my long career as a Big League baseball broadcaster, I've called tens of thousands of innings. One that stands out is the bottom of the ninth inning at Yankee Stadium on April 14, 1967. Some 14,375 fans were on hand, including Jackie Kennedy and her son

John. Whitey Ford started for the Yankees for the 432nd time in his Hall of Fame career. Rohr was making start No. 1.

The game was low scoring. Joe Foy had driven in a couple of runs, and leadoff man and second baseman Reggie Smith knocked in one (people forget that Reggie, and not Mike Andrews, opened the season at second). The Red Sox held a 3-0 lead when the Yanks came up in the bottom of the ninth. Everybody in the stands was on their feet.

"Bill Rohr, on the threshold of immortality…" was how I characterized the captivating image of this young man standing tall on the mound, staring history in the face.

First up for the Yankees was Tom Tresh, who hit a drive to deep left over the head of Yastrzemski.

There goes the no hitter.

Everybody knew the ball couldn't be caught—everyone that is except Yaz. At the crack of the bat, Carl instinctively broke back, being guided by some kind of internal radar. I've seen the film of that catch many times and I never stop to marvel and wonder how Yaz managed to get himself back into position to make the play.

Running as hard as he could, Yaz dove in full stride and reached out the glove hand in full extension. At the apex of his dive, Yaz speared the ball *as it was going by him.* For one millisecond of time Yaz stood frozen in mid air before coming back down. He landed hard, tumbled, and bounced up quickly to his feet. Triumphantly, he held the ball up to show he had made the catch. I know we use superlatives all the time for great catches, but this was truly an *unbelievable* catch, maybe the best I ever saw. The fans went wild.

Here's how I called it:

"Fly ball, deep left field. Yastrzemski going back, way back…he dives and makes a TREMENDOUS CATCH!! One of the greatest catches we've ever seen by Yastrzemski in left field!"

In making the call, I went from my natural baritone up to alto. The Yankee Stadium crowd gave Yaz a standing ovation. Joe Pepitone followed that with a routine fly to right that Tony Conigliaro easily handled.

Two out, none on. The crowed buzzed with anticipation. It felt like electricity going through the stands.

Elston Howard dug in at the plate in his wide stance. Howard worked a 3-2 count before Rohr came in with a curve, which Ellie drove through the right side for a base hit. The no-hitter was over. The tough New York crowd let out with a groan, then rose to its feet to salute the young lefthander.

Rohr got third baseman Charlie Smith for the final out.

Though Billy Rohr lost his no-hitter, his performance gave us a sense that there was something special about this team. The Red Sox came out of Winter Haven feeling things might be different this year. Rohr's incredible pitching performance convinced them of it. And the fans got their first inkling that something unusual might be happening.

Before his near-historic major-league debut, Rohr had been a nervous wreck. On Thursday, Billy was so jumpy he asked Dick Williams for permission to switch roommates, from catcher Bob Tillman to Jim Lonborg. He wanted to be with another pitcher. He felt that would help him in going over the Yankee hitters.

"When we got to New York," Lonborg recalled, "I took him to Dawson's Pub for a big steak. Then we went to the Biltmore to go to bed. He couldn't sleep. He was tossing and turning all night."

Of course, the irony is what happened to Rohr and Howard later in the year. Rohr went on to win only one more game (his next start at Fenway Park, also against the Yankees) and he wouldn't win again all year. In fact, he got sent down to the minors and was soon out of baseball.

Howard came to Boston in an August 3 deal. General Manager Haywood Sullivan had made inquiries about Ellie for a couple of days. The Yankees seemed favorable. The deal was cinched with a phone call to New York from Tom Yawkey.

Ralph Houk, then Yankee manager who would later go on to manage the Red Sox, told the story.

"The phone in my office rang. It was Mr. Yawkey himself, asking to talk to Ellie. I yelled into the clubhouse, 'Ellie, phone. It's Mr. Yawkey from Boston.' Ellie didn't believe me. He thought I was putting him on, but I said that indeed it was Mr. Yawkey, calling from Boston. He comes to the phone, and they talk for fifteen minutes and just like that, Ellie's on the Red Sox."

Howard later said of the call, "I've never enjoyed a telephone call more in my life. Mr. Yawkey said to me, 'Elston, we want you in Boston.'"

Billy Rohr was out of baseball by 1968, but he went on to great success off the field as an attorney in California. On November 20, 1987 at Boston Marriott Copley Place Hotel, the Jimmy Fund, in cooperation with The Bosox Club, held a 20th anniversary celebration of the Impossible Dream for team members. Shortly after that very special evening, Billy wrote me this letter, which I want to share with you.

> *Dear Kenny:*
>
> *How remiss I would be not to thank you for yet another wealth of memories! These words will not—cannot—express the overwhelming sense of love, appreciation, sorrow, and pride I felt at being a part—however small—of the Dream.*
>
> *The love for my teammates and those associated with the Red Sox; the appreciation I feel for the people of New England and their willingness to welcome us once again with their memories; the sorrow I feel when I realize that while the memories need not disappear, they surely must fade as time levels the emotional peaks and valleys into the echoes of our minds; and the pride and thanksgiving I feel at being somehow chosen to be a participant in their little part of history now remembered.*
>
> *My thanks to you for reminding me of my old friends who have gone. I will not believe that they weren't with us Friday night. I will not believe that God is not a fan of this game, nor that Heaven doesn't have a ballpark. And as surely as it does, it must look like that grand old lady at 24 Yawkey Way, Boston, Massachusetts.*
>
> *My thanks for an opportunity to participate in a cause as beautifully as important as the Jimmy Fund. For each of us so blessed as to play this game, there are so many who never play at all. May some portion of those proceeds continue to fuel the flame of Hope for those kids until they too can have their day in the sun.*
>
> *I have not meant for this letter to sound maudlin. I have only tried somehow to capture and relay to you my deepest and*

most sincere thanks for your work, your thoughts, and your love.

The lives of those assembled last week end have gone in many directions. I have been fortunate beyond many—but never more so than when—on those seemingly less and less frequent occasions—I hear the record of the Impossible Dream—and hear Ken Coleman say ...

"Billy Rohr, on the threshold..."

*Thank you, my friend, and may God bless and keep you.
Billy*

"He Said He Heard a Hissing Sound and that was All."

There were so many highs and lows that year—thrilling come-from-behind rallies followed by disheartening defeats. One of the highest highs was a 10-game winning streak on the road in July. When the team's jet landed in Boston, thousands of fans were on hand to meet us. It was as if the Pope or the Beatles had hit town. However, the deepest depression had to be the near-fatal beaning of Tony Conigliaro by Jack Hamilton on August 18 at Fenway Park.

I can still remember looking at the next day's box score in the papers and seeing the last line:

"HBP—Hamilton (Conigliaro), T—2:16, A—31,027."

This cold, antiseptic brevity summed up one of baseball's all-time great tragedies.

He came to the Red Sox in 1964 as a teenager right out of Single A ball. Tony was a local kid, having grown up in nearby Swampscott. He was 6 feet 3, 190 pounds, movie-star handsome, loved to party, had cut some rock and roll records, and was born to hit a baseball. He homered in his first Fenway Park at bat. The following year, he led the American League in home runs with 32 at the ripe old age of 20.

Bill Monbouquette, who won 20 games for the Red Sox in 1963 and hailed from nearby Medford, remembers the first time he saw Tony: "I worked out at Tufts before each year. Tony Conigliaro came by one day. He had just played one year in the minors. I loved what I saw. He had quick, beautiful hands, and the ball jumped off his bat. I knew we had something special" (Peary 613).

Something special indeed.

Tony's early career in Boston was as tumultuous as it was brilliant.

In 1964, Manager Johnny Pesky fined Tony C. $250 for staying out all night in Cleveland. July 1965, Manager Billy Herman fined the fun-loving Tony $1000 for the same thing in New York. Things got worse on that particular road trip when on the flight from New York to Cleveland, Tony got out his portable turntable and began playing rock-and-roll records.

William Jennings Bryan Herman, a man born in 1909, exploded.

"How do you think that thing would sound on a bus between Toronto and Toledo?" he roared. Tony slammed shut his record player (Ragazzi 64).

When the team got back to Boston, Herman, GM Mike Higgins, Tony, and his dad Sal had a long meeting at Fenway Park in Higgins' office. Tony apologized to the Red Sox, issued a statement of apology to the fans, then went out and got five hits including a home run against the Twins.

"This kid has tremendous potential," Herman said. "He can be another Joe DiMaggio, a big superstar. He has tremendous ability, a sound body, and everything to make him great. Maybe he'll mature. It's up to him."

To his credit, Tony did grow up. By 1966, Tony had turned 21 and settled down a little more. He dedicated himself to the hard work and practice required to be a star. In 1967, he became the youngest player in history to reach 100 home runs. And he was just starting to come into his own as a hitter and as a defensive outfielder. He had a strong, accurate arm, and had learned to play Fenway's tricky right field as well as anyone.

Tony started in right for the American League in the 1967 All-Star game, and the baseball world predicted greatness for the young man from Swampscott...if he stayed healthy. That was always the big "if" with Tony. Going into 1967, Conigliaro suffered broken bones four times in his first four years in baseball because he couldn't get away from tight pitches.

One play ominously foreshadowed what was to happen later. It was in a July 26, 1964 game against Cleveland when Tony was hit in the wrist by a Pedro Ramos fastball. The ball broke Tony's ulna and he didn't return to the lineup until September. The Red Sox exonerated Ramos and warned Tony he would have to learn how to move out of the way of brush-back pitches.

Yaz was asked about the play after the game, and from his remarks you could pinpoint the source of the team's concern. Being hit by the pitch is part of the game. That's not what troubled the Red Sox. What bothered the club was that Tony didn't seem to be picking up the ball as it rode in on him, possibly because of his stance, in which he crowded the plate. Tony tended to completely freeze as a ball rode in on him.

"I was in the on-deck circle and I was watching Tony (on the Ramos pitch)," said Yastrzemski after the game. "He never saw the ball. He froze. All he had to do was drop his arms, but he never moved. I don't believe Ramos threw at him, and I don't believe Tony ever saw the ball" (37).

Three years and 23 days later on August 18, 1967, Yaz's words would be conjured up again.

The August 18 game started out quietly enough until the Sox came up in the bottom of the fourth. George Scott led off with a single to center but was out trying to stretch it into a double. Then something happened that I'll never forget. Someone threw a smoke bomb from the stands in left field. It billowed away in thick white clouds. It took ten minutes for the air to clear. It was like an omen.

Reggie Smith flied to deep center for the second out. Up came Tony.

On the first pitch, Hamilton delivered a fastball that rode in on Tony, near his head. Tony froze, then instinctively threw up his hands at the last second to cover his face. Judging by the loud crack audible to everyone in the park, it sounded like the ball had hit Tony's helmet and knocked it off his head. What actually happened, however, was that the helmet flew off as Tony tried to jerk out of the way. The ball struck the young outfielder flush on the top of his left cheekbone, just below the eye socket.

Tony went down in a heap and I remember thinking as he was stretched out motionless in the dirt that maybe he had been fatally beaned. He remained motionless. The crowd gasped and buzzed in concern, then got silent. I've never heard anything like that in a ballpark.

For a brief moment, everything stopped. No one moved or said anything. Then all of a sudden, there was a rush from the Red Sox dugout, led by Dick Williams.

Tony was still lying motionless in the batter's box, and the worst fears crossed everyone's mind. Rico Petrocelli, the on-deck batter, knelt over Tony and whispered in his ear it would be okay. Finally Tony moved and seemed to regain consciousness. The first thing he did was kick his feet in agony.

Trainer Buddy LeRoux brought a stretcher onto the field. Jim Lonborg, Joe Foy, and Mike Ryan lifted Tony's limp body onto the stretcher, and along with LeRoux and Angels' trainer Fred Frederico, carried Tony into the clubhouse.

An ambulance was called. Dr. Thomas Tierney, the Red Sox physician, conducted a preliminary examination. By that time, Tony was awake and in horrendous pain.

"When I got to him," Dr. Tierney said, "Tony said it hurt like hell. He said he heard a hissing sound and that was all."

Tony's face was tough to look at. The left eye was hideously swollen and completely shut. It was an ugly reddish-blue color. Tony was bleeding profusely through the nose. The cheekbone had been shattered and there was a contusion to the scalp.

Dr. Joseph Dorsey, who examined Tony at Sancta Maria Hospital, said that if the ball had struck an inch higher, Tony likely would have died. Dorsey said it was too soon to know if there was permanent eye damage.

Of course, that turned out to be the case. Tony didn't come back that year and missed all of 1968. He went on to play two more seasons with the Red Sox before being traded, ironically to the Angels, in 1971. But his vision problems worsened and he had to retire again. Conigliaro made a brief comeback with the Red Sox in 1975 (in fact, Tony got the first hit of that pennant-winning season), but practically speaking, the beanball from Hamilton shut him down for good.

One of the greatest young stars baseball had ever produced saw his career taken away in a flash. Later, Tony suffered a tragic heart attack in 1982, on the day he auditioned for TV color analyst for the Red Sox. He never recovered and spent the final years of his life bedridden and almost completely incapacitated. Tony died on February 24, 1990.

The Red Sox won the game 3-2, but I'll never forget the clubhouse afterward. The players were silent. Each man just stayed alone with his thoughts. I can still see Yaz sitting on his stool, just staring at the floor and shaking his head.

Tony's injury could have sent the team into a tailspin, but the Red Sox seemed to find inspiration from it. They beat the Angels the next day 12-11, then swept them in a Sunday doubleheader on August 20, 12-1 and 9-8. The second game featured an amazing comeback from an 8-0 deficit, the winning run coming on Jerry Adair's eighth inning home run.

"It's Over! It's over! It's unbelievable!"

It was like that the rest of the year. The Sox played everyone tough and going into the last two games of the season against the Twins at home, they trailed Minnesota by one game. They would need to sweep the first place Twins, then get help from the Angels, who were playing the close-running Detroit Tigers.

The Sox took Saturday's game, 6-4, with Jose Santiago picking up the win, working out of several jams ("I had good stuff. I didn't worry."). Yaz did what he had done all year. He carried the team. Carl went 3-for-4 and drove in four runs, including a huge three-run homer off lefty Jim Merritt that put the game away in the bottom of the seventh.

On the final day of the regular season, Yaz did it again, going 4-for-4 with two RBIs. He also did it in the field in the eighth inning. Harmon Killebrew and Tony Oliva singled. Bob Allison then drilled a liner into the corner in left. Killebrew scored and Oliva stopped at third. When Allison tried to stretch it into a double, Yaz fired a perfect strike to second base to nail the sliding runner.

"Yaz threw about 800 strikes to second base during the season, and that was just one of them," said Dick Williams.

In the two biggest games of his life, Yaz had gone 7-for-8 with six RBIs. Jim Lonborg went all the way for his 22nd win in the delirious 5-3 Sunday victory.

The Sox got all their runs in the sixth inning, a frame Gentleman Jim started with a surprise bunt hit. He caught the Twins' Cesar Tovar napping at third, playing too far back. It was a bold, daring, even audacious move, and it turned the momentum around. Soon after, the 2-0 deficit became a 5-2 lead.

When pinch hitter Rich Rollins (hitting for former Sox catcher Russ Nixon) popped out to Petrocelli at short, the game was over. The Sox were in first place. Later, when California beat Detroit in the second game of a doubleheader at Tiger Stadium, the Red Sox had their first pennant since 1946.

The crowd swarmed onto the field after the final out. The players ran for the dugout out of a sense of self-preservation but Lonborg didn't make it. He was positively engulfed by the pulsating throng of happy fans. People clawed at Jim, patted him on the back, hugged him, kissed him, ripped the buttons off his uniform shirt, and tore his sweatshirt off completely. They even took his cap and shoelaces.

He finally made it into the clubhouse in rags.

In the locker room, players howled, screamed, cried, and laughed. There were actually two celebrations. The first came right after the game. The second and wildest came after the Tigers had lost and the Sox knew they had the pennant and would not have to go to Detroit for a playoff game. Incidentally, before that outcome was secure, Dick Williams announced that if the team had had to fly to Detroit the next day, Lee Stange would have been his starting pitcher. Characteristically thinking ahead, Dick advised Lee to take it easy with the champagne in case he had to pitch in the playoff game.

Players were listening to the Detroit game on radio, and when it was over, bedlam broke out. I was in the clubhouse doing live interviews and watching the amazing scene unfold. I was giddy but also held on to enough of my professionalism to get the interviews done. You've got to remember, I grew up as a Red Sox fan. I was in heaven.

As soon as the Detroit game ended and the Red Sox had won the championship, Dick Williams—the steel-tough, unsentimental tyrant—shot out of his chair, hopped up and down, and yelled, "It's over! It's over! It's unbelievable!"

Williams walked over to Yaz.

"I've never seen a perfect player," Dick said to Carl, "but you were one for us. I never saw a player have a season like that."

And then we witnessed an amazing thing. The tough manager hugged the reticent outfielder, then kissed him. Yaz was genuinely moved. After that, Carl paraded around the locker room dressed only in his underwear and his baseball socks, smoking a big cigar.

"I'm on a trip," he declared. "That's what this is. A trip!"

At one point, Williams was so emotionally overcome that he had to go into the trainer's room to lie down for a couple of minutes. Coach Al Lakeman went in with him to help calm him down. When he came out, Williams said he was okay. He went around the room and hugged each player.

"These are my kids," he said to no one in particular and everyone in general, making a sweeping gesture with his arms. "I was a tough guy in Toronto and a tough guy up here. But I was a winning tough guy."

Joe Foy's high-pitched cackle could be heard above all the noise, cutting through everything and riding on top of the general sound of the celebration. "We win the pennant! Aaaaaaaaaaaaaa-aaaaaaahhhhh!" He then threw coach Eddie Popowski, fully clothed, into the showers.

Yaz got a shower and a shaving cream shampoo courtesy of Jose Tartabull and John Wyatt.

The most emotional moment came when Red Sox owner Tom Yawkey entered the clubhouse, visiting with the players. When he got to Lonborg, he said "Jim, you were terrific. You were…"

Yawkey stopped in mid-sentence, his words halting as tears appeared in his eyes.

The intelligent, articulate Lonborg replied, "Mr. Yawkey, I wish there was something I could say to you to show you how I feel. But I can't think of something appropriate. Isn't that silly?"

"No. You did your talking on the field today," Mr. Yawkey replied. The two men hugged. Yawkey then watched the rest of the celebration alone, from Dick Williams' office. You could see him fighting back his tears.

And so it went, this Impossible Dream. The Red Sox had won a championship. It had occurred not as a conscious effort applied to some preconceived plan but in spite of just about everything.

It was then, and remains today, the greatest thrill I have ever experienced in sports.

CHAPTER 9

Baseball Takes a Strike

THE BIG RED MACHINE AND DIARY OF A SPORTSCASTER

Striking Out

For a long time, sporadically but continuously, I've kept a diary. I've always liked the intimacy of the form, especially the ability to record private thoughts in a safe and secure way. In fact, many of the entries in this book began in the form of diary entries.

A diary is a record of the events of a person's day-to-day life, and the reasons for keeping a diary vary. A diary can be used to help clarify your sense of self and to help you sort out the complications of daily living. Others keep diaries to provide a "laundry list" of events, a series of items from which one can check off and then record the occurrences of a particular day. This checklist jogs the memory months and years down the road, bringing one handily into a reconstruction of the past. For me, a diary has been both of these things.

A diary is the writer's equivalent of a camera. It takes a verbal picture of each day. And just as the creative photographer can alter and compose the image he sees through the camera lens, so the diarist interprets, analyzes, and composes the events of his daily life. In the end, he has a *true* picture, true because it reflects and presents his inner world. Maybe the briefest definition of a diary is this—the inner transcription of one's outer life.

A diary also offers the writer great flexibility. It has the ability to suit the impulses, quirks, tendencies, whims, and predisposition of its creator more than almost any other literary form except possibly the personal letter and certainly e-mail.

When I'm working on a book, I usually begin to tackle my material in diary form. That's how my diary of the 1981 season got started—a series of daily diary entries that with Dan Valenti's help turned into something more than that.

Speaking of DV, let me share this with you. Dan is an intelligent, witty, caring, and self-assured human being who has been a great friend over the years. He's the kind of guy you wouldn't mind hanging out with and talking about baseball, religion, life, or just about anything, and many times we've done that. In the course of collaborating on four books, we've come to forge a unique partnership that blossomed into a friendship, one I value dearly.

It's funny, because as a kid growing up in Western Massachusetts, Dan was both a huge Browns and Red Sox fan. In that way, he got to "know" yours truly years before I got to know him. Dan has a curiosity about people, events, and things that makes him an excellent interviewer, and it did not surprise me when he became host of an award-winning daily radio talk show in Massachusetts. In fact, I've had the pleasure of being on with Dan several times, and I can tell you he does a fine job.

Oh yeah—he can also write the living daylights out of just about any topic he tackles. It's no coincidence that when the National Baseball Hall of Fame in Cooperstown needed a writer to pen the signature words for its popular new "The Great American Home Run Chase" exhibit, they chose words Dan penned for his book *Clout!* about the top home runs in baseball history.

Next time you go to Cooperstown and you're at that exhibit, look up and you'll see these words chiseled in marble, next to Maris, and Ruth, and McGwire:

"Inasmuch as anything can be immortal in this tenuous earthly life, the big home run never dies. It shocks like madness, surprises like magic, and endures like myth.—Baseball writer Dan Valenti."

You can see why I'm proud to have him as my collaborator. So thanks, Dan.

As I said, in 1981 Dan helped me transform a diary I kept of that baseball season. It became a book called *Diary of a Sportscaster,* from which parts of this chapter are loosely adapted. The diary "transcribed" the baseball year as it unfolded to me from my unique perspective of being the Voice of the Boston Red Sox.

My diary proved to be serendipitous, because during that season something happened that had never occurred in all of baseball history. A season already well under way was cancelled because of a players' strike.

Though the strike was sad and unfortunate, it marked the 1981 season as a candidate for posterity, which in turn gave me a sense of urgency about seeing my diary through. The question of how the strike affected me, as well as everyone else in and around baseball, became an important one with which to deal. That question demanded an answer, however incomplete and cursory.

Of course, we're talking 1981 here. Before that, my career as Voice of the Red Sox took an interesting detour right after the 1974 season that I want you to know about.

The Big Red Machine

My four years with the Cincinnati Reds were—personally and professionally—among the finest of my career. After all, it afforded me the chance to be around one of the greatest teams in baseball history, right at the peak of its run.

I went to the Reds after the 1974 season, after my first run in Boston had ended. I found out it was over in the typical way for this business—as a complete surprise and after indications to the contrary. That's just one of the unsavory aspects of the big-time broadcasting business.

After the 1974 baseball season ended, the broadcasting rights to Red Sox baseball changed from Channel 4 (WBZ) to Channel 38 (WSBK). Before that season began, Bill Flynn, general manager of TV-38, said he would be in touch with me after the season was over.

"I think we're getting the rights," Bill told me, "and you certainly fit into our plans."

Well, when the season ended, I still had not heard from Flynn, so I called him and made an appointment to see him in his office at the WSBK studios. When I got there, he told me they had decided to make a change, and that change was to bring in Dick Stockton and Ken Harrelson to be the TV announcers. Johnny Pesky, my TV partner in 1974, was being made a Red Sox coach, and I was out of a job.

Just like that.

After receiving this shocking news from Flynn, I went immediately over to Fenway Park to see my dear friend, Red Sox traveling secretary Jack Rogers and told him I was no longer the announcer for the team. Jack couldn't believe it. He wished me the best and then I left. As I was walking down the hallway in the offices upstairs at Fenway Park, I ran into Tom Yawkey. I had no idea that Mr. Yawkey was still in town.

"Hey, Kenny, how are you?" Mr. Yawkey asked.

"I'm not doing too good, Mr. Yawkey. I just found out that I am no longer the announcer for the Red Sox."

Mr. Yawkey expressed his dismay to hear this. He couldn't believe it. I said goodbye and went home. That night, I got a telephone call from Mr. Yawkey, the only one I ever got from him at home in all my years of doing Red Sox baseball.

"Kenny, I can't tell you how sorry I feel about this," he said. "I just want to let you know I'll be happy to do anything I possibly can do for you. You let me know, and I'll be happy to do anything I possibly can."

I felt like saying, "Well, I'd appreciate it if you could just tell these fellows you want me to continue to do their games." But of course, that was not in Mr. Yawkey's area and he could not do that, nor could I ask him to.

The season was over, I was out of a play-by-play job, and had all of the insecurities that go along with that. Fortunately, during the off season I worked at radio station WEEI doing the weekend sports, and I heard of a possible opening in Cincinnati as the TV voice of the Reds. That was the only broadcasting job available in all of baseball that year.

The only one. That meant there would be a lot of competition. There was also no wiggle room. It was either land that job or it was out of the booth.

Charley Jones had done the Reds games up to that year. As I suspected, there were a lot of applicants, and one of the reasons I got the job was that the Reds wanted someone who already had some rapport with the fans. Back when I did Cleveland Browns football, every Sunday the Browns games were aired in Cincinnati (this was before they had the Bengals). And so through Browns football, I was known throughout the area. It's funny how things work out. My years with the Browns, though even at that time many years in the past, continued to pay off for me.

Incidentally, another candidate who was being seriously considered for the Reds job that year was a young, up-and-coming broadcaster named Jon Miller. So I got the Reds job and spent four great years with a superb organization.

The 1974 Reds were a good team on the verge of becoming great. They had finished four games behind the Dodgers in second place in the NL West. In 1975 and 1976, my first two years with the club, they became the Big Red Machine.

In '75, the Reds played .500 ball through the middle of May but after that, they couldn't be stopped. They ended up winning 108 games and held first place in the West by a whopping 20 games. In 1975, of course, they played the Red Sox in one of the most memorable World Series of all time, taking the Sox in seven games. That Series produced one of baseball's most famous moments—Carlton Fisk's home run to win the historic Game Six for the Red Sox.

In 1976, the Reds followed up with another championship and a four-game sweep of the Yankees in the World Series. It was the first time since the 1921-22 Giants that a National League team had taken two consecutive World Series.

The Big Red Machine featured balanced pitching (in 1975, six pitchers won in double figures), the best defense in the Major Leagues, and speed, leading the National League in stolen bases. In the 34 years that I broadcast Major League baseball, I saw a lot of great teams, and the 1975 and '76 Reds were the best in terms of the starting eight men that were on the field day in, day out.

Look at the lineup: catcher, Johnny Bench; first, Tony Perez; second, Joe Morgan; short, Dave Concepcion; third, Pete Rose; left, George Foster; center, Cesar Geronimo; right, Ken Griffey. These eight men had a combination of speed, power, and defense that was just incredible.

Manager Sparky Anderson, who became a dear friend during my Cincinnati years, once told me, "You know, Kenny, I don't manage this team. The Reds are managed by Johnny Bench, Joe Morgan, Pete Rose, and Tony Perez. I just change the pitchers now and then."

In Cincinnati, our TV schedule included 40 to 45 games a year, all but three of them on the road. It was not a heavy schedule at all, and in my last two years there, I was able to commute between Cincinnati and my home in Cohasset, Massachusetts. But in 1975 and '76, I stayed in Cincinnati as much as I could.

One of my major tasks was learning the National League. I had spent 19 years broadcasting in the American League. My color man that first year was Woody Woodward, the former coach at Florida State who had played shortstop for the Braves and the Reds (who later went on to become the general manager of the Seattle Mariners).

Woody helped me out learning the new league and he was a nice fellow, pleasant to work with and be around, as was the man who followed him as my color analyst, Bill Brown (currently the able voice of the Houston Astros).

I tried to stay in town as much as possible, even though we were broadcasting only three home games. Almost every morning in the hotel where I was staying, the Stouffer's downtown, I would have breakfast with second baseman Joe Morgan, who was on his way to back-to-back seasons in '75/'76 as the National League's Most Valuable Player.

Joe and I would talk about the league. He mentioned, for example, that J. R. Richard of Houston was the toughest pitcher he had to face. He also shared many other thoughts and insights on the various clubs around the circuit.

During one of our breakfast gatherings, Joe once told me something that unlocked the key to understanding Pete Rose.

"When I was with Houston," Joe once said. "I thought that Pete Rose was a hotdog. But when I got over here, I found out that he played ball the only way he knew how, which is all out, all the time. And he made me a better player because some of that attitude rubbed off on me."

Indeed that was true. Pete had this kind of effect, to some degree, on the entire roster.

I spent a ton of time with Joe in my four years doing the Reds and we became dear friends. We were a kind of Odd Couple. Think of it—I'm Irish out of Boston and Joe's black out of Bonham, Texas and mostly Oakland, California—two guys with a world of difference that should have separated them but which only served to draw us closer together. We learned from each other, about baseball, about people, about life. Thank you, Joe.

At 5 feet 7 and 150 pounds, Joe could generate amazing power (he led the National League in slugging percentage in 1976). He once told me about his off-season regimen, including hitting the fast-speed punching bag for hand-eye coordination. I mentioned that to Ted Williams and Ted—the greatest hitter of all time—said with a burst of enthusiasm, "Boy, I wish I had thought of that! What a helluva idea!"

In recent years, of course, Joe has teamed with Jon Miller, my ex-partner, on ESPN baseball telecasts to form the best one-two tandem in the game today. Joe's insights and observations are special. Jon and Joe form what is truly an All-Star broadcasting team.

Speaking of true All Stars, Reds manager Sparky Anderson and I had a very close relationship. Sparky was a sun worshipper during the day and so was I. When we were on the road we'd hang out at the hotel pool for a good portion of the day, usually from 9 a.m. to 2 p.m. in the afternoon. I'd swim some, then spend the rest of the time with Sparky, lounging by the pool, soaking up the sun, and talking baseball for hours. When the team was at home, Sparky made the hour between 4 and 5 p.m. available to me, which was extremely generous, considering we weren't doing many home games.

Sparky was one of those guys who didn't have much of a Major League career as a player but in a long life in the bushes absorbed every lesson he could about the game of baseball. Ralph Houk, Tom Lasorda, and Walt Alston were like this, also. As a result, each became a great manager.

In Sparky's case, he did it with a lot of patience, an excellent understanding and handling of pitching staffs, and the ability to let his best players just play the game without a whole lot of interference from him. Sparky became the only manager in baseball history to win a World Series in both leagues (Tigers, 1984), the first man to win Manager of the Year awards in both leagues, and the first to win more than 100 games in both the National and American leagues. He retired as manager of the Tigers in 1995 and became a color commentator for the Angels.

In 1975, I walked into Sparky's office one day and learned what kind of man he was and what made him a great manager. We had just returned from a road trip to Montreal and Philadelphia. When I walked in the office, Sparky was sitting at his desk looking really down—glum and dejected, not at all his usual upbeat self.

We were alone. Sparky looked up at me and said, "Kenny, let me tell you what lousy managing is all about. Here we have a bad series in Montreal then we go to Philadelphia. I've got a young kid from the Dominican Republic with a language barrier (Cesar Geronimo) and he's playing center field for me. He makes an error that loses a ball game.

"The next night," Sparky continued, "I start Merv Rettenmund in center because I want a right-handed batter in the lineup to face Steve Carlton. I don't say anything to the kid. We come home and we have an off day. So here is this young man, really down, his tail between his legs for three days, and he's thinking the reason he didn't play the next night in Philadelphia was because of his error the night before.

"What I should have done was talk to him the night I started Rettenmund. I should have explained that I wanted Rettenmund in there for his right-handed bat and that it had nothing to do with the previous night's loss. I should have also said that it had nothing to do with him (Cesar) or the error because we all make errors in this game. But I didn't do that, and Ken, that's lousy managing. That kid was real down and I'm the guy who put him there, and I feel bad about that. I got it straightened out now, but that's not the way you manage a baseball team. I'll learn from this mistake."

And indeed, he did.

In my final two years in Cincinnati, the Reds finished in second both years, and the Reds replaced Sparky with John McNamara. Sparky went on to manage the Tigers. I also jumped leagues, heading back to Boston in 1979, where I teamed up on the radio doing Red Sox games with Rico Petrocelli. That was the year that saw Carl Yastrzemski become the first man in American League history to amass 400 home runs and 3,000 hits. Just two years later, we were in the middle of that Twilight Zone season, 1981, The Year of the Strike.

A Ringside View

By the early 1980s, I became increasingly aware of what was happening around me, especially the fact that what I was doing wasn't just another job, simply because baseball isn't just another sport. The game is one of the country's grand traditions, a part of our national character, literally comprising a portion of the country's identity. Forget all the talk about big money and greed and all of that for a moment and you will see that baseball remains largely what it always has been, and that is a part of the collective unconscious that makes America the great land it is. For this entire century, baseball has sent a message our way. Quite simply, Americans "get" this tradition called baseball.

Writer Thomas Boswell put it best when he said that "More than any other American sport, baseball creates the magnetic, addictive illusion that it can be almost understood."

The 1981 Boston Red Sox were an interesting baseball team playing in the historic, strike-shortened season, and I had the ringside view.

The '81 Red Sox had lost their backbone of catcher Carlton Fisk, shortstop Rick Burleson, and center fielder Fred Lynn. The manager was Ralph Houk, who took over after having been two full years out of baseball. The team had a much-maligned ownership and a Big League identity problem. And yet it was a year in which they led the Major Leagues in hitting, put on a thrilling drive for the American League's Eastern Division flag that carried them into the final weekend of the season, and solidified themselves into a true team. But it was the strike that made 1981 memorable. That's why I want to share my diary with you. If you want to fully understand the nature of the game today, you have to get a feeling for the 1981 strike.

Let me start with the entry I made on Opening Day, 1981.

Friday, April 10

Opening Day! There's no feeling like it. The first game of the season conveys a sense of timelessness and magic that's indescribable. Everyone feels it. Opening Day brings you back to your roots as a fan. You feel like a kid again, let out of school early. Your childhood seems tangible because you feel childlike once more, with another baseball season about to begin.

The day—a beautiful one, cold but lots of sunshine—started early. Broadcast partner Jon Miller and I were on with Pat Whitley during his Opening Day special on WITS at 10:15 a.m. After that, we went right to the ballpark. We cut some commercials and promos, then had lunch in a crowded pressroom. Faces we would be seeing all year long were on hand, as well as many who just show up for the Grand Opening—the faithful and the fickle.

In the game, Dennis Eckersley and Britt Burns of the White Sox hooked up in a great pitchers duel. Some 35,149 attended, the second largest Opening Day crowd in club history. Dwight Evans and Gary Allenson gave the Red Sox a 2-0 lead with solo home runs, but a three-run homer by returning hero Carlton Fisk put the White Sox ahead. The blow was as dramatic as they come, since Fisk was making his first start in something other than a Red Sox uniform.

Fisk's homer was not so much a four-bagger but a fable. The crowd didn't know how to react. They loved Fisk and probably still do, but he's now on the other side. Talk about mixed emotions. Momentum, Old Mo, had shifted dugouts with one swing of Fisk's bat.

The Red Sox stranded a bunch of runners in this game, something that's also been a problem all spring. Stranded. I like that word. It conjures up thoughts of shipwrecks and desert isles, a sense of hopelessness and waiting to be rescued. A base runner must wait to be moved along and home, or else he is stranded. It's a perfect word.

Failure to hit in the clutch is baseball's equivalent of betrayal. It's not that the hitter fails out of intention to get the run in—he only fails in the results, which in a game of statistics counts for just about everything. When the day is done, no one's going to doubt that Jim Rice wasn't trying to deliver Rick Miller from third. All they remember is that he didn't do it. The final measure is this: did the run score? If you're the home team and your guys were left on second and third in a one-run game, that's all you care about. That's how the fans look at it.

When the Sox went out in the ninth, you could hear the collective groan. I heard it through my headphones and also from the stands, and it produced a fascinating effect, something like "aural 3-D."

After the game, Fisk made a remarkable observation when he discussed his home run, without even realizing it.

"Everything just fell into place, like it was a bit unreal. I felt that home run coming on. I hit that one perfectly. Early on, I didn't feel comfortable. I've had that problem all spring. It was my footwork in the box. When I came up (for the home run), I consciously remembered something Ted Williams once told me about overstriding. Ted always preached a short stride into the pitch."

"...something Ted Williams once told me." In one sentence, Fisk spanned baseball history, back to Ted Williams, whose coach was Hugh Duffy, whose rookie year was 1888. That's right, the nineteenth century. It lives. Baseball lives.

Now the season has started. The game takes on a new meaning after today. April baseball is odd. Nothing, in fact, is so misleading as the first few weeks of a new baseball season—not a political promise, not an ad campaign for a new movie, nothing. The season is 162 games long. Patterns won't emerge until June. Until that time, we can only take the individual games and box scores and give them our weightless attention. For example, both catchers homered today, Fisk and Allenson. At this rate, you could make the following valid statement: "Each man will end up hitting 162 home runs." That's a valid statement, but it's not true. The season will catch up not only to Pudge and Gary but every other player.

There's a gravity that pulls on all of April's statistics. Some guy's not going to drive in 350 runs, though in a particular game, he may drive in five. The stats will round out and assume their proper number. It is this succession of games—always a tomorrow, always a tomorrow—that makes any early discussions of pennant races, batting titles, and the like meaningless. Baseball needs about eight weeks to find the new season's rhythm.

Right now, as always in April, baseball lies on a 38th parallel of interpretation and extrapolation, where what happens on a diamond on any given day means nothing more than what it means on that one day. Baseball as absurdity. Today, the Red Sox got beat by the White Sox, 5-3. But cheer up—they won't go 0-162!

After the game, WITS hosted a party at 1200 Beacon St. It was one of those "must" affairs, and I got through it, though to tell the truth I wasn't in much of a partying mood after the Sox 5-3 loss. The thing that gets to me about these kinds of affairs is all the fatuous small talk you have to make. Still, I understand from a business reason why these things are important and that's what gets me through. That and being around Jon Miller.

Jon is an immense talent, and I know he won't be contained or satisfied for too long by his current job as No. 2 man in the Red Sox booth. He's too good. He's going to be a No. 1 someday. But I'm going to be selfish about it and hope that Jon stays with me for a long time. I love working with him. After the party, I dropped Jon off at The Chalet in Newton. I got home after 10 p.m. It was a long, tense, ultimately disappointing day.

♦♦♦

The strike lasted seven weeks and one day. Nothing like that had ever happened before or has happened since.

Interestingly, I recorded most of my thoughts on the strike only after it had ended. I kept a series of contiguous notes, almost in shorthand, to later jog my memory, but I remember consciously wanting to wait until I could see how it all turned out before commenting in depth on the weird experience.

♦♦♦

A Startling String of Zeroes

August 1981 (the strike has ended)

In many ways, the just-concluded baseball strike is an imponderable subject for me. As I write this, it's over now. I'm not sure we'll fully get the grasp of it, get our hands around it, until some time has passed. However, I want to record some initial impressions.

During the long duration of the strike, the days merged into one another like the colors of the rainbow. Where exactly does one color begin and another end? You can't say. The strike seemed like a fabric draped over my cold shoulders, only it couldn't provide heat or warmth, just awkwardness and bulk.

You have to remember. I had been doing Major League baseball since 1954. I've never had a summer off. At first, I didn't know what to do. Sure, I filled my days with things—Jimmy Fund work, golf, charity events, speaking engagements, long days at the beach, looking for different ways to keep busy. But I'll tell you, it didn't feel right. Jon Miller put it this way one day when we went to the beach together: "It's like I'm playing hooky. I'm here, but I know I shouldn't be here."

Part of me wants to avoid writing about the strike. I feel like the great writer Roger Angell, who wrote that the strike has been "so ugly, and dull, and diminishing that I am tempted to skip over it altogether." Dan Valenti had this great line: "If, as the proverb says, a dream grants what one covets when awake, then a nightmare permits what one fears. Baseball has long feared this strike, and now its nightmare has come true." Both Angell and Valenti wrote exactly what I've been thinking.

What did the strike mean to baseball? I don't think that question can really be answered. It's impossible to tell how many fans walked away during the strike, not to return at all or to come back with suspicions. Only time will tell if the game and the players have broken faith with the fans. I fear that at some level it has. How can fans return to the old feeling? Can they just pretend that this didn't happen?

The easiest way to measure the effect of the strike is in economic terms. According to estimates published by *U. S. News and World Report,* each day without baseball cost the 26 Big League clubs $1.25 million. The 650 players lost about $600,000 daily. Also hit hard were city and state governments, which lost tax money normally collected from baseball. For example, Pittsburgh Mayor Richard Caliguiri estimated that his city lost about $1 million on the first three games cancelled by the strike, a Pirates-Dodgers series. In Boston, City Hall guessed that the city was out a quarter of a million each day.

The players walked out because of the owners' demands for compensation for losing players to free agency. There was a lot of talk from lawyers on both sides. That's all you saw on the sports pages in the weeks leading up to the strike. Stories about money, legalities, contracts, threats, injunctions, and lawsuits. It was like watching a messy and very public divorce being aired in the papers. I think this turned the fans off more than anything else. The games were secondary. At least that's how it felt. And the closer we got to the strike, the more attention it drew. The game almost became irrelevant. It was like, "Oh, by the way, the Red Sox beat the Yankees, 6-2."

The fans weren't really interested in the economic and personnel issues. All they cared about was the game itself, that is, what went on between the white lines. How could a guy with a wife and a couple of kids making $15,000 working for the gas company or on a construction crew rally behind someone making upwards of one million dollars a year for playing a game for eight months a year? He couldn't. Many fans would play for nothing, just because they love the game so much. For the fans, there were no good guys, no one to root for, and no one to cheer home.

Where will all this money business end? Jon was joking around about a player making someday $10 million a year. The trouble is, I think he was only half kidding.

Leonard Koppett published some interesting statistics related to this last point. From 1971 to 1980, gross revenues for Major League teams rose from $160 million to $300 million, players' salaries went from $18 million to $85 million, and the percentage of salaries as a ratio to the clubs' incomes went from 11 to 28 percent.

It seems there's a money spiral. It's sucking the game down.

♦♦♦

Now with that overview, let me include some other entries. The first is one that I made the day players called the strike. The second is the one I made that dealt with the actual six weeks of being off.

♦♦♦

Friday, June 12

Anaheim, California. Things look grim. The strike is on. I went to Laguna Beach again with Jon (Miller) and John Guerin of the Worcester Telegram. We finally got back to the hotel after getting caught in a horrendous L.A.-type traffic jam. (Red Sox Traveling Secretary) Jack Rogers wanted the bags down in the hotel lobby as soon as possible. Jack got limousines for Manager Ralph Houk, the coaches, the writers, and the broadcasters.

Jack addressed the players, telling them that as of the moment they went on strike, the team had no obligation to assist them with their travel plans. He was legally bound to say this, but I'm sure he wanted to say it as well. It's just frustration. The last thing he said to the team was: "Fellas, you're on your own. Good luck."

The players were indeed on their own to get back to Boston or wherever they were going. Many fished about. These guys aren't used to making these kinds of travel plans on their own.

Later, we had dinner at the Hyatt Regency near the L.A. airport. We talked about the strike, and no one wanted to believe it had come to this. We boarded the plane for a 10 p.m. flight. Hydraulic problems forced us to change planes. It seemed fitting, a nice symbol for the condition baseball is in—going nowhere.

As I write this, it's 2:26 a.m. Boston time, and I'm still sitting in a plane at the L.A. airport. I can't picture what it will be like spending a summer weekend at home with no games to do, but that will be the case. Everyone, including me, expects a long strike. It is comprehended by very few people and related to by hardly anyone except the people directly involved. I really fear this will hurt the game. How can it help?

The Strike: Saturday, June 13 to Friday, August 1, 1981

The strike, the first in Major League history to occur after a season had started, cancelled 580 games or 38 percent of the season. I am beginning this entry on Saturday, August 2. The strike has been settled, and we resume the season on Monday, August10. I will use some of that time to work on this entry.

I arrived in Boston from Anaheim on Saturday, June 13 with Ralph Houk, the Red Sox coaches, and a few players, including

Carney Lansford and Rick Miller. Carney and Rick were quiet, almost as if they felt guilty. I told them that while I didn't agree with their actions, I nonetheless respected their position, doing what they felt they had to do. They seemed relieved to hear that.

We waited in Ralph's office for a long time for the bags to come in. We were pretty much quiet. Houk had the look of someone who was hurt. "Can you believe it?" he asked rhetorically, to no one in particular. He asked this several times. Ralph is old school. He earned the nickname "The Iron Major" because of his heroics in World War II. As a player, he waited on the bench for years behind Yogi Berra. He rarely played. He knew what it was like to struggle and to be thankful he was in the Big Leagues. He managed in the minors, and when he made it as a Big League skipper, he said he always had a sense of gratitude. A guy like Ralph Houk just can't understand players walking out like this. Nether can I, to be honest. There's got to be a better way to make their point rather than to hijack this great game and hold it for ransom. That's what this feels like—a kidnapping.

As we sat there in Ralph's office, just off the clubhouse, I think the implications of the strike—no baseball—were starting to hit us, each in his own way. We were all baseball lifers. We didn't know what to do, what to say, or how to act.

Ralph had a great line: "I ran into a fan and he told me 'Don't worry.' That's fine, but how do you 'don't'?"

How do you "don't?" This almost sounds like something Yogi Berra would say, but Ralph's right. How do you put this out of your mind? You can't.

I walked out of the clubhouse and down the tunnel that connects the locker room to the dugout. As I was doing it, my steps echoed. It was a hollow sound. The park also "sounded" lonely. I then thought of all the great Red Sox ballplayers who walked that tunnel in joyful expectation of playing ball, guys like Tris Speaker, Babe Ruth, Jimmy Foxx, Ted Williams, Yaz.

I walked onto the field. Fenway Park looked absolutely pristine, beautiful, and jewel-like. It was a shame, I thought, that we couldn't play on this beautiful diamond. Fenway looked like a radiant bride who was left standing at the altar. I felt badly about it. I walked around the field a little bit, thinking about all the games I had seen there as a kid and all the games I had done as a broadcaster. I could see my dad and me in the bleachers, cheering for Ted and Bobby Doerr and Dominic DiMaggio. I wonder what dad would have made of this strike? I ask that rhetorically.

I walked to the tunnel and back into Ralph's office. He kept saying, "I can't believe this." We all concurred. Ralph went on, "I kept thinking somebody was going to come up on a big, white horse and say it's over, that we're gonna play ball."

I went home to Cohasset and went to bed at 11 a.m. (the reversal of hours didn't help my mood) after reading a story by Bob Cubie in the *Quincy Ledger*. Cubie mentioned that a group of men averaging $173,000 a year for a little more than half a year's work were walking off the job while three members of the Abington police force took voluntary pay cuts so that two of their colleagues could stay on the job.

(Wife) Ellen was in Cleveland visiting friends. On Sunday, June 14, I went to the beach with my daughter Susan. It was one of the few times in 26 years that I was not in a broadcasting booth on a Sunday doing a game somewhere. I loved being with Susie, but I felt strange, empty. I later played some golf. A leisurely day, but I didn't enjoy it. I felt I should be at the ballpark, doing a game.

♦♦♦

During the fifty-day strike, I had some experiences I'll never forget. One was a trip to Charleston, West Virginia to do two International League games between the Charleston Charlies and the Pawtucket Red Sox on Saturday, June 20 and Sunday the 21st, which was Father's Day.

♦♦♦

Back in the minor leagues and heading to Charleston. Engineer Art Roberts and I just barely made the plane at Logan (International Airport in Boston) at 4 p.m. that Friday. We changed planes in Pittsburgh and got on a plane that we discovered, only after boarding, was destined for Buffalo, New York. We had just enough time to get off and find the right plane. That's what happens when you're used to having a traveling secretary do all the arrangements.

I always heard from countless people that flying into the Charleston airport is a hairy experience. On the flight from Pittsburgh to Charleston, the fellow (a businessman) who sat next to me —a Charleston native who must have earned combat pay for flying into the town so many times—told me the pilot would really grind it down and indeed he did. You see, the airport sits on the top of the mountain and landing is scary.

We planned it so Jon Miller would meet us in Charleston. There were no cabs at the airport, something that just doesn't happen in the Big Leagues. We called one, and Art and I waited twenty minutes. It arrived and the cabbie took us to the Executive Inn on the outskirts of Charleston. I walked into the motel to register, and I asked the girl, "Where is the cocktail lounge?"

"We don't have one," she replied.

"Okay, then how about the dining room. I'd like to eat."

"Well, sir, we don't have a dining room either."

"No dining room? Is there a coffee shop?" I asked, amazed.

"No," the answer came back.

"Then can you tell me where I can get something to eat?" Ah-ha! I figured I had her there. Surely, they must eat in Charleston. The girl directed me to a Greek restaurant a half mile down the road.

Welcome to the minor leagues.

Broadcasting from Watt Powell Park, we were informed that WITS sportscaster and long-time *Boston Record-American* columnist Larry Claflin had been taken to the hospital after apparently suffering a heart attack. It sounded serious. I immediately asked our producer in Boston, John Queeney, not to tell us another word about it until the game was over. I didn't want it weighing on my mind if the news was real bad. Without knowing, I could hold on to hope and put it out of my mind so I could do the game. When the game ended, we learned that Larry had died at 1 p.m. I felt like someone had given me a hard, fisted punch in the solar plexus.

The game between the Charlies and the PawSox started at 2 p.m. The contest was punctuated by long rain delays. The Charleston general manager was in charge of the tarpaulin, make that two tarpaulins (one for the mound and one for the plate). Pawtucket manager Joe Morgan helped him out.

The crowd was sparse, and to top it all off there was a tornado watch in effect. The rain and winds fiercely laced the park throughout the game, rocking the press booth. Several times, Jon and I looked at each other in astonishment and fear, thinking we were about to topple along with the booth into the stands. At one point, we actually thought we would go down. I bolted up and tried to open the door of the booth but couldn't because of the force of the wind. I sat down and looked at Jon. We were absolutely beside ourselves over what was happening.

When we got to the airport after the Sunday game, Father's Day, the plane left late. We missed our connecting flight to Boston, forcing us to partake of the hospitalities of the Pittsburgh Airport Hilton. To top it all off, the threat of an air traffic controllers' strike hung over our heads. President Reagan says he will fire them before they strike. What a mess. But I gave it my best shot not to get discouraged by all of this, trying unsuccessfully to get a flight to Providence. Happy Father's Day!

♦♦♦

We didn't do any more minor league games, but Jon and I stayed in touch, going out to eat and talking baseball. We did, however, have one other interesting experience in a minor league ballpark. We got to see history.

♦♦♦

The other event of note during the strike was the fabled 33-inning game between the Pawtucket Red Sox and the Rochester Red Wings on June 23. Jon and I were there doing the game for the Red Sox network. We were joined by half the press from the civilized world to broadcast the continuation of the game that was suspended at 4:07 a.m. after the 32nd inning on a cold Easter Sunday morning with the score tied 2-2. Eight hours and seven minutes of baseball produced what Roger Angell called "a startling string of zeroes."

Because of the crunch of media types that descended on Pawtucket's McCoy Stadium, the game was late in resuming. Jon and I had a long time to fill before the top of the 33rd began. We even ended up describing a ten-man softball game we could see going on beyond the stadium. Jon had me in stitches. He did some improvisations worthy of another Jon: Jonathan Winters. Jon came up with these hilarious names for some of the guys in the softball game. One big guy with the proverbial softball beer-belly gut was dubbed Jocko Clownpecker. Another guy, a small man, was Freddy Floborkto, I guess as in Freddy Patek. Another big man Jon named Rump Rebozo. Jon was just cooking.

Pawtucket owner Ben Mondor and General Manager Mike Tamburro showed their class by giving the regular Pawtucket media their usual places in the press box. All of the extras, drawn to the game because of its freak, circus-like quality, had to use the temporary press facilities. Press types from all over the world were there.

The resumption of the game was an anticlimax, ending after just one inning of play when Red Sox second baseman Marty Barrett scored the winning run. When history's longest baseball game was over, the record book had been rewritten:

- most putouts, one team (Pawtucket, 99);
- most putouts, both teams (195);
- time (8 hours, 25 minutes);
- most at bats, one team (Pawtucket, 114);
- most at bats, both teams (219);
- most strikeouts, one team (34 Rochester batters);
- most strikeouts, both teams (60);
- most assists, both teams (98);
- most pitches thrown in a game (882 – 459 by Pawtucket pitchers, 423 by Rochester pitchers).

It was a game of instant slumps (just add water and stir). Pawtucket DH Russ Laribee went 0-for-11. Left fielder Chico Walker was 1-13. Barrett, despite scoring the winning run, went 2-12. Center fielder Lee Graham, 1-14. Right fielder Sam Bowen, 2-12. Shortstop Julio Valdez, 2-13.

As a footnote to history and the answer to a future trivia question, Bobby Ojeda was the winning pitcher.

After our fling with minor league baseball, Jon and I looked for something, anything, we could do to bring baseball to our listeners. We wanted to do this not only to appease a baseball-hungry public but also to keep working out behind the microphone. However, after experiencing life on the road in the minor leagues, we didn't want to do much traveling. What a dilemma. What could we do?

We turned to Strat-O-Matic baseball.

This came about after Jon had the idea of recreating games the way they used to in the old days. We experimented with it and actually recreated the second game of the 1967 World Series featuring Jim Lonborg's one-hitter and Carl Yastrzemski's two home runs against the St. Louis Cardinals. Our intentions were good but the recreation was a disaster. We had no script, no rehearsal time, and the sound effects hadn't been perfected. Also, there was no suspense. Everyone who listened knew what was coming.

This spurred us into Strat-O-Matic baseball, where we "resumed" the 1981 season. Coincidentally, Dan Valenti came to Boston to do an article on the baseball strike and heard about our Strat-O-Matic games. Dan, a Strat-O-Matic player himself, was curious about what we were doing.

Dan's article gets at what the Strat-O-Matic season was all about. I like it because it also tells you a lot about Jon Miller, the Man of a Thousand Voices. You can see some of the playfulness, inventiveness, and creativity that makes working with Jon such a tremendous joy.

Here is the piece that Dan wrote:

It's been 80 years since Boston has had a summer like this one…that is, a summer without American League baseball. And this time around, the city's being caught with its Sox down to the tune of $275,000 a day, an innocent victim of the Major League players' strike. Yet the baseball-crazy Hub is managing better than you would expect, in part because of a throwback of a different sort devised by the Red Sox radio team of Ken Coleman and Jon Miller. They've gone back some 50 years to pull a page out of the game's past: the radio recreation of baseball.

Coleman and Miller began by recreating the second game of the 1967 World Series between the Red Sox and the St. Louis Cardinals, the game in which Jim Lonborg threw his celebrated one-hitter. But for all the drama of the game, for all the meticulous research Coleman and Miller did to recreate the game as authentically as possible, something was missing.

"The fans knew the result before we even started," Miller says. "Not only did they know the final score, but also when Julian Javier was going to get his hit and that Yaz would hit two homers. And that took much of the enjoyment out of it. There was just no suspense. It was also technically ragged. We just weren't ready."

Enter Miller's childhood and a game called Strat-O-Matic baseball.

Strat-O-Matic is an ingenious table baseball game that statistically reproduces a player's performance based on his actual hitting or pitching records. Thus, Jim Rice can be expected to hit with much more power than most players, and Dennis Eckersley will give up more home runs than most starting pitchers.

As Miller explains, "The whole idea is that if you've played the season over again, with the same schedule and the same teams used in the actual season, the results would be very similar, the key difference being how the teams were managed."

Miller has been a Strat-O-Matic devotee since 1962 and got the idea of resuming the strike-interrupted 1981 season with Strat-O-Matic games, which could then be broadcast as recreations.

"I figured that if Strat-O-Matic could be used to play the previous season over again, then why not use it to continue the interrupted season," Miller says.

Miller played a similar Strat-O-Matic (SOM) game during the off-season between two Red Sox championship teams—the '46 Sox and the '67 Impossible Dream team. He produced a highlights tape, complete with cheering crowds that he dubbed in from one tape recorder to another. He then mailed the tape to Coleman as a joke. Coleman liked it, and during a rain delay in Milwaukee this year (1981), Ken aired the tape. WITS, the flagship station of the Red Sox radio network, received a favorable response from listeners— enough of a response to keep SOM in the minds of the two broadcasters, especially as the talk of a strike got serious.

No "sell" was needed when it came to backing from WITS management. They enthusiastically backed the project as a way to recoup some of the advertising dollars lost because of the end of Red Sox broadcasts. No one kidded themselves that this would make up for all the lost revenue, but it could salvage a portion of the money. Plus, it would once again give the fans baseball…of a sort.

To make the SOM season as realistic as possible, Miller spent some time listening to original recordings of recreations of baseball games done in the 1930s. Again for realism, Miller also updated his set of 1980 cards (SOM cards for any current season actually contain the statistical results of the previous year, thus, in 1981, SOM players were playing out the 1980 season). He made all the trades and roster changes that occurred during the off season (remember, SOM rates a player based on his previous year's stats).

After working out the technical problems of doing the recreations, the "season" was ready to continue. The first series, aired over WITS beginning the night of July 1, featured the Red Sox hosting the Yankees at Fenway.

Guest managers, invited by the station to fulfill that great fantasy of managing a Big League club, play the games at the WITS studios in Boston. The first series pitted Boston Bruins president Paul Mooney managing the Red Sox against Bruins' front office man Nate Greenberg at the helm of the Yankees.

Miller scores the game and also advises on procedural points relating to SOM ("How do I send a guy from first to third on a single?" "How do I sacrifice?" "How do I move the infield in?"). Miller's scorecard in effect becomes the script from which he and Coleman recreate the game on the air. It's shades of Ronald Reagan recreating Cubs games by using Teletype reports.

All of the games originate in a small studio in WITS' new location at 24 Lansdowne St., near Fenway Park. Miller and Coleman sit with headphones on facing engineer/producer John Queeney, who rides herd on a console with numerous colored lights, fluctuating needles, and large, black dials. The dials are numbered with makeshift labels of white adhesive tape:

Dial 1 – Clapping crowd.
Dial 2 – Wildly cheering crowd.
Dial 3 – Booing crowd.
Dial 4 – General crowd noise.

There are also switches that control sound effects such as organ music, rhythmic hand clapping, an assortment of National Anthems, and even the voice of storied Red Sox P.A. announcer Sherm Feller, imitated by the multitalented Miller, who in a previous life must have been a stand-up comic.

When calling his innings (third, fourth, seventh, and eighth), Miller constantly shifts his eyes from the scorecard to Queeney to Coleman, who sits at his left. When a home team player makes a good play, Miller holds up two fingers to Queeney, who then turns Dial 2. A home-team error produces three fingers from Miller, and Queeney tugs Dial 3. When Coleman does his innings, Miller adds color and continues his gestures to the producer.

It all somehow comes together on a finished tape as a self-contained, well-orchestrated, improvisational baseball symphony. When you close your eyes and listen to the playback, you can almost fool yourself into thinking an actual game is going on.

The re-creation of a nine-inning game takes anywhere from 90 minutes to two hours without commercials, which are dubbed in later. The tapings can be tiresome and exhausting. Sessions can last eight hours straight.

"It's tough for me to take time to do the games," Coleman says. "I have to be at the Sidney Farber Cancer Institute so much (where he is chairman and executive director of Boston's famed Jimmy Fund). But it's even tougher on Jon because he has to be there when the guest managers play the series. It takes time. Then he has to come into the studio for the broadcasts."

And then there's the suspense factor. The listeners don't know how a particular game will turn out, but Coleman and Miller do. They are much like actors in a play knowing that, in fact, the butler did do it (or that Eddie Murray does win the game for the Orioles in the bottom of the ninth).

"Real games can be hard enough to call, such as a one-sided affair where the outcome isn't much in doubt," Miller says. "But at least there you can get caught up in the live action, having it there to describe. With SOM games, though, we have to invent just about everything. I just don't know how we're going to hold up if we have to recreate a 12-0 game."

The grind probably explains why the SOM Red Sox broadcasts feature so much of the dry, bizarre, give-and-take comedy that punctuates the regular season broadcasts of this singular announcing team. Miller is a born comedian and he can improvise better than Lionel Hampton. Moreover, it helps to have as his Number 1 guy the Bud Abbott of broadcasting—Coleman is a born straight man.

It's the comedy and humor that keeps listeners tuned in, much as if they are hearing Abbott and Costello do "Who's on First?" for the first…or 100th time. It's always funny.

Sometimes Miller instigates the banter with a perfect straight-line feed from Coleman:

COLEMAN: The National Anthem is always rather special here in Baltimore, when you consider that Francis Scott Key wrote it out here at the harbor. There's a ball to Evans and the count runs to 1-and-2.

MILLER: Have any other events of historical significance occurred in Baltimore that you can think of? You know, events that make it a special place for you. I'm fond of crab cakes, myself.

COLEMAN: Well yes. Of course, this is the Babe's hometown. Babe Ruth was born here. Foul back.

MILLER: Oh yeah, that's right. A close personal friend of yours, the Babe. I understand he used to let you put mustard on his hot dog.

COLEMAN: Oh, my (STIFLING A LAUGH). Right, and the Babe could really put away those franks (STILL TRYING TO CONTAIN LAUGHTER).

MILLER: Frank? Frank Malzone? Frank Robinson? He used to be with Baltimore too.

COLEMAN: And…(BOTH MEN LAUGHING) and I was here… (LAUGHING)… and I was here in Memorial Stadium and did the game the night Rocky Colavito hit four home runs for the Cleveland Indians.

MILLER: I remember that. I did a paper on it in my 20th Century American History class.

COLEMAN: You did? (VOICE TREMBLING TO CONTAIN HIS LAUGHTER) There's a ball outside.

MILLER: Yeah. I was a problem child (BOTH MEN BURST OUT LAUGHING).

COLEMAN: Evans swings and lines a base hit into left field, and he's on with one out. That will bring up Allenson, who struck out his first time up. (PAUSE) You know, Jon, you mentioned crab cakes. And it just so happens that I just had some crab cakes with Brooks upstairs in the press box.

MILLER: Brooks? Brooke Shields.

COLEMAN: No (LAUGHING). Brooks Robinson.

MILLER: (FEIGNING DISAPPOINTMENT) Oh, the old ballplayer, huh? Good friend of yours?

COLEMAN: Oh yeah, a great guy.

MILLER: He *is* a great guy.

COLEMAN: I didn't say he wasn't.

MILLER: A great guy…unlike most of your friends (BOTH MEN LOSE IT).

Later on in the game, Coleman starts the fun.

COLEMAN: The umpires for tonight's game: Billy Martin is calling the balls and strikes, Ron Luciano at first, Larry Holmes at second, and Marvin Hagler at third. (PAUSE) Red Sox baseball is brought to you by Natural Lite. Taste (MILLER TRYING TO SUPPRESS A HUGE LAUGH). Taste (COLEMAN'S VOICE QUIVERING WITH LAUGHTER)…Taste is why you'll (CRACKING WITH LAUGHTER) switch.

MILLER: Sounds like you've had a few Lite beers.

COLEMAN: No, Jon.

MILLER: You'd kill for one, though, wouldn't you?

COLEMAN: (STILL LAUGHING) Maybe after the game is over. It's that kind of night in Baltimore.

During this particular broadcast, which airs on July 6, 1981, they break it up some more with Miller's impersonations of Baltimore announcer Chuck Thompson and NBC newsman David Brinkley.
Yes, it's a grind, but clearly, these two men are having fun grinding.

♦♦♦

That was Dan's article, and he's right about the grind of doing the recreated games. As the strike went on, each "game" became just another reminder of what we were all missing.
For the record, the SOM Red Sox finished at 17-13.
Then the strike ended. Here's what I wrote on that day.

♦♦♦

Friday Aug. 1, 1981
Finally, a break came in the talks. They've ended the strike. I can't describe what a huge relief this is, but at the same time there's

no forgetting what has happened. The owners and players made up (but they didn't kiss). They didn't reach an agreement. They reached a settlement. In that fine distinction you can find all you need to know about the mistrust that has affected both sides. I'm afraid it will linger.

Major League Baseball has announced the season will resume on August 10, preceded by a week or so of workouts and exhibition games. So now we get a second season. A second training camp, a second round of exhibition games, and a second pennant race.

◆ ◆ ◆

After the games resumed, I wrote this:

Friday August 15, 1981

Fittingly, the first run of baseball's so-called Second Season came in on a balk by Chicago Cubs pitcher Mike Krukow. You couldn't have scripted it any better or more appropriately. *Time* magazine wrote in its story on the resumption of play: "The national pastime returned, not with a bang but with a balk."

The incongruities were appalling. All teams started out with 0-0 records. The New York Mets, 17-34 before the strike, spent a couple of glorious days in first place in the National League East. The Cincinnati Reds, half a game out of first place before the strike, found themselves even with the San Diego Padres, who were 12 ½ out.

The fans seem both relieved and skeptical. A crowd of 72,086 attended the All-Star Game in Cleveland, the first game held after play resumed. The next night, on "opening day" in Cleveland, 4,773 fans showed up in a ballpark that sits 80,000.

In San Diego, owner Ray Kroc, in a bury-the-hatchet gesture to the fans, let everyone into the park free on "opening day" and 52,608 took him up on the offer. The next night, when they had to pay their way in, only 5,360 were willing to dig into their pockets to watch the Padres. Throughout all of baseball, crowds were light.

Maybe the players, owners, and even the fans have learned something because of the strike. Experience is a great teacher, but so is inexperience. No one ever had dealt with an in-season strike until this year. We all found we weren't very good at handling it. Let us hope we are all wiser now.

Monday, November 22, 1999

I write this looking at the 2000 baseball season fast heading our way (maybe by the time you read this the new season will have started; maybe it's even over). We *did* learn a lot during the 1981 strike. We all learned that baseball is a business. It's not a sport masquerading as a business, as it was many years ago, but now a business masquerading as a sport. We've seen player salaries routinely topping eight figures. Yearly salaries of $10 million, $12 million don't even raise an eyebrow anymore. Multiyear contracts topping $100 million barely make headlines. TV revenues are up, but all is not well. In 1999, for example, overall attendance was down.

When you take a look at team payrolls, you notice something interesting. Here are the top 10 teams and their 1999 total payrolls (figures supplied by the commissioner's office):

- New York Yankees, $91,990,955.
- Texas Rangers, $80,801,598.
- Atlanta Braves, $79,256,599.
- Los Angeles Dodgers, $76,607,247.
- Baltimore Orioles, $75,443,363.
- Cleveland Indians, $73,531,692.
- Boston Red Sox, $72,330,656
- New York Mets, $71,510,523.
- Arizona Diamondbacks, $70,046,818.
- Houston Astros, $56,389,000.

Eight teams made the playoffs in 1999. You'll notice that all eight are in the top ten in payroll. Look at the bottom 10 of the list: working up from the cellar, you have Florida, Montreal, Minnesota, Kansas City, Pittsburgh, White Sox, Oakland, Philadelphia, Detroit, and Tampa Bay. These are franchises that generally have been economically shut out from being competitive. That's not right. You have to worry about the future with such a financial set-up.

Another thing we learned about the strike in 1981 is that once the genie gets out of the bottle, it's hard to put it back in. From that moment on, the game didn't have the same feel as before. I've talked to scores of people on this point, and they all agree. Players are now driven almost solely by economics, and you can hardly blame them. As for the fans, those who remember the game before the strike understand this sense of loss.

The newer fans are much more casual about their loyalties. That's because there are so many other attractions competing for their time and money—the rapid development of the Internet, cell phones, video games, and so on. The extremely speedy pace of high technology and its impact on life today provide a plethora of choices not available before. Increasingly, when the choice is baseball, it's made with the same passion and conviction as you would make to go see a movie or play Pokemon.

One very positive development has been the return to classic baseball architecture, the kind you will find in Camden Yards in Baltimore and in many of the other new stadiums that have been built recently or are going up now. I'm glad for that, and I see this architectural trend as proof that the so-called "purist" version of baseball is the one that is most deeply felt by fans and those who still have a true love of the game.

I'm not denying there is primarily a commercial thrust to this use of bricks, mortar, steel, and stone, but there comes a point where you have to put that out of your mind if you are to be able to enjoy a baseball game today, which, incidentally, I still very much do. You see, I'm still a Red Sox fan.

Let's face it—we live in a different world. Change is inevitable, and you either move along with it or you find yourself left behind. For baseball, and I think sports in general, moving along as a fan means investing little of your time, less of your attention, and still less of your loyalty. I'm not saying this is good or bad. I'm only acknowledging what is and is likely to be for some time to come. As I said, the genie never wants to go back into the bottle.

Setting the New Tone

I think a case could be made for the argument that the 1981 strike injected a strident, businesslike tone in baseball that even affected the way the game is played on the field. I think with so much money at stake, players are less apt to "take one for the team." They are not as inclined to play injured. They may be more likely to play to pad their own statistics rather than sacrifice for the team. For example, when a manager wants to move a player to a new position to make room for someone else, that player as often as not will go to his agent and lodge a formal complaint to the team.

Years ago, players accepted changes without complaint. I think of how Pete Rose moved from second, to third, to the outfield, and to first base, all because he knew the team would benefit from it. With the Red Sox, shortstop Johnny Pesky moved to third to make way for Junior Stephens in 1948. Similarly, in early 1970s, Rico Petrocelli went to third so that newly acquired Luis Aparicio could play short. Today, it's different. Players will often complain when asked to move around for the good of the team.

Or look at how pitching has changed since 1981. Pitchers are groomed now as specialists, and many of them honestly believe they can't throw more than a certain number of pitches without risk of arm injury. I'm not saying you can directly link this trend to the strike, but I would submit that because of the shift in attitude that took place in the minds of both players and management, this kind of specialization would be more likely to occur.

Why? Because once you declare that the season itself can be cancelled, you're basically saying that all other assumptions can be called into question.

At one time, of course, a pitcher's worth was measured in complete games. The manager gave the pitcher the baseball and expected him to go nine. As recently as the 1970s, you'd routinely find staffs with three and four pitchers with 200 or more innings pitched. You'd even see guys throw 300 or more innings. In 1974, for example, the following pitchers threw for 300 or more innings:

- •Luis Tiant, Red Sox, 311;
- •Gaylord Perry, Indians, 322;
- •Mickey Lolich, Tigers, 308;
- •Catfish Hunter, Athletics, 318;
- •Ferguson Jenkins, Rangers, 328;
- •Wilbur Wood, White Sox, 320;
- •Nolan Ryan, Angels, 333
- •Phil Niekro, Braves, 302.

Twenty-six pitchers that year threw 250 or more innings.

Today, it makes headlines when a pitcher goes the distance, as if he had completed a grueling marathon. The development of relief pitching has reduced the starter's job to just another role, a role that's almost as specific as a closer. The starter no longer worries about going nine. He's concerned with so-called quality starts, defined as an outing that lasts six innings in which the pitcher gives up three runs or less.

I don't know what will happen as the game looks ahead in this new century and new millennium, but I can't imagine the prohibitive costs can continue to spiral upward, unchecked, without serious consequences. Somewhere there has to be an end. A family of four can't get out of a Big League Game without spending $200 or more. Ticket prices are pushing $50 and $60 apiece in some cases. As a result, baseball is no longer a routine part of a fan's life but has become a Special Event, big-time entertainment like a concert in a stadium. I think that explains why you see so much rowdy behavior in the stands and how quick fans are to rain boos when a player doesn't perform. It's the only refuge fans have right now—to expect that these guys go out and win every game, which of course they cannot do.

Picture this: You're sitting there in your $45 seat. The game is more than three hours old and you're in the bottom of the 7th inning. It's 10:45 p.m. You have to get up in the morning to go to work. It's a chilly late April night. Your team is trailing by four runs. The $11 million cleanup hitter comes up with runners on second and third. He gets fooled by the pitch and sends a room-service ground ball to second base.

And he doesn't bother to run it out.

He just flips his bat, takes a few token steps down the line, then stops. Now let me ask you—will you cheer a guy like this?

The Heart of an Optimist

Already, an entire generation of young people are growing up who really don't care about baseball, at least not with the passion that for so long attended the game and its youth. They don't really play the game in the sandlots the way we used to, they don't know its past, and they have never experienced the tranquility of a day at the park. They have been robbed.

But you know what? People don't fundamentally change. If these kids could be taught how to play, taught about Ted Williams and Babe Ruth, and given a brand of baseball that would be more concerned about itself as a pastime and less as a blind pursuit of big money, they'd love the heck out of it. That's the greatest area of hope, and it would be my one suggestion to consider for the future good of the game—get the kids involved again. Put the biggest games on when they can see them. Play more day baseball. Throw in some single-admission doubleheaders.

Baseball might rediscover its soul again.

I have no other concrete suggestions to offer for how this could come about, no blueprint that will save baseball from itself. I'm just a broadcaster. It is not my place to become the architect of the New Baseball, whatever, wherever, and however that will be. But I do know that if a way is not found to bring the game more in line with the lives of the everyday fans and to get kids interested, the game will continue to take the wrong direction. At some point, it really will stop being baseball at all. The disconnect between the game and its fans will reach the breaking point. I hope this doesn't happen.

I know this. I'm an optimist by nature and I remain an optimist about baseball. As Charles Einstein once wrote, "To enjoy baseball, you do not need violence in your heart." As long as this holds true, I'll always be a believer.

TED WILLIAMS

("Too many people go for the Ultimate Hit before they're ready to do it")

Any book about my long life as a sports broadcaster must contain a section on Ted Williams, the greatest hitter of all time. This is true for a number of reasons. First, I watched Ted in the first few spectacular years of his career strictly as a fan. There was no bigger Ted Williams fan than Ken Coleman.

Later, when I was the Voice of the Cleveland Indians, I had the privilege of broadcasting many games in which Ted Williams appeared during the last seven years of his storied career. From 1954 to 1960, the Indians and Red Sox played each other 22 times a year. In other words, while Ted was still active during his last seven seasons and my first seven, the Red Sox and Indians played each other 154 times—the equivalent of one full season. During the course of that time, I got to interview Ted several times and came to know him a little.

Following my retirement from Major League broadcasting in 1989, I got to know Ted even better, as we were involved in a number of Jimmy Fund events and other special projects together. He came as advertised—larger than life but always down to earth, easily one of the most knowledgeable, intelligent, and giving men I have ever encountered, in or out of sports. Ted is modest about the amount of time he has spent helping others. Let me just say that when it comes to human beings, Ted is a .400 hitter. Naturally, Dan Valenti and I were delighted when he agreed to do the foreword to this book. We'd like to give you a taste of Ted, mainly in his own words in a couple of interviews we did with him, but first, more about this incredible man and his great career.

It was Ted Williams' determination as a young man not only to be a great Major League hitter but to become the greatest of all time. Few can argue that he didn't make it.

Williams finished his long career with a .344 lifetime batting average, 521 home runs, 1,839 RBIs, six batting crowns, two MVP Awards, and two Triple Crowns. He appeared in innumerable All-Star games and led the Red Sox to a league championship in 1946.

However, a mere statistical summary can only go so far in suggesting Ted's prowess as a hitter. The numbers must be taken into context of the five prime years he lost to military service, serving both in World War II and in the Korean conflict. Other factors that must be weighed in looking at Ted's numbers include the elbow injury suffered in the 1950 All-Star game, which took away some of his power; his lack of speed, especially in his later years, and the weak lineups he played in for the last five years of his career.

Controversy also marked Ted's career, from his famous spitting incident to his running feud with Boston sportswriters. Williams was a walking headline, guaranteed to sell papers in Boston.

Ted hit for power and average and stood in the batter's box with intelligence unmatched before or since. He knew more about pitchers and pitching than they did themselves. Ted is the leader, all time, in lifetime on-base percentage, .483 to Babe Ruth's .474. Think of it: just about half the time Ted Williams came up to the plate in a Big League game against Big League pitching, he reached base. That's phenomenal.

Dick Donovan, who grew up in my hometown of Quincy, grew up idolizing Ted. Later, Dick became one of the American League's finest pitchers.

"It was sort of an eerie feeling," Donovan once said, "standing out there on the mound and thinking that Williams knows exactly how you are going to pitch him. To put it briefly, you have mixed emotions about turning the ball loose" (Pope 61).

There's a great story I love about Dick and Ted. Donovan was warming up before a game. He spotted Williams talking to a couple of Dick's White Sox teammates, catcher Sherm Lollar and outfielder Jim Rivera. Dick overheard a bit of the conversation, with Ted's booming John Wayne voice finishing off a sentence, "…like Donovan over there. He's a perfect example of what I mean."

Curious, Dick wandered over and asked Ted what he was saying.

"Dick," Williams replied, "I'm going to tell you exactly how you're going to try to pitch me today."

Ted then went through the entire game plan. He had it down, cold.

"I couldn't believe it. Ted would pick a situation and tell me exactly what I'd try to do. It was amazing. Here was this guy who knew everything I was thinking" (61, 62).

There was an amazing unofficial statistic on Ted. I've never actually confirmed it, but I've heard it said a number of times and have no reason to doubt its truth. It's this—he struck out three times in one game only twice in his career, once in his rookie year in 1939 against Detroit's Bobo Newsom and in 1957 on May 16 against Jim Bunning. The Bunning one really got him.

"The Bunning thing bugged Williams so much that he took to walking around the clubhouse before games and pantomiming situations in which he would be facing Bunning again. 'The score is tied in the ninth inning in Detroit,' Ted would drone. 'There's a man on and Williams is up. The count of 3-and-2 between Bunning and Williams. There's the pitch. BOOM! There it goes! IT'S OUTTA HERE!'" (68).

The next time Williams faced Bunning was on July 12, 1957 in Detroit. In the top of the first inning, Ted launched a Bunning pitch up on the right-field roof of the stadium.

Add the many competing dailies operating in Boston for much of Ted's early and middle career plus Ted's flair for the dramatic and his larger-than-life personality, and it's easy to see why Ted dominated the sports pages for two decades. His dramatics included the game-winning home run in the 1941 All-Star game in Detroit, his 6-for-8 hitting performance in the last two games of that year to finish over .400 (.406), and his last at bat.

Fittingly, Williams bowed out in spectacular fashion. On his last time up in the Major Leagues on September 28, 1960, Ted hit a towering home run off Baltimore's Jack Fisher at Fenway, what Dan Valenti once called in an essay, "the last thunderbolt of an ancient God." Ted had willed a home run.

Ted could be irascible and engaging, brusque and charming, but always, he radiated a fierce intelligence that was driven by an enormous curiosity about life. He tackled everything with energy and enthusiasm. That's how he became one of the world's greatest fishermen, and is in fact a member of the fishing Hall of Fame.

Ted also was a great hunter and insatiably fascinated by many different things. He soaked up knowledge and mastered just about everything he tried, from photography to flight. When a photographer would pose Ted in front of the batting cage or beside a 100-pound tarpon, Ted could, and sometimes would, tell him what lens setting to use.

Ted, elected to baseball's Hall of Fame in 1966, later went on to manage the Washington Senators beginning in 1969. He was named Manager of the Year that season. Following his managerial stint, he worked for years as a hitting instructor for the Red Sox, working with the team in spring training.

There are so many Ted Williams stories that come to my mind, but one sticks out and it's one that no one has ever heard before. A few years back, in the mid 1980s, Ted and I were doing a promotional seminar at the Marriott Hotel in Newton, Mass. for the Citrus Hills, Florida, retirement community. Ted was staying at the Marriott. Ted always liked to eat early, but on the night of our presentation he didn't have the chance. After the seminar was over, Ted asked me to dinner.

"Kenny, there's something I want to talk to you about."

Naturally, I accepted Ted's invitation. Who wouldn't? We went into the restaurant and they wisely put us in a quiet corner where we would not be disturbed. We talked politics, art, boxing, and of course, baseball.

It was a great evening, the longest conversation we ever had. When I was driving home to Cohasset, I got to thinking. Ted had said there was something he had to talk with me about. What was it? Suddenly, I realized there was nothing special Ted had to tell me.

He was alone that night at the Marriott and what he really wanted was some company. He was alone and on the road. Ted knew me, so I became his company. You see, ordinary people can walk into a bar and sit down. Ted couldn't possibly do that. People would have been all over him in an instant. It is the price of fame, which many people would never understand, but I did. Ted may not remember that night but I will never forget it, and I take this opportunity to thank Ted Williams for a most special evening in my life.

In this interview, recorded during spring training 1982, Ted talks about his favorite subject: hitting. He also discusses the top pitchers he played against.

KEN COLEMAN: Ted, I'm going to start in a somewhat unorthodox manner by showing you three pictures for your reaction. The first photo shows the right-field roof at Tiger Stadium in Detroit. And I can't help but say that if you played your home games at Tiger Stadium, you might have ended with 821 home runs instead of 521.

TED WILLIAMS: Well, no question, Detroit was one of the very best parks to hit in. But you know, another thing that was a contributing factor there is that the Detroit pitchers were always the daring type. It seemed like every pitcher they had in the starting rotation over the years that I played had extreme confidence in himself. Like a Newhouser or a Trucks or a Trout or a Bunning. Trucks was tough. I'd tell myself not to overswing against Trucks. Just be quick. You had to be against him. In that respect, he was a lot like Score.

Those guys threw hard, and when you made contact, the ball just took off. But those Detroit pitchers were always real confident that they were just as good as you were. They pretty near defied any hitter, including me. It may have cost them a little bit in the long run with hitters like DiMaggio or Mantle or some of the other good hitters, but for some reason, that staff was always a defiant staff. I think that's one of the reasons why I got balls to hit that I didn't get in some of the other close parks.

KEN: The second photo is going to bring back some memories, because it's of a guy who's very special to me and to you. I'm speaking of Bobby Doerr, the Red Sox all-time best second baseman.

TED: You're absolutely right. There's nobody who's ever been closer to me or that I ever had more affection for in my baseball life than Bobby Doerr. He's an absolutely perfect gentleman, and he was a hell of a ballplayer. He is a very close friend. I really believe Bobby's close to going into the Hall of Fame and rightly so. I love him.

KEN: As a hitter, quite the opposite of the way you hit most of the time, Bobby was a great one for changing his batting stance. He seemed to have a new stance for each new at bat. Now being as close as you were to Bobby, and with you being a great student of hitting, did you ever talk to Bobby or get on him about that?

TED: Yes I did, and I shook my head as you asked the question. I first saw Bobby in the Pacific Coast League, and I don't think I ever saw a better hitter than he was. He hit the ball all around. Right center, left center, everywhere. He could pull balls, hit line drives into left field. Then he got to Fenway Park. It's awful hard for a right-handed batter to ignore The Wall.

I've seen a lot of hitters hurt themselves trying to pull everything in Fenway. Instead of just hitting the ball straightaway, they tried to pull everything. And I said this in my book *The Science of Hitting*: you pull only when you get the type of pitcher that you see real good and you feel you can pull. And you pull when you got the count. Batting practice is a good time to work on pulling, because you know what pitch is coming. Hitting 2-and-0 or 3-and-1, or on the first pitch of the game—these are excellent situations to try to pull. But a lot of guys don't take advantage of that, and as a result, they're hitting like they got two strikes on them all the time instead of taking advantage of the count or the pitcher. But again, you can hurt yourself thinking in terms of pulling all the time. And Bobby and I would talk all the time about it. He'd say, "I know I'm hurting myself trying to pull so much, but what a temptation."

KEN: The last photograph shows Ted Williams bunting. What's your reaction here, Ted?

TED: I used to bunt now and then, more than people remember. Everybody else bunted, so I thought I'd better do it too, to keep the defense honest. But even more important that that, and it's one of the keys to hitting, is that you never swing at a ball until you get a chance to appraise the speed. That will give you information on what the ball might be doing that given day for that given pitcher. You do that very thing when you're trying to bunt a ball. You're just trying to get your bat on it. You can see the ball better because you're just looking for it. You then watch it, following it all the way into the bat. You see the ball much better when you bunt, and often I'd shorten up just to get a look at the pitcher's speed.

But swinging away is a little different because when you swing at a ball, you don't see it quite as well as you would on a bunt. And one of the things I tell young players is the first time up against a pitcher, try and see as much as you can. Well, certainly you're not gonna swing at the first pitch if that is a rule. Fifty percent of the time it won't be a strike. If you take it, you can judge it. When you've seen one pitch, you've seen the speed. That's all you need.

You can see if the ball rides. You might even be able to judge if a pitcher has or hasn't got it on that particular day. So why give away that first time at bat when you haven't seen a pitch? You may have never seen the pitcher before. He could be off or on, and you might get a sign of that by seeing as many pitches as you can the first time up. When you first come up in a game, you have to try and learn as much as you can about the pitcher in as short a time as possible. There's no better time than on that first pitch or two.

KEN: Wade Boggs of the Red Sox has really studied your book The Science of Hitting. In that book, you make the point that, in the strike zone, there are areas where you're going to hit .220 and also areas where you'll hit .400. And one of the things Boggs says he's gotten out of the book in that regard is patience at the plate. And you don't see it that much with today's hitters, it seems to me.

TED: Well, let me tell you. Of all the things in my career, I was criticized for my patience at the plate as much as for any other thing. Now, all of a sudden, they realize that being patient at the plate is pretty important. Why is it important? Because you get a better ball to hit, that's why. Something that wasn't said in *The Science of Hitting*, and I've never said it before, is that most hitters—I should say pretty near all hitters—are incapable of handling the full 17 inches of the plate. Consequently, a good hitter should gear on the two-thirds of the plate he can handle. Now against some pitchers, you're gonna have to move the two-thirds you're interested in, because you know you're not gonna get anything on the inside of the plate, for example. And you know you're gonna get 80 or 90 percent of the pitches on the outer two-thirds. So why not think of *that* two thirds of the plate?

Covering the full 17 inches of the plate is pretty hard to do, but that's exactly what you've got to do, especially with two strikes. So you gotta concede someplace. What should you do with two strikes, and especially when you're down on the count? You make up your mind: "I'm going to hit everything through the middle." Why is that best? Because the bat is at right angles to the direction of the pitch, and your hitting area on the bat will be at its longest. So there's all the percentage in the world in telling a guy to go to the middle. If you're down on the count, hit through the middle. If you're in trouble against a tough pitcher, hit through the middle. If you're in a slump, think of the middle. One of the things I'm sure people don't know about me as a hitter is how much I thought about the middle, especially when I was down.

KEN: You once made an interesting observation. You said if you wanted to find out about hitting, you talk to pitchers because they're the guys trying to get you out. You like to talk to good pitchers, don't you? You mentioned Warren Spahn, a great pitcher.

TED: You bet he was. And I'll tell you. I think a pitcher can learn an awful lot if they get a good rapport going with a tough hitter. A smart hitter, get going with him, and he can learn an awful lot. I feel the same way about hitters. You get a hitter talking with a great pitcher like a Spahn or a Ford, and that hitter will learn an awful lot, particularly about how pitchers think and how they try to set you up at the plate. That was one of the things I did in my career, in my education as a hitter that made me a better hitter. I couldn't learn enough from them, so I was always pestering them: what would you do here? How would you react in this situation?

KEN: Former American League umpire Hank Soar has been around a long time, and he's a very straightforward man, like you are when it comes to talking about people. I did an interview with Hank and asked him to rate the best he's ever seen. When I said fastball, he came right back and said, "Herb Score." Do you agree?

TED: Herb Score I think had a little better velocity than any lefthander I ever saw. I saw Newhouser. He was a great pitcher, a hell of a pitcher. But I think that Score threw just a might harder. He grunted more. He reared up more. Newhouser was fast but smooth, with less apparent effort. I didn't hit against Koufax. He was in the other league. But I'd have to say that, just for speed, I'd have to pick Score.

KEN: Now when it comes to curveballs, Hank selected Bob Lemon.

TED: Well, the best curveball I ever saw in the Big Leagues was Washington's Camillo Pascual, though Lemon was tough and must rank right up there. Pascual's curve was just plain nasty, because it broke so sharply. The thing that made Lemon so tough was that all his stuff was quick. His fastball had a little quick dip to it. His curveball was sharp and quick. His slider was quick, down and in. His stuff was quick and hard to get a hold of. I thought that, overall, Lemon was one of the toughest pitchers I hit against. He didn't strike me out that much, but that's because I had good luck guessing against him.

KEN: For the best slider, Hank named a man who didn't stand the test of time all that well. He picked Bob Grim.

TED: Well, Bob Grim had a good slider, no doubt. But I can think of quite a few pitchers better than him. One almost nobody mentions was Dick Donovan, who was always tough on me. Donovan had one fault. He went a little too much with one pitch, his slider. He had an excellent curve. He had a good sinking fastball, not too far away as far as I'm concerned from Lemon. But he wasn't quite as versatile as Lemon because he didn't use all his pitches to as good a degree. And as a result, he was an easier pitcher to hit. I simply laid in wait for his slider all the time. You couldn't do that against Lemon. Another tough pitcher was Don Larsen. When he was right, he was a great pitcher. You can talk about Raschi, Reynolds, Garcia, Trucks, Trout, and all those guys, but I think Donovan could have been as good as any of them. Except for Mr. Feller. He's the number-one right hander I ever saw.

KEN: Ted, you have a very successful boys' baseball camp in Lakeville, Massachusetts, and you spend time with the youngsters there. You also work with professional ballplayers, minor and major leagues. What's the difference in teaching a young boy as opposed to a professional hitter? What do you stress?

TED: You get a little more fundamental with the kids. The guys in professional ball all have talent, but many youngsters don't have talent, so you dwell on the basics. You put yourself mentally back in those years they are in and say to yourself, "Here's what I'd like to know." And then I start talking to them about things like "Do you hit a curve differently than you do a fastball?" The answer is, you don't hit it any differently, but you do wait on it longer. I also talk about the importance of hip action in the swing and about putting your hands in a better position to hit the ball. I emphasize not pulling. I try to teach them to hit through the middle and show them why that's the most important way to hit when you're starting out. Then, after they get the middle down, they can start working towards the homer, the Ultimate Hit. Too many people go for the Ultimate Hit before they're ready to do it. They go for the Ultimate Hit, and that means pulling the ball and getting it into the air. When they try to do that before they get the basics down, it usually means trouble.

KEN: Ted, you're a great fisherman. Do you think there's a correlation between fishing and hitting?

TED: Hitting you gotta practice, fishing you gotta practice. You gotta study hitting, you gotta study fishing. I'd like to put the parallel this way and I did once at a little talk I gave up at a small private school in New England. I correlated hitting in sports to studying in the academic world. And the two are exactly the same, really, because the more you practice, the better you get. The more confident you get. And if you have the desire and the willingness to put out a little bit more at practice, you're gonna succeed. Now if you study, which I didn't do that much of in school, and you take that desire to want to get a good grade and you're striving to show everybody you can be the best, you won't have to worry about that test. You won't have to be biting your nails wondering if you're gonna pass it.

KEN: Ted, you had a long, distinguished career with the Red Sox, spanning parts of four decades. How do you know when it's time to quit?

TED: A lot of circumstances determine when you should hang 'em up. Ballplayers are making big money now, so I think there's a tendency to hang in there longer than you should. By the end of my career in Boston, I was absolutely fed up with playing. I made up my mind in 1960 that I had just had it. The year before in '59 I had a bad year. I hit .254, the only time in my life that I didn't hit .300. But I had a pinched nerve in my neck that bothered me all year. It hurt so bad I couldn't even turn my head. Every time I swung, it hurt. I was encouraged by everyone, even Mr. Yawkey, to quit. But I wasn't ready to give it up then. I knew I could still hit, and I wanted to go out and show it. So I played for one more year, hit .316 with 29 homers, and that was it. I was going on 43 when I quit. I think a player should consider quitting when the game gets too hard to play, when it's no fun. When you look from second to third and it looks like a long way, it's time to quit. When you see great hitters like Mays, Mantle, Aaron hitting .260, it's a shame.

KEN: That last at bat surely had to be one of your greatest thrills.

TED: Yes it was. I knew it was going to be my last game. The thing I remember to this day was how cold, damp, and raw Fenway was that day (September 28, 1960). It was a miserable, gray day. There was a wind blowing in from center, and I said before the game that nothing was going out of the park. We had the pre-game ceremonies, I made my speech (see below), and the game began. There were only about 10,000 people in the stands because of the weather, but they cheered every move I made.

Early in the game, I scored from third on a sacrifice fly that Lu Clinton hit. Then on my next time up, I really caught hold of one and sent it deep. I thought it had a chance but it didn't make it. Trotting back to the dugout, I thought to myself, "If this one didn't make it, nothing would." I told Vic Wertz something to that effect. I came up for the last time in the bottom of the eighth. Willie Tasby led off and I waited in the on-deck circle. They just cheered me. When I got into the box, they gave me a standing ovation for several minutes. I had my head down, just trying to concentrate on the pitcher, Jack Fisher, a young, hard thrower, part of that Baby Birds staff they had in the late 50s, early 60s. On a 1-and-1 pitch, Fisher tried to throw a fastball by me, but I was on it. I swung and was lucky enough to drive it over Al Pilarcik's head in the bullpen in right-center. I got one more big hit out of my bat. Manager Mike Higgins had me go out to left in the top of the ninth, and he immediately sent (Carroll) Hardy out to get me. And then I ran in for the last time. I'll never forget that last, great ovation.

◆ ◆ ◆

On March 7, 1988, Dan Valenti caught up with Ted in Winter Haven, Florida, where the Red Sox used to train in the spring. Ted and Dan talked about hitting, and Ted amplified on some of his ideas.

DAN VALENTI: Ted, If you had to isolate one factor in hitting that stands apart from all the others in terms of importance, what would it be?

TED: The most important aspect of hitting, of the swing, particularly as far as generating power is concerned, is the hips. A hitter absolutely needs to open up his hips to fully get his arms and hands into the swing. I've said it before and I'll say a million times: hips before hands. Hips before hands. In other words, the hips have to fly open before the hands come around. It sounds like a simple piece of advice, but if a hitter doesn't instinctively have good hip action, it's an awful hard thing to teach.

DAN: Why is that so difficult to teach?

TED: Because when you try to teach something that's not there in the first place, you're going against the hitter's instincts, his habits, how he's been hitting all his life. So you try to point out that the habit's not a good one. You then must get a hitter aware of what he's doing at the plate at all times. Once he's in that batter's box, each movement of his body will do something either for or against his swing. You can't waste any motion. The timing is unforgivable in that sense. The balls coming in on you at 90 miles an hour from sixty feet, six inches away. So it's obvious that all of a hitter's movements must be efficient and therefore monitored, because all the movements are important. And the most important of those is the hip action.

DAN: Is that where power comes from?

TED: Exactly! You can't hit with power unless you're able to turn your hips into the pitch. The hip rotation, done at precisely the right time, then allows the arms to come through to meet the ball. Like I say, it's a hard thing to teach, because actually you're trying to teach the hitter to be more aware of what he's doing. Awareness sounds simple, but not many people can do it. It takes tremendous concentration and focus. It's not the same thing as thinking. In fact, it's the opposite.

DAN: Ted, you work a lot with young hitters here in the minor league camp. When you're sizing up a hitter, what's the first thing you look for?

TED: The first thing I look at in a swing is the batter's quickness, because if he's not quick, you can bet your ass and be damned sure about it that he doesn't have good hip action. So I look at how quick he is. Is he always on the ball? If he's behind everything or he's overmatched, you can be damned sure the problem's in the hips. He's not getting enough hip movement. I can't emphasize this enough. Hips move the hands through the ball. Hitting through the hips—that is, hitting with good hip action—initiates everything in a batter's swing. Everything else is secondary.

DAN: Is that why you had that little rocking action just before you hit a ball?

TED: Yes. It was a timing device for me. It gave me a good rocking action of the hips to get my swing started. If you don't have something like that to get you started, you're not going to get your hips into the swing properly. And you're not going to hit in the Big Leagues. And you certainly won't generate enough power to hit home runs. Home run hitting doesn't just come from bulk. It comes more from speed and being quick. Look at Aaron. He wasn't that big. You see a lot of big kids who can't put one out, but a smaller guy can. Why? Look at the hips and his quickness.

DAN: And you say that's a tough thing to coach.

TED: The toughest, actually. To coach that takes a lot of time and patience. Basically, your biggest battle is just trying to get the hitter see the importance of it, because as I said, he's not been doing it that way and you're now going against his ingrained hitting instincts. That's tough, but smart hitters will have the dedication and persistence to stay with you. What you do is try to incorporate good hip action into the player's particular swing. I don't like changing the swing itself. It should be one that a batter is comfortable with. As long as the hips are working properly, it doesn't matter what the swing looks like. The swing will take care of itself.

DAN: What else do you look for?

TED: Beyond that, the feet should keep in balance at all times. This is also crucial. Having good balance will enable you to get the proper weight shift on contact with the ball. That shift, by the way, is another facet of the swing that falls into place—takes care of itself —once proper hip action is established. You look at all the great hitters and you'll see what I mean.

◆◆◆

In May of 1984 at Fenway Park, I emceed the ceremonies in which the Red Sox officially retired Ted Williams' famous No. 9 uniform. They also retired the No. 4 of Joe Cronin, who played shortstop for the Sox, managed them, and was their general manager before going on to the presidency of the American League. Ted was asked to come to the field microphone and address the crowd. He hadn't done so since September 28, 1960, the day he retired. During that speech on his final day as an active player, Ted got in one last dig at the Boston writers and praised the Boston fans:

> "Despite some of the terrible things written about me by the Knights of the Keyboard up there (TED NODS TO THE PRESS BOX), and they were terrible things—I'd like to forget them but I can't—my stay in Boston has been the most wonder-

ful part of my life. If someone should ask me the one place I'd want to play if I had to do it all over again, I would say Boston, for it has the greatest owner in baseball and the greatest fans in America."

In his 1984 speech, a mellower Ted again expressed his allegiance to Boston and his love for Joe Cronin. Here's what he said on that historic occasion:

"Thank you commissioner for your kind words tonight. I wish I had the ability to be able to express what's in my heart tonight. And indeed the fellow who can't realize how lucky he has been in a long career is a very unfortunate person. One of the greatest breaks I ever got in my life was when a great former second baseman came out to California. And he was out there to pick up the option of a young second baseman, my dear, wonderful friend and teammate for so long, who was 19 years old, and the Red Sox had an option on him. His name was Bobby Doerr (APPLAUSE).

"Eddie Collins, who I'm speaking of, came out there and decided, 'Yeah, this kid's gonna be a second baseman, all right.' And Bobby was here for 15 years. In the meantime, Eddie Collins also saw a young left handed hitter hit in practice, and he decided, 'I think this guy can hit.' As a result, I came as far as anybody could come in this United States to play in a city as distant as San Diego, California, was from Boston, Massachusetts. I certainly know this was one of the greatest breaks I ever got.

"But following that, I got to play for a manager by the name of Joe Cronin. I can't tell you how important he was to me. I know there are a lot of stories about the things I said, did, and acted. But I had understanding from a very, very wonderful man. He taught all the young players so much. I was with him over the course of 15 years in the Boston Red Sox organization. So I came up, and I'm about ten years younger than Joe, and he was getting toward the end of his career, and I said, 'Joe, you know you've got some gray hairs on your head.' He looked at me and said, 'Yeah, and you know who put them there, (THE PARK ERUPTS IN LAUGHTER)

"Joe Cronin was a great player, a great manager, a wonderful father, and nobody respects you more than I do, Joe, and I love you. I'll always remember the fond memories we shared. In my book, you're great, and I have the greatest respect and love in my heart for you. (APPLAUSE)

(TO THE FANS) "I know you want to see the ballgame. And I'm just gonna say that this is a memorable night for me, especially because I'm with Joe Cronin, and our numbers are being retired together. I want to tell you something. It's really been a lousy day. It's been raining. Even our club isn't going as good as they can do. But I'd just like to say that you people in the stands really show me something. You are truly great baseball fans (LOUD APPLAUSE). And I will always be cognizant of the fact that as far as Ted Williams is concerned, baseball is the greatest in Boston and its fans are the greatest. I salute you."

Of course, some 15 years after that speech, the fans in Boston as well as the rest of the world got a chance to return the favor and then some during Ted's ceremonial appearance at the start of the 1999 All-Star game at Fenway Park on Tuesday, July 13. The Game's Greatest Living Player (Joe DiMaggio had died earlier in the year, ending that debate) rode in on a cart from the centerfield garage door, and Fenway exploded in what was arguably the loudest, longest, most emotional ovation the old ballpark has ever heard or maybe will ever hear as long as baseball is played there.

Greats of both the past (Aaron, Spahn, Mays, Yaz) and the present (Sosa, McGwire, Gwynn, Ripken) gathered around The Kid like they were themselves kids. The love-in for Father Baseball, as one writer called Ted that night, continued for many minutes, going well past the orchestrated, scripted pre-game ceremonies. When the P.A. announcer tried to get the players back to their dugouts, they wouldn't go.

Players on the field, fans in the stands, people watching at home felt the bittersweet chills of this emotional scene. There were many wet eyes, including Ted's.

Perhaps the most wistful and in a way most heart-wrenching moment occurred when it came time for Ted to throw the ceremonial first pitch into the plate, where Carlton Fisk was waiting. Ted rose slowly out of the golf cart, helped and supported by Tony Gwynn. He gripped the baseball, the fingers following the form instinctively.

Ted then looked for the plate.

"Where is it?" he asked Gwynn.

The man who once had 20-10 eyesight, who now has to deal with tunnel vision as the result of a mild stroke, squeezed the ball. Tony pointed Ted in the right direction. Ted located it and threw a surprisingly strong and accurate ball in to Fisk. Again, the crowd cheered impossibly loud and long. There were more tears.

The Kid had come home.

CHAPTER 10

Broadcasting and Beyond

"BASEBALL, LIKE IT OUGHT TO BE"

Game Seven

Of course, the decade of the 1980s provided a lot of thrills and good times. The Red Sox contended for many of those years. In 1983, Yaz played his last game. He said goodbye in fitting fashion, with a lap around the park, reaching out and both physically and psychically touching the fans. Fittingly, Yaz played left that day, and he even made one last great play off the Green Monster, fielding a ball and holding the batter to a single.

In 1984, Roger Clemens made his debut, and Roger blossomed into a star. In 1986, he struck out 20 batters in a game, he was the winning pitcher in the All-Star Game, and he propelled the Sox into the World Series following a heart-pulsing comeback against the California Angels in the Championship Series. That was the series that made Dave Henderson famous. It was Henderson's home run with two outs in the ninth inning in Game Four against the Angels that brought the Red Sox back from oblivion.

The Red Sox played the New York Mets in a thrilling World Series and came within one pitch of winning their first World Title since 1918, but it was not to be. The Mets rallied to come back in Game Six and Game Seven.

Boston's Bruce Hurst was the pitching star of the 1986 World Series. He shut out the Mets 1-0 in Game One at Shea Stadium and pitched a complete game 4-2 win in Game Five at Fenway to once again put the Red Sox up, three games to two. Bruce was the starter in the all-important Game Seven.

Before Game Seven, I remember sitting on the team bus in front of the Grand Hyatt Hotel at Grand Central Station, where the Red Sox stayed. Hurst was sitting directly behind me. We were ready to go to the stadium for the final game. The bus was only half filled, because a lot of the guys had gone out early to Shea. The ride was silent, completely silent, and it was already dark when we left the hotel.

As we were going through Queens, I was tempted to mention that a high school I spotted through the window was where former Red Sox player and Twins manager Sam Mele used to attend and where a kid named Whitey Ford used to go to watch him play.

But I didn't think it was appropriate to say anything. Bruce was the starting pitcher that night in a game that would be played in front of the entire nation and many parts of the world, and I thought it best to leave him alone with his mental preparations.

I had watched Bruce Hurst throughout his career and seen him go through some tough times, struggling early on before blossoming into a fine Major League pitcher. Early in his career, Bruce, a Mormon from the little town of St. George, Utah, had difficulty with the profanity that was part of a Major League clubhouse. It's always been that way in clubhouses, I guess since the early days of baseball—men horsing around, rough housing, and swearing.

The trip from the Grand Hyatt to Shea Stadium seemed to take forever, but then suddenly we were there. The bus slowed down, then began inching forward toward the entrance where we would get off. A large, boisterous crowd had gathered. They were yelling and screaming, and the scene was chaotic. There was a huge lit-up sign that provided a totally intended, though completely ironic caption. The sign read: "Baseball, Like It Ought To Be."

Finally, we got to the entrance and the bus stopped. There were police officers and security police on horseback, all with guns and billy clubs ready. They rushed to form a cordon in which we could safely make it into the clubhouse. Their body language made it clear that they were there to enforce the peace. They weren't messing around. People were screaming, making gestures, and going crazy. It was a truly bizarre scene.

Hurst leaned forward from his seat behind me and tapped me on the shoulder. I turned around. He nodded to the sign.

"Ken," he said, "maybe this is baseball like it ought to be, but this is definitely not baseball the way it is in St. George, Utah."

Bruce pitched brilliantly that night through five innings, and the Red Sox led 3-0 after five. He left in the sixth, having done his job. He gave it all he had in that pressure cooker of a game, and I will always be proud of what Bruce Hurst accomplished, not just in that game, but in his career. In 15 Major League seasons (11 full-time, four part-time) Bruce went 145-113 for a .562 winning percentage and a 3.92 ERA.

The pitching dropped off in 1987, and the Red Sox finished with their first losing record since 1966. In 1988, the team started slowly and was struggling to stay at .500 at the All-Star break when manager John McNamara was fired and replaced by Joe Morgan from Walpole, Massachusetts. That began Morgan Magic. The team won 19 of 20 games and set a record for most consecutive home wins. The team went on to win a Division Crown.

Then came 1989. It was to be a fateful year for me.

My Last Game

I'm a broadcaster, not a writer. I don't know how many times real writers rewrite. Kurt Vonnegut said he became a writer because editing and revision allowed him to upgrade his stupidity into something approaching cleverness, his cleverness into wisdom. I know that Hemingway wrote six pages a day, no more, no less, and each one rewritten. My friend Robert Parker, author of the splendid "Spenser" detective novels, once told me his output was about the same. On the other hand, Thomas Wolfe wrote compulsively for long, long hours. Dan Valenti has talked to me about the endless revisions involved in the writing process. Contrarily, the prolific

Isaac Asimov claimed never to have revised. I find that hard to believe, but even if it is, he's the exception that proves the rule.

Don't get the idea for even a moment that I'm comparing myself as a writer to these guys. I couldn't get up to the plate against guys like that; they would strike me out on three pitches. Here's what I'm getting at. This is the eighth time I've rewritten this section. I think it has to do with the incident I'm about to describe. This incident is troubling. It happened more than ten years ago, and it still bothers me. I know what I want to say but can't seem to find the right words.

This is about the day I was let go as the Voice of the Boston Red Sox. For me, it was the day the music died. It felt like a death in the family.

From the early 1950s until 1989, there were only two Voices of the Red Sox—Curt Gowdy and me. That's almost 40 years. Curt left because the network came calling. I left under far different circumstances.

Let me tell you what happened.

The Boston Red Sox ended the 1989 regular season on October 1. There had been rumors that year in the Boston papers of a shakeup involving the radio broadcasting team, since the broadcasting rights for next season were up for grabs. I paid no mind to the gossip. I never did, really, for in my business, rumors are ripe. There's always scuttlebutt, and my policy was not to pay attention, because it tended to blur your focus. Whenever I went behind the microphone, I wanted to be fully present in that moment, not worrying about some unfounded rumors but worrying about describing the action to the best of my abilities.

During the season, I had expressed the thought to a few close friends that I was contemplating retirement at the end of the year. I had suffered a mild heart attack the previous January and was going through the usual physical and mental recovery. The thought of not working had some appeal to me, particularly early in the season. Who needed all the stress and aggravation, especially the incessant travel? Life on the road had become tiresome. Looking back on it now, this frustration of being away from home was only a natural part of my recovery. Medically, I was on fresh turf. Emotionally, I needed the comfort and security of home.

But by the season's end, I felt stronger and more refreshed. I would tape my games and listen to them on the drive home, and I felt great about the way I sounded. I could hear the energy in my voice. This was also the result of my illness, or rather, my recovery. As I got my full health back, everything brightened, and I returned to work with a renewed sense of optimism. I found myself looking forward to the 1990 season. The issue was resolved in my mind: I wanted to come back.

Despite my heart attack, I missed just one game for the entire season in 1989, a night game in Chicago. At the suggestion of my broadcast partner Joe Castiglione, I did not work the final game of that series. It would allow me a small break, a bit of R & R. I had also received permission from my employer, Campbell Sports Network, to miss the game. No problem.

Joe, incidentally, had the tough job of following Jon Miller. After Jon left to take the job as No. 1 play-by-play man with the Orioles, we were flooded with applications for the job. I had heard some fine things about Joe Castiglione and had met him once or twice. I thought he was a very nice man. In fact, I was instrumental in helping Joe land the Red Sox job. Castiglione dedicated himself to working hard and it showed in his performance. When I left, Bob Starr, a fine broadcaster with a great voice, took over for me. After Bob left, Joe got the No. 1 job, which he holds to this day.

In any case, as the 1989 season progressed, the matter of next year's broadcasting rights and the announcers just lingered, like a bad cough that accompanies the flu. It didn't get better or worse. It just hung around. The powers that be simply decided to do nothing. We were left hanging.

Bidding was going on for the rights to broadcast Red Sox baseball for 1990, but according to the papers and from what I gathered on the inside, the sides were making no progress. Frankly, this is an area of my business about which I know little, other than the fact that a deal such as this all comes down to the bottom line. The broadcasting rights go to the company that will pay the most money. Campbell Sports Network had taken over Red Sox games seven years earlier, making it one of the best-run radio networks in Major League Baseball.

Finally, a deal was announced near the end of the season, in late September. Campbell was out and Atlantic Ventures was in.

When Atlantic Ventures (WRKO) won the broadcast rights for 1990, there was the usual speculation about changes in the broadcasting booth. I had been through this many times before in my long career in what can be an unyielding and unsentimental business. It's funny. When an engineer or a machinist faces being let go, it's a private matter. When the broadcasting rights to a Major League baseball team change hands, it makes the papers. People mention in print that you are rumored to be history. That's just the nature of the broadcasting beast. I accepted that.

Joe Wynn of Atlantic Ventures called me a couple days after winning the rights to say that the newspapers would not be making these decisions and not to worry about my job. He said the same thing to Joe Castiglione. Wynn set up a meeting with me, at which Mel Miller and Eric Schultz, both then with WRKO, were present. I told them I very much wanted to return. At the meeting, I also expressed my preference to work on a "one year at a time" basis. I said it would be in WRKO's best interests and mine if they signed me year by year during the four years they had the Red Sox rights. I also suggested I would like an occasional day off, somewhere between seven and 10 days, spread out over the course of the 162-game regular season.

This was common practice in recent years in radio and similar to an arrangement I had when I worked with WITS, the Red Sox rights holder prior to Campbell. It was a request, not a demand. They listened politely and gave me no reason to believe there was a problem or that they were considering a change of any kind. In short, I felt the meeting went well. I was not at all concerned for myself. To be honest, I worried more that Joe might not be asked back.

Meanwhile, I had spoken with John Harrington, the man who calls the shots in the Red Sox front office, and told him the same thing: I would like to return for 1990. While the season was still going on, a meeting was called in late September involving Atlantic Ventures, the Red Sox, and me. It was quickly postponed with no explanation. A second meeting was called and then similarly postponed. Finally, the meeting was set for 10 a.m. Tuesday, October 3, two days after the end of the season, early in the morning. Castiglione also was to meet with them separately the same day at 9 a.m.

Finally, the day came for the final game of the season, on Sunday October 1. The net effect of all the happenings was this: when I went on the air for the final game, I had no way of knowing it would be the last time I would broadcast a Major League baseball game.

As it developed, they had already made their decision but couldn't see fit to let me know. I had been hung out to dry in that final broadcast, though I didn't have a clue.

That left me in an awkward spot. It certainly would have been presumptuous of me to say anything about returning or not during that last broadcast. I just didn't know.

My pregame show reflected that. Here's what I said in the last such show I ever did:

> "Good afternoon, everybody, and welcome to our dugout show. During today's game, I'm going to be reminiscing about the 34 years that I've been covering Major League baseball, recalling some of the highlights of those years that have come and gone in the hope that you will enjoy it and the knowledge that I certainly will.
>
> "For months now, people have been asking me whether I will be returning to broadcast Red Sox baseball next year, and the only answer I can give you is: I don't know.
>
> "Let me say quite simply how I feel about that, looking with a mixture of the pragmatic and yet sentimental soul of the Bostonian of Irish heritage. If I return, that will be fine. It is not my decision to make. If I do not, consider this, and I hope that it applies to your professional life as it has to mine.
>
> "For 20 years I have been a broadcaster for the Boston Red Sox. And I've had some other great jobs as well, with the Cleveland Indians, and the Browns, and the Big Red Machine of the Reds, and Ohio State and Harvard and so on. But this is the one I always wanted, and I've been fortunate enough to do it for 20 seasons. I know a lot of men and a lot of women, and you do, too, who have held jobs that are just that—jobs. A method of earning money in order to simply raise a family. They've not en-

joyed any of it. And those are the people to feel for. That is where life is tough.

"Me? I've been fortunate, and I say that not out of pride but with gratitude. Forgive me if I sound like I'm indulging myself, because when you broadcast baseball games or any time you're in the public eye, you're subject to criticism, and sometimes very deservedly so. But I would like to simply say that the best compliment I've ever received publicly was from the famed poet Donald Hall, who in a long *New York Times* essay stated, among other things, 'We trust the man.'

"With that I want to thank Jim Biangini of the *Newburyport Daily News*, who was kind enough to say, 'His voice is as much a part of the good old summer time in Boston as picnics on the Charles, children playing in parks, and the smell of freshly mowed grass.' I thank Jim for those words, and also Mr. Hall for his.

"A young broadcaster three years ago in Winter Haven asked me how I would like to be remembered, and I had no idea because the thought had never occurred to me. But Mr. Hall and Mr. Biangini have put it better than I ever could, and I thank them very much for that.

"One final word if I may. If this is indeed the last game that I ever broadcast on radio in Boston, and if I provided some enjoyment for you over the course of the years, I would appreciate it very much if you wouldn't mind sending a contribution to the Jimmy Fund of the Dana-Farber Cancer Institute. It would be very meaningful to me."

During the broadcast of the game itself, I did what I had done for many years in the season's last game. I reminisced about the year and all the years and thanked everybody from Al Fiorello in the Fenway Park parking lot to Helen Robinson on the Fenway switchboard for their cooperation.

"This Too Shall Pass"

That last game was a quick one, as are most final games when nothing is riding in terms of a pennant. It ended around 3 p.m. Some 33 hours later, I walked into the twice-postponed meeting where I would learn my fate.

In the meeting, after the usual amenities, I heard the euphemism: "We've decided to make a change. We want to go in another direction." The network wanted to have someone who would commit to the broadcasts for four years.

I wanted to go on a year-to-year basis, because if I wanted out after a year or two, I would be free to tell them. Also if during that time they felt I wasn't doing the job well enough, they could let me know and it would have been more comfortable from my point of view as well as their standpoint. I was given no explanation as to why I no longer fit into their plans.

I know enough about the broadcasting business to recognize that talent is its own worst judge. I also knew that I was on top of my game. I knew that my voice, which is an instrument, had realized its maturity. I had the confidence to know that a little silence and pausing can make the delivery more effective. I had reached the point, at least from my view, that in this intangible endeavor called broadcasting, I was the best I could be.

However, I had lost my job.

I was completely undone by the decision to drop me as Voice of the Boston Red Sox, and I reacted in a way that I regret to this day. What I should have done was stand up and say, "Okay, it's your decision. You deal with it," and then left. Instead, because of my very deep love for the Jimmy Fund, I felt that if I reacted like that it would cause problems with the Jimmy Fund's relationship with the network and the Red Sox. So I tried to be the brave soldier.

I said, "I'll just say that I'm retiring and even write a press release saying that."

That's what I did. That press release was fiction. Columnists wrote and people said I stepped out with class, but in my heart I didn't feel that way at all. It took me a long time to get over the shock.

My lovely Irish mother used to say to me, "This too shall pass." On my "Ken's Corner" program of poetry and thoughts for the day, I came across something that helped me: "If you go to the feast of anger, you'll discover the skeleton at the feast is you."

My dear mother was right. It did pass.

So the anger is gone, and as I have been all my life, I remain an avid Red Sox fan. I'm also very proud to say that I am now, along with my dear friend Ned Martin, a member of the Red Sox Hall of Fame.

An incident comes to mind here. I was playing in a Jimmy Fund Golf Tournament with my son Casey and two police officers from Blackstone, Massachusetts, in the summer of 1992. When we finished, one of the officers said to me:

"I want to tell you something, Ken."

"What's that?" I asked.

"Thank you." he said.

"For what?"

"My son is now 11. Thank you for teaching him the game of baseball."

When I got to bed that night, I thought of those words and cried.

Kevin Convey, writing in the *Boston Herald* not long after I left, captured the thoughts and feelings of so many people who reacted to the situation of my leaving:

> "It is late on a hot summer night in 1967. The house is dark except for the flashlight beside my bed. It is quiet except for the transistor radio set just above a whisper. Tonight, they are playing on the coast and I am 3,000 miles away, long past my bedtime. As sure as the voice of Ken Coleman I know the Red Sox will win this game. And the pennant. And the World Series, of course. The great season will never end. And I will never grow up. I am 11 years old. The summer seems infinite and full of promise. The voice of Ken Coleman whispering to me alone in the darkness tells me it is so.
>
> "Summer without Ken Coleman? Never. How could it be? Ken Coleman didn't just call baseball games. He called my summers.
>
> "There will be other summers. And I will listen to other announcers. But I will never stop hearing Ken Coleman."

I have this dream. I'm ready to go on the air, just before the first pitch. But at the last second, someone takes the microphone away from me.

This too is passing.

The Jimmy Fund and Beyond

One of the things I've discovered since then is that some people look forward to retirement . . . but I'm not one of those people. I will never retire, unless for some reason I am forced to, and the only reason I can think of that will cause that would be the aging process, which can bring on poor health.

Through my adult life, I've been active physically, which I think is extremely important, because it adds to the quality of life. Each day, or as often as I can, I do 30 minutes on a treadmill and/or 30 minutes of swimming. I also play golf, though I don't consider golf exercise. I just enjoy it, and think it's a great source of relaxation and camaraderie.

Most of my golfing actually involves work. I play in about 35 to 40 Jimmy Fund golf tournaments each year throughout New England and Florida. Sometimes, these involve very long days. I might have to leave the house at 6 a.m., travel to the site of the tournament, play 18 holes of golf, then speak afterward at the dinner. By the time I get home, it's often past 11 p.m.

Those are long hours. If you do that two or three times a week, as is often the case, it's sometimes not all the fun it's cracked up to be. Of course, the reason for my being there has little to do with golf. I'm there on behalf of the Dana-Farber Cancer Institute, to help raise money for the Jimmy Fund, and that shall always keep me going, no matter how tired I am.

We hear the word courage used a lot in sports. Well, let me tell you—courage is what I see when I visit the children and their parents at the Dana-Farber Cancer Institute.

Almost everyone in New England and many people from all over the world have heard of the Jimmy Fund. They know it has something to do with helping kids with cancer. But exactly what and where is the Jimmy Fund?

Here's how the Jimmy Fund introduces itself. For children with cancer and their families, the Jimmy Fund is a clinic in Boston, where vintage Disney paintings adorn the walls and caring doctors work to take the terrible fear out of cancer, replacing it with hope.

For researchers and treatment specialists worldwide, the Jimmy Fund is the Dana-Farber Cancer Institute, which made history with the first remissions in childhood leukemia almost 50 years ago and never looked back. Dana-Farber's Jimmy Fund Clinic remains one of the world's premier centers for pediatric cancer treatment and research, part of a medical complex that has made many advances in adult cancers as well.

"Jimmy," by the way, was a little boy who had leukemia. Jimmy (not his real name) loved baseball and captured the hearts of the Boston Braves. During a 1948 radio broadcast, millions heard this courageous child visit with his baseball heroes. Contributions poured in from people everywhere who wanted to help him. This launched an effort that has brought hope to thousand of kids and adults.

The Jimmy Fund and Fenway Park have become synonymous; the Red Sox adopted the Fund in 1952 as the team's official charity. But the Jimmy Fund also means collections in movie theaters, golf tournaments, bake sales, bicycle tours, and much more. And it consists of the countless hours given by countless numbers of volunteers.

The Jimmy Fund has certainly made a difference. For every three children who have cancer today, two will survive thanks to the pioneering work done by the Jimmy Fund. As many as 80 percent will completely recover from certain types of leukemia. And children and adults of all ages with other forms of cancer will live longer and more comfortably.

In 1948, when the Jimmy Fund was formed, patients were rarely told they had cancer. The diagnosis was considered too difficult to bear. Today, in the Jimmy Fund Clinic, doctors and nurses speak openly and honestly with their young patients. They can afford to, because today there is hope.

And I'll say that the remarkable examples of courage I have seen on the part of young cancer patients and their parents will stay with me the rest of my life. It certainly helped me put into perspective the challenges and obstacles that I had to face.

In addition to my Jimmy Fund work, these last ten years have been filled with "Ken's Corner," a five-minute radio program of poetry, inspirational essays, and thoughts for the day. I've done "Ken's Corner" since 1967. I also give many speeches and do numerous voice-overs for commercials, videos, and the like. For example, the National Baseball Hall of Fame in Cooperstown used my voice to record the information on the plaques for those who are blind or whose vision is impaired to the point where they can't read the plaques for themselves. From 1990 to 1994, I did play-by-play for Harvard Football, followed by two years of Boston University football.

It's a busy life but with enough downtime so that I can enjoy the quiet.

I'm glad now that I have, after all these years, come to the quiet.

CHAPTER *11*

An Appreciation

LOOK TO THE SUN

I look back on my career and recognize how fortunate I am. I made a good living doing something I loved. I was entrusted with a God-given gift, my voice, and I tried to use it to the best of my abilities. I didn't always succeed, but I worked hard so that I could always look myself in the mirror, knowing that I had given it my best.

It's funny—when you finish doing a game, you react to the broadcast you just did. Sometimes I felt that "this was a good one. I was sharp. I was on top of everything." At other times, I felt that, "I was struggling tonight. I was not what I should have been."

Very often, especially when the Red Sox were at home, I would have my engineer—Al Walker, the best ever, or the second best, John Mullaney—tape my innings. I would listen to the tape on the way home from Fenway. I'd do it for several reasons. On radio, there is—has to be—a lot of repetition. So I'd listen to the tape and ask myself: was I using too many phrases too often? Was I dull? Was I enthusiastic? Were there too many pauses? Pauses, by the way, are okay on radio. They give the listeners a chance to breath a little.

In my first book, *So You Want to be a Sportscaster*, I suggested that one way to learn how to speak and how to realize the full capabilities of your voice was to read poetry aloud to yourself. When you read poetry, you are doing more than just reading. You are into expressing thoughts as opposed to saying words, and there is a vast difference.

I guess every performer—whether it's an entertainer, a dancer, a ball player, or a broadcaster—always has the desire to do one more show. There's a yearning to practice the craft that identified you and set you apart, to utilize the gift that came to you on loan from God. When you are not using that gift to its fullest extent, there's a sense of frustration that goes along with that. But having been allowed to use that gift for so many years, as I have, there is also a great sense of fulfillment.

It's a huge relief that I'm not "in the booth" any longer because I don't miss the travel, the pressure, and the business side of broadcasting. It's a relief because my schedule is entirely my own. I don't have production meetings to attend, no sponsors to please, no one clamoring for me to be here, do this, address that. It's also a relief because I've come to enjoy the easier pace of my life now. Though I am busy with many activities, I have enjoyed settling into a more thoughtful and deliberate way of living, where I'm controlling the pace and not completely at the mercy of a travel schedule.

I have always loved the beach. There's something about a long walk on the shoreline of the ocean that has a calming effect, and I do it often. You look at the tides coming in, going out—the vastness and expanse of the water, the waves reaching in or moving away one by one—and you can see why it has become such a popular metaphor for the comings and goings of life.

That's how the years pass, moving in, then moving out, like those ocean waves. In sports, there's always next year. With people, eventually there's not. We run out of time. That's how it is, and I believe that's how it should be. We all need to make peace with that, and maybe that's why a setback like losing a job or having to say goodbye are so difficult: they are reminders that our stay on this good earth is a limited one. But the years pass only that something else, something better, can take their place. That's not anything I can or even need to "prove," just something I feel and believe. It's not something you can explain but can only experience.

I look back today and wonder how the years could have passed so quickly. Then I realize, in an instant, that perceptions like these matter very little. In the end, I can truly say of my ride as a professional broadcaster: it was all worth it.

I write these words just days into the new millennium. It's a natural time to take stock.

I can honestly look back on my career with satisfaction—not because I handled all that came my way perfectly, but because I made an honest effort to do so. God knows there have been mistakes, but He also knows that when the heart is in the right place, the results are secondary. Providence will take whatever we have to give, especially when it is our best, and work with it. Indeed, I feel that some of our worst moments and greatest failures become the means to our greatest personal triumphs.

I can hear my all-time favorite singer articulating the words I used in the opening of this book. I hear Frank Sinatra's beautiful and haunting phrasing, "Regrets? I've had a few, but then again, too few to mention."

Me too, Frank.

Thomas Merton once wrote, "It is the silence of the world that is real…All of our fatuous statements about our purposes, our business, and our noise—these are all illusion."

I am off the air now, no longer in a Big League broadcasting booth, and more and more I am learning to appreciate this silence. Merton was right: it is the silence that is real.

And it is good.

I enjoy and at times even relish the quiet, but I will continue to use my voice when and where I can, and in all of it, I will look to the sun, because I believe it is yet still rising.

WORKS CONSULTED

Anderson, Dave. "Yaz: Superstar or Little Hero?" *Dell Sports*, Vol. 1, No. 61, March 1968.

Andre, Lee. "The Dream Game that Can be a Nightmare for the N.F.L." *Sport World*, Vol. 6 No. 1, February 1967.

Appel, Marty. "The Making of Mr. October." *The Diamond*, October 1993.

Berry, Henry. *Baseball's Greatest Teams: Boston Red Sox*. New York: Collier Books, 1975.

Berkow, Ira and Jim Kaplan. *The Gospel According to Casey*. New York: St. Martin's Press, 1992.

"Bob Feller: The Green Kid Dazzled the Fans." *A Treasury of Sports Stars In Action*, No. 3, 1962.

Cartwright, Gary. "Frank Ryan: The Unwanted Quarterback Made Good." *Sport*, Vol. 39 No. 6, June 1965.

"The Coach Wants to See You, and Bring Your Playbook." *Maco's All Pro Football*, 1966 Edition. Also consulted, Cleveland Browns team outlook.

Cobbledick, Gordon. "Herb Score is Back!" *Sport*, Vol. 26 No. 1, July 1958.

Coleman, Ken and Dan Valenti. *The Impossible Dream Remembered: The 1967 Red Sox*. Lexington: The Stephen Greene Press, 1987.

Coleman, Ken and Dan Valenti. *Diary of a Sportscaster*. Pittsfield: Literations, 1982.

Cope, Myron. "Baseball's Biggest Trade Two Years Later." *Sport*, Vol. 34 No. 2, August 1962.

Donley, Paul. "Jimmy Brown—Why He Can't Quit." *Pro Sports*, Vol. 2 No. 2, March 1966.

Donley, Paul. "The Top Secret Plan to Stop Jimmy Brown." *Sport World,* Vol. 3 No. 6, December 1964.

"Even a Tank Couldn't Get by Huff." *Sports Action Magazine,* Fall 1961, Vol. 1 No. 3.

"The Game's Greatest Toes." *Sports Action Magazine,* Fall 1961, Vol. 1 No. 3.

Gelman, Steve. "The Twilight Crisis of Y. A. Tittle." *Sport,* Vol. 34 No. 6, December 1962.

Goodenough, Tap. "Ted Williams, Hunter." *Sport,* Vol. 36 No. 2.

Hand, Jack. "Inside Football's Biggest Brains." *Pro Sports,* Vol. 2 No. 1, January 1966.

Hirshberg, Al. *What's the Matter with the Red Sox?* New York: Dodd Mead and Co., 1973.

Izenberg, Jerry. "Eight Days to Daylight." *Pro Football Illustrated,* Vol. 2 No. 3, Fall 1966.

John, Tommy and Dan Valenti. *TJ: My 26 Years in Baseball.* New York: Bantam, 1990.

Kalman, Davey. "The Rock the Indians Lean On." *Pro Sports,* Vol. 2 No. 4, July 1966.

"Lenny Moore—Automation on the Gridiron." *Sports Action Magazine,* Vol. 1 No. 3., Fall 1961.

Mantle, Mickey. "The Unknown Yogi Berra." *Inside Sports: Mickey Mantle's Baseball,* Vol. 1 No. 2, August 1962.

Maule, Tex. "A Man for This Season." *Sports Illustrated,* Vol. 17 No. 11, Sept. 10, 1962.

"NFL Debate: Who Should Call the Plays—Quarterback or Coach?" *Sports Action Magazine,* Fall 1961, Vol. 1 No. 3.

Neft, David S. and Richard M. Cohen. *The Sports Encyclopedia: Baseball.* 11th ed. New York: St. Martin's Press, 1991.

Nutter, Buzz (as told to Ernie Salvatore). "Jim Brown: Too Tough to Hurt?" *Pro Football Illustrated 1965,* Vol. 1 No. 5.

Olderman, Murray. "Who's More Important, the Passer or the Runner?" *Sport,* Vol. 34 No. 6., December 1962.

Olderman, Murray. "What About the Johnny Unitas Rumors?" *Sport,* Vol. 36 No. 2., August 1963.

"Paul Hornung Gets His Big Chance." *A Treasury of Sports Stars in Action,* No. 3, 1962.

Peary, Danny, ed. *We Played the Game: 65 Players Remember Baseball's Greatest Era 1947-1964.* New York: Hyperion, 1994.

Pope, Edwin. *Ted Williams: The Golden Year 1957.* New York: Manor Books, 1972.

Ragazzi, Reno. "Is Tony Conigliaro Tossing Away His Career?" *Pro Sports,* Vol. 2 No. 4, July 1966.

Riger, Robert. *Best Plays of the Year 1963.* New York: Prentice-Hall, 1964.

Rosenthal, Harold. *Fifty Faces of Football.* New York: Atheneum, 1981.

Saunders, Brad. "I Don't Want to be a Walking Mess of Scars." *Pro Football Illustrated,* Vol. 2 No. 3, Fall 1966.

Scholl, Bill. "Browns Build Nation-Wide Television Network." *The Cleveland Press* 19 Nov. 1959, p. 63.

Sisti, Tony. "Yastrzemski: Superstar at Last." *Sports Quarterly Presents Baseball,* 1968 Edition.

Smith, Curt. "How About That!" *The Diamond,* October 1993.

Stainback, Barry. "How Lou Groza Came Back." *Sport,* Vol. 32 No. 6, December 1961.

"Steelers' Iron Man: Bobby Lane." *Sports Action Magazine*, Vol. 1 No. 3, Fall 1961.

"Streamlining Football's Scouting." *Sports Action Magazine,* Vol. 1 No. 3, Fall 1961.

Sweet, Ozzie. *Legends of the Field: The Classic Sports Photography of Ozzie Sweet.* New York: Viking Penguin, 1993.

Total Baseball: The Official Encyclopedia of Major League Baseball. 6th ed. Kingston: Total Sports, 1999.

Total Football II: The Official Encyclopedia of the National Football League. New York: Harper Collins, 1999.

"Why They Can't Stop Jimmy Brown." *Sports Action Magazine,* Vol. 1, No. 3, Fall 1961.

Valenti, Dan. *Clout! The Top Home Runs in Baseball History.* Lexington: Stephen Greene Press, 1989.

Valenti, Dan. *From Florida to Fenway.* Pittsfield: Literations, 1981.

Valenti, Dan. *Red Sox: A Reckoning.* Wilkes-Barre: Stallion Books, 1979.

Valenti, Dan. *Cactus League Roadtrip.* Lexington: Stephen Greene Press, 1990.

Vanderberg, Bob. *'59 Summer of the Sox: The Year the World Series Came To Chicago.* Champaign: Sports Publishing Inc., 1999.

Vescey, George. "How Long Can Mantle Last?" *True's Baseball Yearbook,* 1963 Edition.

Willliams, Ted with John Underwood. *The Science of Hitting.* New York: Pocket Books, 1972.

Williams, Ted with John Underwood. *My Turn at Bat.* New York: Pocket Books, 1970.

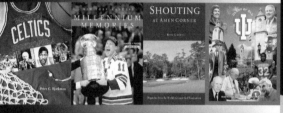